DONALD TRUMP JR.

#1 *NEW YORK TIMES* BEST-SELLING AUTHOR

LIBERAL PRIVILEGE

JOE BIDEN AND THE DEMOCRATS' DEFENSE OF THE INDEFENSIBLE

ENDORSEMENTS

"Turning the tables on Joe Biden, exposing his radical associations and family's self-dealing, Don Trump Jr. provides searing insights and critical information for Americans who still believe we deserve a leader who puts America first."

—**Laura Ingraham,** Host of *The Ingraham Angle* on Fox News Channel

"If you care about this nation, you must read *Liberal Privilege*. Donald Trump Jr. excavates Joe Biden's past unlike anyone else. This is a powerful book the fake news doesn't want you to read. So get a copy now and spread the word!"

—**Mark Levin,** National TV and Radio Broadcaster

"In his latest book, *Liberal Privilege*, Donald Trump Jr. reveals how Joe Biden used the government to enrich his family. A must-read for anyone who wants to learn about the inner workings of the swamp!"

—**Senator Rand Paul**

"For decades the media has given Joe Biden a pass. Scandals, terrible policies, and self-enrichment have defined his fifty-year career in Washington. Donald Trump Jr. defines Joe Biden. An absolute must-read!"

—**Charlie Kirk,** Author of *The MAGA Doctrine*

"Donald Trump Jr. doesn't care about anything but the truth. After reading *Liberal Privilege*, one thing is clear: I thought Congress is bad right now—luckily, I never served with sleazy Joe Biden!"

—**Congressman Matt Gaetz**

DEDICATION

I am proud to dedicate my book to
the Founding Fathers, American greatness,
our heroic military, United States exceptionalism,
the brave members of law enforcement who keep this nation great,
and stopping the radical Left from destroying our great country.
We won before, and we will win again!

CONTENTS

PART I

NO JOE

CHAPTER 1

Fake News, You're Fired!

I never thought I would write one political book, let alone two, but after seeing the activist media do such a disservice to our country, I have to fight and write. I have to supply you with the truth because I would not be able to live with myself until these frauds are exposed, and the facts are out there.

There is a lot of talk these days about privilege, and the only kind that gets no mention is liberal privilege, the title of this book. Liberal privilege is the ability to rewrite history, neglect facts, and alter the news in a one-sided fashion to further the liberal agenda. I'm writing this because no one in the fake news media is willing to do their damn jobs. I'm doing this because mainstream media is *dead*—they are no longer journalists. They have abdicated that role to be left-wing activists. They don't report the news anymore; they make up the news. And they won't even question the Democratic National Committee (DNC) talking points, even when they make absolutely no sense.

Since "today's journalists," a.k.a. the media arm of the DNC, won't do their jobs by reporting the truth, it falls on concerned citizens to step up. I am one of those concerned citizens. I'm happy to help voice the frustrations of so many Americans who have watched in shock and horror as the Left has swallowed and consumed media—whether mainstream television, newspapers, and even more flagrant these days, the censorship on social media platforms. It would be nice to see some of the thousands of sanctimonious hacks in the media, who preach about journalistic integrity on a daily basis, do some actual work, but that's not who they "identify" as anymore. There is a reason why even during the peak of the Trump economy boom, there was still an average of 96 percent negative reporting.[1] When the economy was at an all-time high, when unemployment was at an all-time low for every group, when wages went up for every group in the nation—liberal privilege allowed the media to continuously cover the accomplishments in an overwhelmingly negative light! That is liberal privilege!

They're activists, not journalists.

Journalism on the Left is dead. Rest in peace. They are bought and paid for. We should at least be asking questions about Biden's perilous health history and his corrupt family deals, learning the real story of China and the WHO, and discovering the truth of the robust economy my father, Donald J. Trump, built from the shambles of failed Obama-Biden-era policies.

If the liberal media wasn't simply the Left's propaganda machine, you would know all about these things. You would see people from both sides of the aisle willing to ask the hard questions and dig for answers. But you don't—you just see what the DNC wants you to see through their distorted fake news prism.

If you really stop to listen to their words as the outrage cycles flow, you can hear the DNC talking points repeated, nearly verbatim, from one leftist media outlet to another. It's a cacophony of fake news screechers. I've sat and watched as various networks picked up the exact same catchphrase within an hour of each other—straight from the mouths of their Democrat propaganda masters.

"Manufactured crisis" is one popular accusation toward President Trump. From the very same party that said, "never let a good crisis go to waste," they simultaneously spew half-truths from the mouths of Nancy Pelosi, Chuck Schumer, Bernie Sanders, and nearly every talking head on the Left-owned media. There is no clearer example of this liberal-privilege class distorting the truth to fit their narrative than what happened on a tragic, sunny morning in April 2019: Islamic extremists slaughtered hundreds of Roman Catholics in Sri Lanka and, instead of the Left saying Christians were murdered, they used the term "Easter worshippers." Former President Barack Obama used this term. Is it just me or is there an echo in here, because Hillary Clinton also used the same term in her own condolence tweet mere hours apart?[2]

Suddenly, every talking head in the media was using the phrase "Easter worshippers" instead of Christians—normal people don't talk that way. Yet magically, everyone on the Left starts wording things similarly.

The problem is that these people weren't just "Easter worshippers"—what does that even mean? People who worship Easter? They were *Christians*. The DNC-coined phrase served the leftist media in wanting to minimize the fact that Christians are persecuted all over the world and to dehumanize the people slaughtered in Sri Lanka and tame the view of Islamic extremism. The same way that Obama never wanted to label Islamic extremists as Muslims. Two sides of the same coin. Political correctness run amok.

Hillary Clinton can blast "Islamophobia and racism," call one individual "despicable," and call out white supremacists, for a fraction of the Sri Lanka death toll, when a mosque is attacked in New Zealand. But we certainly can't mention how Christians are slaughtered nearly every single day in countries from Syria to Somalia to Iran.

You think you get the truth from the media? The name of the game is this: if it hurts Trump, it sells, and people spread it—doesn't matter if it's true or false. If it would help Trump, they don't share the information. They suppress any information that doesn't further their agenda, and I guarantee as you read this book, you're going to wonder why you haven't heard some of these facts before.

Don't believe me? Every now and then, the information they want to suppress slips out. When Mike Bloomberg was running for president, he directed his entire news organization not to cover anything controversial for Democrats. They announced they would continue to investigate Trump, but they wouldn't dig into anything regarding Bloomberg—or any of the other Democrat candidates.[3]

Here's the truly frightening part—Michael Bloomberg himself directed his news agency to do this, and the Media Research Center, a media watchdog, reported that *none* of the major news networks said "a single word—positive or negative or neutral—on their major morning or evening or Sunday interview shows"[4] about Bloomberg's policy. Totally acceptable—no problem, right? Let's just change the rules about reporting on presidential candidates to suit one guy's campaign and hurt another. That's completely fine.

If you're like me, the power one man could possess to utterly alter the way campaign news is covered should make you mad. *Furious!* This is but one example of the double standard the media gets by with *every single day*. If you just blindly watch the major fake news outlets, you would miss this—and you would definitely miss it now since nearly all Bloomberg's propagandists (not reporters) no longer get press credentials at Trump rallies because "they have declared their bias openly."[5]

Why should we give them access? They're not there to report the news; they're going to push anything negative against the president while ignoring the very obvious flaws of the Democrat candidates.

By the way, it was during a family Christmas dinner at Mar-a-Lago where I was seated with Jared, Eric, Barron, Ivanka, my girlfriend Kimberly Guilfoyle, Melania, Tiffany, and my dad when we played our favorite game. While my father is pretty good at coming up with nicknames on his own, he asked for input on Michael Bloomberg. Since we are New Yorkers, it was no secret to any of us that Bloomberg has always been self-conscious about his lack of height. While there were some great nicknames suggested, I stated, "Mini Mike." The table went silent. Dad looked at me and said laughingly, "That's *great!* Don't use that one, that's mine."

While Michael Bloomberg used to compliment my father regularly, and even begged to appear on *The Apprentice*, things rapidly changed upon the presidential election of my father. In contrast to my father, "Mini Mike" was a terrible politician. Spending $1 billion only to win American Samoa[6] in the Democrat primaries is likely the most expensive disaster in modern political history. It seems the only thing Donald J. Trump and Mike Bloomberg had in common is that they were businessmen. I know it may come as a surprise to the other side, but my father and I were international businessmen for decades before he ran for office. I ran our international book of business, which is why I got so involved in politics—because once Trump won, we immediately decided not to do any new international business deals so there would be no potential conflicts of interest. Even though we had no obligation to give up international deals by any rule or law, we proactively did so to avoid any possible notion of impropriety. Suddenly, I had some extra time on my hands.

Contrast that with Hunter Biden for a minute. He miraculously became an international businessman the second people saw Vice President Joe Biden on the international stage. Not once before did Hunter work in international deals until his father got elected. Not once before did he sit on Ukrainian energy boards. Hunter Biden wasn't going to pass on a good thing once the opportunity presented itself. Call him the talented Mr. Ripley because he sure as hell reinvented himself for profit every single time. But you'll only hear predictable silence from the media on that—we're not supposed to talk about Hunter Biden. It's fine to come after me, but we can't touch little fifty-year-old Hunter. It's also totally immaterial that his father was the senator from Delaware and "Amtrak Joe" Biden rode the train every day for decades,[7] so, of course, Hunter mysteriously found himself on the board of directors for Amtrak at a young age. No hint of cronyism or conflict of interest there!

There's nothing to see here, folks—or so the fake news marketers say. In this book we're going to look at little Hunter's business dealings in some detail, along with those of his father, and let's just see if you think there's a reason to talk about Biden family corruption when we're done.

As you read all the facts I've uncovered while business is shut down because of the China Virus, hold this thought in your head: *What if Trump or anyone connected with him (like me) did it?* I'm going to tell you information that often doesn't get any press at all and unreported news that will make you cringe. As you read, imagine the outrage cycles, the endless headlines, and the allegations and investigations if my father said or did these things, and then you tell me if you think there may be a double standard.

This past winter I gave an interview to Jim VandeHei of Axios—not exactly a conservative voice—and volunteered to debate Hunter Biden on live television. Let's get it all out there, full open books—tax return to tax return. I even volunteered to let Jim moderate so no one could claim it was a biased conservative discussion. No one took me up on it; it was barely covered. They'll call us corrupt; they'll say we're profiteering, and they'll attack us mercilessly, but when I volunteer to go, toe to toe, full disclosure with Hunter, no one's interested. Crickets.

So, we're going to set the record straight right here and right now. I'm saying the things no one else is going to say, and we're going to force the Left to deal with it.

Here's one of the worst tragedies of all—it's not just the liberals turning their backs on this corruption. Failed conservative sycophants out there will carry the liberal talking points because they still want to get invited to the cool Hollywood parties and want to be loved by the very people who hate conservatives and what we stand for the most. We need to push back.

When my last book, *Triggered*, was coming out, I had the opportunity to go on *The View*. I know it's not exactly a bastion for conservative thought, but this is how the book-publicity game works—you go on, take a few lumps, and get a few minutes to talk about your book. I've met Whoopi Goldberg numerous times, and she even came to the finale of *The Apprentice*. My girlfriend, Kimberly Guilfoyle, and I knew several of the hosts from prior professional experience, including Abby, Sunny, and Meghan. While Kimberly had been on the show before, this was my first time. We had realistic expectations. I mean, I'm not naive—even the supposed conservatives on the show aren't exactly part of the Trump fan club. I knew it was going to be rough, but I can play that game. I'm quick on my feet, and I don't get intimidated.

Well, it turns out, even my modest expectations were too high. I thought, since they had us on for three segments (about forty-five minutes) of the show, I would get at least one chance to talk about the book. I was wrong.

The entire appearance was the definition of "triggered"— they were after blood from the moment Whoopi started the show, where she refused to even say out loud my last name. Meghan McCain then seemed to have an absolute nervous breakdown. She was distressed as she talked about character.

I was glad to have Kimberly with me. It was a little "good cop, bad cop," because she was a calming presence while I wanted to go on offense. She was the voice of reason, helping to moderate, so the whole powder keg didn't explode too soon. They always attack any conservative guest who comes on the show and make them the bad guy. With Kimberly there to calm things down, she could talk about areas I couldn't touch.

Kimberly wanted them to see me for who I am—tough but also a loving dad and a son who will fight for my father. Meghan McCain obviously loves her father, and, speaking of me, Kimberly said, "You know what, he loves his father too." A sincere comment like that was their chance to see that we're all just people; we all have different viewpoints, and we have a right to our opinions.

I came on the show in good faith, thinking we would talk about the book during a segment or two of the show, but they didn't want to do that. The entire pretense of me being on the show was to discuss my book—they didn't even ask me one question about it. There is real content in my book we all could have openly discussed, but then as things went downhill and they kept badgering, perhaps having me on wasn't such a good idea.

Someone brought up mistakes and I seized the initiative. "I get it, we've all made mistakes." And then I pulled the nuclear option out of my back pocket I had prepared just in case a situation like this happened. I let *The View* and the world know Joy Behar had dressed up as an African queen in blackface, and Whoopi had stood up for Hollywood director Roman Polanski, saying he had not committed "rape-rape."[8] I had someone on my team standing by who had my Twitter account burning, posting facts to Twitter in real time as I confronted *The View* hosts.

When I challenged Whoopi on defending Polanski for sodomizing a thirteen-year-old child and then hiding from prosecution in Europe, a guest in the audience shouted at her, "Is that true?" I think it's what pissed her off. During a break, Whoopi said that she wasn't defending rape and that we didn't know what we know now. The guest in the audience countered by saying, "What did you have to know? She was thirteen!" Whoopi was *livid*. She and the others had come out with guns blazing, and I hadn't fallen into their trap. I came prepared.

Joy was a total professional, but Meghan McCain was the most surprising. She was nearly quivering, and I thought they were going to have to give her juice and snacks during the breaks. Whoopi took the cake, however, by being so angry she wouldn't look me in the eye or shake my hand afterward.

I was told later that an email had circulated before the show saying they were going to set me up and destroy me. Should I be shocked that they went into this in bad faith? Would anyone who has watched the show be surprised at what happened? They tried. Except it didn't work. *The View* ladies came in with a false sense of security, thinking I would be easy meat like all the rest of the conservatives they jump on and dismantle. They're used to always winning. This show was their five thousandth episode doing this crap, and in five thousand episodes, no one had pushed back at them at all like Kimberly and I did.

Sergio Gor, who helped me with my first best-selling book, *Triggered*, organized some friends to join us in person while we were on *The View*. We received ten tickets, and I gave two to my friends Donna and Greg Mosing. Greg is a big, boisterous guy from Louisiana. He's about 6'3" and came wearing camo and a red MAGA hat. He started cheering for the good points I made and was so loud you could hear him over the crowd. People started having fun with him as he won the group over. Whoopi was outraged. "This is not a fucking MAGA rally!" she shouted at her crowd during the break. Sometimes you need the guy who opens the door for you, and that was Greg. He had people having fun who typically wouldn't have had the courage to be supportive in that crowd, which seemed 95 percent "home team" for the liberal hosts. Greg certainly helped us to win the popular vote with the audience!

That day, the hosts came in unaware of the most significant difference between the rest of their guests and me. All the other people they have on the show are hungry for their acceptance, but their opinion doesn't mean anything to me. Most guests who go on *The View* need their platform to sell a product. I don't. I don't need to be invited again, and I don't need them to like me. I was able to come on, be myself, tell the truth, and burn the place down. If only we had more conservatives who would actually stand up and fight.

Later during the book tour, it amazed me how many people, especially men, came up to me and mentioned this appearance on *The View*. People would tell me, "Don, you were awesome on *The View*. Someone had to stand up to them finally." I always joked with the men who whispered their comments to me with my reply, "What the hell were you watching *The* for?" To which they would respond, "Oh, we only saw it online, we'd never watch it on TV." Sure, buddy.

This is capitalism—there was a market for someone to finally push back, and people loved it.

My father sometimes says I get too amped up, too aggressive. At Mar-a-Lago for the holidays, the show came up. Melania said it was amazing. My father, who is very difficult to impress, said, "When I heard you were going on that show, I thought you were out of your mind." Usually, he would give me some pointers for the next time. Instead, he said, "I wouldn't change a thing" about how we handled ourselves. "You're good. That was amazing." He hadn't initially watched it because he thought it would be a disaster, but this is one of the few times he was genuinely impressed.

I don't think I'll be getting a Christmas card from Whoopi anytime soon.

When you're done reading *Liberal Privilege*, you're going to know the true voting records and the untold stories, and you will have peeked behind the curtain to the truth the liberal media refuses to report. And while we're doing that, let's look at the gift that keeps on giving: Joe Biden. Every time the guy opens his mouth, we get a new gaffe sound bite. He would do our work for us if the media wasn't covering for him 24-7. I've read up on Creepy Uncle Joe, the fifty-year politician who is the embodiment of the DC swamp establishment yet claims to be the one who can fix the problems. As I write this book, the *New York Times* today opined on why Joe Biden shouldn't be debating President Trump; you can't make this shit up. While I was in quarantine researching this book with Kimberly Guilfoyle, Joe Biden was hiding in his basement, grateful not to be on the stump. Name one political campaign in history that was elated when their potential constituency couldn't *see* or *hear* their candidate—and in Biden's case, I'm not sure which is worse. The man doesn't know where he is half the time, stumbles with everything he tries to say, constantly dribbles racial "microaggressions" (to steal their own word), and can't even tell his wife from his sister. I've got to give it to him—he's a political first. It's never been seen in American politics, or in politics anywhere for that matter, that it's better for the candidate to stay silent and in hiding than talk to the people.

During the first Democrat debate, Biden's feeble performance inspired David Axelrod to question his mental capacity. "At times the Vice President seemed somewhat confused to me in handling some of the questions and following some of the action."[9] Other pundits on the Left called it out for the "weak performance" it was,[10] and nothing has changed since that first debate. It's so bad, his handlers keep him in "bubble wrap"[11] and ensure he doesn't speak with certain reporters when he goes out.[12]

One good thing—Biden wearing a mask keeps him from sniffing children's or women's hair in that weird way he does. Yes, we'll talk about that, too, though it's sure to get me in even more trouble. At least eight brave women *have* accused good old Uncle Joe of inappropriate touching. Several other ladies have complained of suggestive and bizarre and uncomfortable words said to them by the presumptive nominee.[13] If you watch nothing but the mainstream fake news, you may never have known that. Contrast this with how these organizations have handled Justice Kavanaugh or the Covington Catholic students.

Would you leave your daughter alone with a guy who does the things Biden does? Just watch a few clips of him touching girls and women and decide. When I've pointed out the videos we see of Biden's creepy behavior, instead of slamming him for being weird, they crucify *me* in their outrage cycle. As I write this, the media is writing yet another piece slamming me—their retribution for me having the guts to point out on Twitter and Instagram exactly how disturbing Uncle Joe's behavior really is. They're not after truth; they want to make me or anyone else pay for bucking their narrative. God forbid that someone refuses to take the beating from CNN or the *New York Times* and bravely fight back. It would be political suicide.

But that's where it's good to be me. I don't give a shit.

I'm not a politician, and I have not thought past getting my father reelected in 2020. That allows me to say the stuff I truly feel and believe. I'm not bought and paid for like these guys are, and I'm not some weak Republican In Name Only (RINO) who rolls over because they can't handle being seen in a negative light by the two people actually watching CNN while stuck in an airport somewhere.

I can say what people are thinking but are too scared to voice. I can ask the questions you want to ask, and I have the audacity to give you the answers that violate the DNC's duplicitous rules. I've been "canceled"—the new buzzword—1,500 times this week; I don't care anymore. It's cathartic for me.

I'm doing the journalists' job for them because *they won't do it.* There's not a fact they won't manipulate to suit their needs.

Compare my father's response to the threat of COVID-19 as opposed to Joe Biden's and Obama's response to swine flu. They took much longer to declare a national emergency, even though thousands of Americans were infected. Thank God COVID-19 didn't hit under Joe Biden's lackluster watch, or, in reality, we may have seen the death toll numbers rise to 2.2 million, the number some experts predicted would happen.[14]

President Donald Trump shut down travel over what would become a globe-spanning viral pandemic, and any reasonable human being would say it was a commonsense solution to stop travel from the *epicenter* of a deadly viral outbreak. But no—that's not what Joe Biden, Nancy Pelosi, or Chuck Schumer said. Biden called it hysterical and *xenophobic.* (Liberal privilege: when all else fails, scream racism.)[15] Approximately one month after President Trump shut down travel, Pelosi is on record inviting people to come visit, to celebrate Chinatown, and to congregate in mass gatherings—no problem. "We feel safe and sound, so many of us coming here," she said as she crowded together with lots of people.[16]

Donald Trump started out right away, without hesitation, to flatten the curve and protect Americans, and he was *roasted* for it! He knew he would take a hit from them, because that's what they always do, but he did the right thing despite their criticism.

Only liberal privilege would allow the very same people who attacked him for quickly shutting down travel from the epicenter of the pandemic to, only a short two months later, scream criticisms for acting too slowly.[17] How can you have it both ways? Either he was an outrageous xenophobe for shutting down travel, or he acted too slowly—at least pick one and stick with it.

But they don't have to pick one—they *can* have it both ways, because the media is their lapdog and won't call them on their idiocy. Hypocrisy. They have given liberals the superpower to re-write history by changing the narrative at will to suit their political objective. No corrections, no withdrawals—once a situation no longer furthers their agenda, they make up a new one and go on to the next outrage cycle.

Speaking of fake outrage cycles, during all the "Russia, Russia, Russia" fake news drama, they attacked me repeatedly. Three different times they tried to drop outrage "bombshells," and not a single time were they correct. Once their attacks clearly proved to be wrong, they just moved on like nothing ever happened. Worse yet, they pretended they were right because they reported it. Some stories proven false still stood, the damage already done, with no actual attempt at correction. Most outlets made no effort to even walk back previous reporting because they accomplished their goal in distorting the truth. That is terrifying. They think they can predetermine the outcome, and they do it every day.

That is why we have to take this so seriously. We're not in a fair fight. The fake news media provides billions worth of free advertising that bolsters the Left's agenda, and if you're going to fight them, you have to be all in.

That's me, and that's my father also—100 percent. I don't know about you, but I want the guy who built the greatest economy the world has ever known, against all odds, to get back in office for another four years and do it again. It took a globe-reaching pandemic to damage the Trump economy, and there is not a single person on the Left who can turn our country around like Donald J. Trump.

They said he couldn't do it the first time, but he did. They told him he could never make a trade deal with China, but he did. They claimed he could never get unemployment to record lows, especially for minorities, but he did. Obama himself said there was no magic wand to bring back American manufacturing jobs for hardworking Americans who want to lead the world, but my father proved him totally wrong—again.[18] Obama and Biden failed 2.3 million American manufacturing workers as they presided over the slowest recovery in economic history, abandoning jobs they left for dead during two terms.[19] Incredibly, Barack Obama, the president of the United States, told dejected manufacturing workers their jobs were "just not going to come back."[20] In fact, our only export under Barack Obama and other swamp creatures before him has been the American dream. Donald J. Trump has changed all that, letting Americans live their dream once again.

And those same manufacturing jobs came roaring back under Donald J. Trump's economic policies—a 399 percent increase in manufacturing jobs during Trump's first twenty-six months in office over Obama's last twenty-six![21]

Just contrast that with Joe Biden who wants to eliminate coal production, telling coal workers they should "learn to code."[22] Let's be honest, Joe Biden doesn't know how to code, so who is he kidding? I would pay good money to watch Joe Biden attempt to code. Hell, I would pay good money to watch him use a microwave. When some in the media lost their jobs and conservatives said, "Learn to code," they were thrown off social media platforms for hate speech.[23] The Left can dish it, but they can't take it. It's liberal privilege.

It took a *worldwide pandemic* to slow down my father's economy—a result I see people on the Left gleefully cheer because it could possibly hurt his reelection chances. When nothing else worked in stopping President Trump, their only hope now rides on this global pandemic, which put a dent in the economy. Even if it destroys your livelihood or your 401K, for Democrats it would be a small price to pay, and they are fine with you paying it. They don't care if millions lose their jobs, as long as it casts my father in a negative light. If you think they care about you, you obviously haven't been watching.

Donald Trump made America great again, just like he promised, and he will do it again. I know it, because he kept his campaign promises to Americans despite a three-year Russia hoax investigation, sham impeachment, and all the rest of the bullshit. He was still able to perform and deliver on promise after promise, despite the pressure, despite incoming fire no president has ever faced—and he still won, for us.

Think about it—Congress was claiming that his son (me) was guilty of treason, a crime punishable by death! Can you imagine trying to function when your oldest child's life is a national headline about treason with possible ramifications of a death sentence? I would think most people might have difficulty concentrating and getting things done with people threatening a family member's life with a little thing like being strapped to a gurney and receiving a lethal injection. But my father pushed through the unequaled shitstorm they threw at him, all the distractions and pushback and threats, to start delivering on his campaign promises.

The media also attacked my little brother Barron, who was thirteen at the time, my sister Tiffany, who was twenty-five, and anyone else they could. But we're not supposed to fight back or point out that fifty-year-old alleged crackhead Hunter Biden and his father are corrupt—that's off-limits. We're not supposed to look at Biden's Senate papers or his voting record. We're not supposed to look at his racist comments or hair sniffing, because he's part of the liberal privilege class.

This is how the Democrats play the game. They gin up identity politics, change their position, rewrite history whenever they feel like it, and try to destroy good people—like they tried with Brett Kavanaugh, Dr. Ronny Jackson, and countless others like the Covington Catholic High School kid, Nicholas Sandmann.

Okay, so spoiler—I'm going to give you this story's ending first, so you know it's a happy one, because in January 2020 Nicholas settled a lawsuit with CNN that *may* have awarded him *$275 million in damages*.[24] Regardless of the final amount, it probably makes him the highest paid CNN "employee" of all time.

Why? Because CNN tried to assassinate a sixteen-year-old kid. And why did they try to destroy a child? Because *he was wearing a Trump hat. He was white. He was male. He was a Christian. He was from the South. And he was a Trump supporter*—it's like the holy trifecta for a liberal attack dog, except that's five things, not three. It was a Leftist's fantasy, because all these things are fair game for unlimited attacks if you're a liberal. They tried to make this kid out to be the ultimate enemy of everyone good and moral, and even though there was no evidence, it didn't stop them from immediately and ruthlessly attacking Nick, who, honestly, kept his cool way better than I would have.

Think about it—he was *sixteen*. They tried to destroy his life *for wearing a hat*. They had no qualms about it.

And, turns out, they got it really, *really* wrong. We'll never know the exact amount since the settlement was handled behind closed doors. Instead, they bolstered a guy who was full of crap and lied about his service, among other things, because he looked like their dream activist. He was a Native American, but he wasn't a war hero or much of anything else he claimed to be. God forbid that they had—oh, I don't know—*fact-checked* him before they jumped on Sandmann. It was too good to be true for the media and the Left, so they just ran with it.

And this is the double standard we deal with on a daily basis. Isn't it funny that with all the bombshell revelations, in nearly four years, not one inaccurate story that broke about Trump was later corrected? That's because they "Sandmann" it every time—they go for the kill shot, they get it wrong, and then they go on to the next lie. Time after time. Strange how that happens—you would think that maybe 50 percent of the time they would issue a retraction. But they never do, because it's a coordinated effort from the marketing arm of the Democrat Party.

Most people don't know I published this book on my own, independent of traditional publishers, because I didn't want anyone to change what I'm telling you. I turned down a very substantial offer from a major publisher in order to keep it raw and unfiltered. I wanted to speak directly to you.

No one else was going to write *this* book. I knew that it was vital to get you the facts so that you could see clearly around the biased filter in which America receives its "truth." What you're told is reality doesn't match up to the truth, and I'm going to expose the propaganda machine for what it is.

They say perception is reality. The Left has done their best to twist and manipulate reality, and for too long we've let them. Well, your reality is about to change, my friend.

Fake news, "You're fired, and I'm telling the world why!"

Next in line—Joe Biden.

CHAPTER 2
Unfit to Serve

Joe Biden might be the original swamp monster. He's been part of the establishment for so long, he's put down roots—*fifty years* as a Washington insider. That's pretty incredible longevity, I'll give him that. But is today's gaffe-prone Biden the same one who started his liberal crusade? The guy we have now can't even remember what *state* he's in half the time (and for the half he does, I'm betting he's in front of a teleprompter). He confuses his wife and his sister, which I hope doesn't happen at home.[1] And to make matters worse, while running for President, Biden told voters in South Carolina he was running for a United States Senate seat.[2]

The media has no problem overanalyzing anything Trump does. Heaven forbid the president wears the wrong tie—you'll see that on the front page. But it seems that the media conveniently goes out of its way to forget some of the most important things about Joe Biden. Make no mistake, I have friends who have survived very traumatic brain injuries. I don't wish ill on anyone. Before the Left takes this chapter out of context, I am not passing judgment on anyone, but given what we have seen, can we really pretend that Joe Biden would be capable of fully executing his duties?

You may not even know that over thirty years ago, Joe Biden had not one but *two* aneurysms. Why don't people know? Because the liberal press doesn't want us to talk about it. From everything I've learned about aneurysms, he's very lucky to be alive at all.[3] There wasn't even a single event—they were two separate events: one on the right side of his brain, the other on his left side. Folks, we call that a *history* of aneurysms.

In February 1988, Biden had emergency surgery for an intracranial berry aneurysm that had begun to leak. He wrote in his autobiography, *Promises to Keep*, the pain that sent him to the hospital was so great, he curled up in a fetal position on the floor and then lay unconscious for five hours.[4]

He had to have another surgery on a second cranial aneurysm in May 1988 that knocked him out for months. They literally had to cut his head open and rummage around in there hoping to find and fix these deadly problems in Joe's brain.

Just how dangerous is even one cranial aneurysm? Biden's first one ruptured, and approximately 30 percent of those with aneurysmal ruptures *die on the spot*. Another 30 percent die from complications in the first six months.

It's crazy how few live through even a single aneurysmal rupture and how many people suffer a serious, lifelong impairment.[5] According to the Brain Aneurysm Foundation, 66 percent of those who survive an aneurysm experience some permanent neurological deficit.[6] Biden himself told a White House audience about his conversation with his neurosurgeon right before surgery. "What are my chances of getting off this table and being completely normal?" he asked.

His doctor replied, "Well, your chances of living are a lot better. They're in the 35 to 50 percent range." Hearing that would scare the hell out of me! No problem—there's just a 50 percent chance you're going to die from having "the top of your head cut off" (Biden's words, not mine) during exploratory surgery to fix a bleeding aneurysm. Biden shared with the audience a joke among neurosurgeons: "How do you know someone's had a cranial aneurysm? On the autopsy table."[7]

Now, I am always happy for anyone to come out healthy from a major health issue—Biden beat the odds and survived. But his own question keeps going through my head: He asked what were the chances of getting off the table *normal*? And what's "normal"? Does anyone come out of this kind of trauma normal? When you go through open-heart surgery, a stroke, or any kind of major trauma, it changes your life. Think about it, not one but *two* brain aneurysms, the surgery and anesthesia, and the recovery process. I think it's impossible to say that you come out of that the same— you can't. No matter how great your recovery, you're never going to go back to exactly who you were.

I'm not trying to be disrespectful, because I don't wish for anyone to be ill or have a life-threatening disease. Do you think that maybe the confused, stumbling Joe Biden we have today— who is so vastly different than the one we see in old videos speaking from the pulpit of the Senate twenty years ago—is suffering the complications of his cranial aneurysms? Remember, 66 percent of those who survive have some permanent neurological deficit—problems like difficulty communicating. Something like, say, perhaps getting confused and saying the wrong things. Or confusing your wife and sister. Or what state you're in. Or which office you're running for. Should I go on?

When asking the neurosurgeon about what might be affected, Biden said he learned that "the side of the brain that the first aneurysm is on controls your ability to speak." Seriously, stop right now and go read the article by Terence P. Jeffrey in CNSNews from 2013,[8] written before the DNC told their marketing arm—the media—that Biden's health was not to be discussed. Do we honestly believe that Donald J. Trump could have had multiple brain aneurisms and no one thinks that his health today or cognitive ability would be impacted? Could anyone reading this right now, with a straight face, tell me it wouldn't be an issue for Donald Trump? Or is this just another example of liberal privilege? An incredibly glaring example. The media would have long ago disqualified Donald Trump for this, yet they aren't even willing to acknowledge it on the other side with Joe Biden. They have staked their reputations on President Trump's mental health, with no proof and no evidence . . . it must be nice to be a Democrat.

Does this not bother anyone else? I don't know—I might want to find out if my presidential candidate has lasting brain damage from multiple aneurysms! Because it sure as hell would concern me if I was thinking about voting for the man! I think no one in their right mind can dismiss the probability that Biden's medical history could be responsible for his frequent gaffes and speaking problems. I often wonder where the concern is. Where is the regard from those close to him, his family, his wife, to step in and stop this insanity? The world can see he is stumbling, he is faltering, he is incapable. I guess they have all been too busy profiteering from his political offices to step in.

The problem is, the fake news media will do everything in their power to cover for him, minimize his screwups, and destroy anyone who even thinks about mentioning Biden's health and mental condition. Never mind that it was actually a point of open discussion during the Obama years. It might interest you to know that one of Barack Obama's personal physicians, Dr. David

Scheiner, who is a die-hard liberal and known for being a big advocate of a single-payer system,[9] thought Joe Biden was unhealthy and questioned his ability to make it for four years as president. Those are his words, not mine—and before everyone jumps in fake outrage over me asking a question regarding his mental capacity, let us also keep in mind what Obama's physician had to say.

In fact, he said, *"He's not a healthy guy."*[10] Go back and read that description again. In fact, read it three or four times. I'll wait.

Fox News ran the story and quoted Scheiner extensively. "He's not in bad shape for his age," Scheiner admitted, "but I wouldn't say he's in outstanding health. Could I guarantee he won't have issues for the next four years? He has a lot of issues that are just sort of sitting there." The good doctor went on to say, "I sort of got the feeling he wasn't very strong . . ."[11]

Unlike those attacking President Trump, who have been partisan hacks, this is President Obama's own doctor—in his own words. I imagine he would give Joe Biden any benefit of the doubt. Do you see the media reporting this anywhere today? I don't. Seriously, we aren't even supposed to question this topic? That's why I had to write this book.

Scheiner's comments directly contradict statements made by Dr. Kevin O'Connor, who gave Biden a clean bill of health despite Joe being treated for an irregular heartbeat—oh, and, you know, a history of deadly aneurysms. And let's not forget Biden's nearly constant gaffes caught on camera like when he didn't seem to know the difference between D-Day and Pearl Harbor Day.[12]

Repeat Biden's neurosurgeon's own words with me: "The side of the brain that the first aneurysm is on controls your ability to speak."[13]

His defenders blame stuttering—they say he's battled it his whole life. That may or may not be true (it doesn't seem to have affected him fifteen or twenty years ago—go back and watch the videos, I suggest you do). But stuttering doesn't make you forget who your wife is during your Super Tuesday speech! Stuttering doesn't have an effect on your memory! I'm not trying to diagnose Biden because I'm not a psychiatrist or a neurosurgeon. I *do* have ethics unlike others who many times have tried to diagnose my father without ever meeting him. I'm saying it's simply not okay for us to ignore these warning signs in someone running for president of the United States (unsuccessfully for the third time, I might add). Think about it—this is the man who wants to be in charge of the nuclear football. When the fate of the free world may be on the line, do you want the man who confuses Nevada and New Hampshire[14] and who forgets which office he's running for?[15]

Sure, no problem! Give that guy the briefcase, and let's just hope he gets it right.

So why don't we hear more about Biden's health? Simple—it's off-limits in the liberal media, so they won't touch it. It's verboten. Oh, there may be a couple of friendly chuckles when he really bumbles something—"That's just Joe being Joe." You won't hear anyone question his fitness to be president—no, sir, that just wouldn't be respectful. (At least not on the record—behind closed doors, it's very different.)

Which is total hypocrisy, since the Left has no problem questioning President Trump's health every day. We should *absolutely* question Biden's fitness. In fact, we must!

They think it's okay to endlessly harass my father with fake news cycle after fake news cycle regarding his health and mental fitness. Once again, this highlights the glaring discrepancy between the treatment Trump receives and literally any liberal receives. If you question Biden's health, you will be ruthlessly attacked—I'm just begging for it by mentioning it in this book. Yet after seeing a couple press conferences, it's okay for every armchair pop psychologist in their mother's basement to diagnose my father with a host of fictitious problems. Never Trumper S. E. Cupp is a perfect example of someone who believes she's qualified to analyze President Trump's mental state when she drops gems of brilliance such as it "isn't that Trump's impaired judgment might cost him the election; it's that it may well have already cost American lives."[16] Who is she to diagnose anyone?

The double standard is sickening. The American Psychiatric Association CEO and Medical Director Saul Levin, M.D., M.P.A., states that it is "unethical for a psychiatrist to render a professional opinion to the media about a public figure unless the psychiatrist has examined the person and has proper authorization to provide the statement."[17] This is the Goldwater Rule. But those kind of rules about medical ethics don't apply when trying to hurt conservatives, especially President Trump! Have I mentioned liberal privilege?

Yet unethical behavior didn't stop 350 half-witted shrinks from writing that Trump's mental health was deteriorating. No matter that they never examined him—that's just a meaningless detail. I would say that anyone could find 350 people of any group to make a certain conclusion they had predetermined. But that's not quite true, because *conservatives don't do that shit*. On the Left, that's acceptable behavior.

So the story persists despite incontrovertible evidence to the contrary. When United States Navy Rear Admiral Ronny Jackson, Obama's appointed presidential physician, briefed the nation on

Donald Trump's health, he reported about my father's good genes and great cardiac health. My father told him to answer anything the media threw at him, and he did so during an unprecedented briefing. Apart from urging President Trump to lay off the burgers and become more physically active, he didn't have a single negative thing to say about my father's health. In fact, he repeatedly used the word "excellent" when fielding obviously loaded questions, and ended by saying, "absolutely he [Trump] is fit for duty."[18] But don't let that fool you—the media narrative after this sterling report was a sickeningly morbid fascination with the possibility my dad could die in office. They hounded Jackson during the interview, and the storyline quickly went from the truth of my father's good health to a fake narrative that he was about to *die*! Possibly right then—maybe he would just keel over after one too many cheeseburgers. You could practically see them salivate at the thought.

It reminds me of the scene from *Dumb and Dumber* where Jim Carrey asks a girl out. She tells him his chances are one in a million, and he immediately pauses, thinks it over, and blurts out, "So you're telling me there's a chance!" Frankly, when I watched that press conference, I could almost see the clown show that was Lloyd and Harry in their baby blue and orange tuxedos.

Of course, my dad didn't die—much to their disappointment. Like I said, dumb and dumber.

They try so hard to find anything they can use against my father. When speaking at the US Military Academy at West Point, DJT had to navigate a wet, slippery ramp in slick, leather-soled shoes. He took his time going down, and then he resumed his normal walking pace. But even after all the previous medical certifications, the media still couldn't resist wondering if my father has Parkinson's! Everyone else had rubber-soled shoes, and he was just being careful not to wipe out and give the media the photo op they want. They obviously pretend to have never witnessed this man on the move or his unrelenting pace. In fact, the most common remark I get while traveling is, "How does your father do it? How does he keep up his pace?" Even the *New York Times* couldn't resist speculating whether my father has Parkinson's! Why the double standard? Why don't they grill Biden like this? It's simple—they are deeply invested in one outcome. That is why they perpetuate a false narrative every single day.

And let's not forget one minor little piece of this story that has received virtually no coverage at all. Dr. Ronny Jackson also performed a Montreal Cognitive Assessment test on my dad. This is a thirty-point screening technique to aid in the detection of even minor cognitive impairment, dementia, or Alzheimer's disease.

How did my father do? Thirty for thirty—a *perfect* score. "I have absolutely no concerns about his cognitive ability," Dr. Ronny Jackson reported. Yes, my father does tend to speak his mind—I think we can all agree that's very true, especially if it's on social media—but Obama's doctor "found no reason whatso-ever to think that the President has any issues whatsoever with his thought process."[19] Naturally, Dr. Jackson's report did nothing to stem the tide of fake news questioning my father's health and mental fitness. Of course, not—it's the *truth*, and the media is never interested in the truth.

So, let's hear some more truth.

CHAPTER 3

Puppet on a String

A great patriot who didn't get the benefit of liberal privilege despite being promoted by President Obama is Rear Admiral Doctor Ronny Jackson. As an immensely qualified doctor brought on during the Bush administration, a physician who has actually examined my father, and someone who has been in close proximity and spent extensive time around Joe Biden, he has some unique insights.

I befriended Dr. Jackson largely due to his proximity to my father during the first two years of the Trump presidency. He is one of the most decent individuals to have worked in the White House. My entire Secret Service detail can attest to it, too, and their word always means a lot more to me than a gratuitous back-slapping politician. They always spoke very highly of Dr. Ronny—having traveled the world together, noting his character and witnessing his work ethic at all hours. He always went out of his way to be available. So as I was writing this book, I called Dr. Jackson and asked for his input on his experiences with the media, double standards, Obama, Biden, and more, since he has such a clear perspective. I was shocked at what he had to say.

"I couldn't believe they were all over me every single day," Dr. Jackson told me of the criticism he received after performing the test on my father. They were "tearing me up from the far Left and the liberal press because I got out there and did my job." He noted how Dr. Bandy Lee, a psychiatrist from Yale, kind of led the charge, criticizing his work and demanding that President Trump be examined by a panel of psychiatrists.[1] "When I did it [the Montreal Cognitive Assessment], it kind of took that argument away," Dr. Jackson told me, but it didn't last long.

"The double standard is incredible," Dr. Jackson told me regarding the difference between the way the media treats Trump as opposed to Biden. "One day when Biden was having one of his episodes where he couldn't figure out where he was or what office he was running for and instead was talking about running for the Senate, I was listening on the radio. . . . I just got sick of the double standard, so I picked up my phone and tweeted out, saying, 'Hey, does anybody remember the cognitive test that I gave President Trump—the one that he aced? Looks like somebody else needs a test.' I referenced an article where Biden was making these [mistakes]. Oh my God! You should have seen [it]—that thing went crazy. I started getting hate mail like you wouldn't believe."

Just for being brave enough to ask the question, Dr. Jackson quickly received a personal email from former President Barack Obama ripping into him and expressing his disappointment and more. Obama couldn't believe that Dr. Jackson wouldn't play along with the Left's narrative. It shows the incredible hypocrisy of the Left that Obama would roast Dr. Jackson over even *questioning* Biden, yet they wouldn't say a thing about the media circus around Trump, even when the cognitive test should've put it all to rest!

When we were talking about Biden's cognitive ability, Dr.

Jackson wondered, "Where were all these liberal psychiatrists and all these Harvard professors that were coming after me and attacking me and my credentials and everything else just because I did my job and did the president's physical?" Surely, if they really cared about our leaders' fitness, they should be asking at least as many questions about Biden as Trump. But they don't. "I was on active duty as a navy admiral serving as a physician of the president. I was super objective about it. I did a thorough physical exam on President Trump—by the way, which he crushed." Yet the media still questioned Trump's fitness and Dr. Jackson's professionalism and sterling record.

I asked the former rear admiral if there was anything from the exam my father "crushed" that he didn't get a chance to share. "His cardiac performance was impressive. I put him on the treadmill for a routine cardiac stress test and it was incredible what he could do on that treadmill. He was in the top 10 percent of the entire nation for his age and probably would have been in the top 2 or 3 percent if I had let him keep going. When I told him we were done, he was still going strong. He has fantastic cardiac conditioning and cardiac endurance." He went on say, "From a physical standpoint, he's in phenomenal shape. . . . They just cannot stand to hear me say that, but it's a fact. I had all the objective data to prove it."

Regarding the cognitive test Dr. Jackson performed, he told me, "There were a lot of them that were very, very basic compared to the one we did. The one we did was considered one of the more thorough ones. It's a screening test." Normally, with these tests, doctors want to have some indication that the individual may need to be evaluated, but Dr. Jackson said, "There was absolutely zero indication to do it, and if we were going to do it, it was going to be strictly just to do it to have it done" to answer the questions about the president's mental fitness. "I knew he was going to do well. I knew it was going to be within the normal range; I just didn't know he was going to get thirty out of thirty on it! So, he crushed it!"

That didn't prevent CNN, MSNBC, and others from sending "assassins" to try to take Dr. Jackson down and undermine the president's physical during the briefing. "They were not expecting when I went into that press briefing room for me to have done any of" the cognitive testing, Dr. Jackson told me. He was expecting a ten-minute press briefing; instead, "They just started asking me crazy questions. Just ridiculous stuff." After a while, they ran out of things to ask.

The day he executed his duties as an appointed presidential physician and revealed the actual results of a scientific exam, Dr. Jackson realized the media had stamped him as a Trump supporter. He had impartially done his job for three different presidents, from two different parties, and since he didn't follow their narrative, the liberal-Left media "canceled" this man—or tried to.

The same people who questioned Dr. Jackson's credibility are some of the very same ones who unethically diagnosed my father on TV with zero contact and zero actual testing. It's beyond idiotic that the media would say these armchair telepsychiatrists are somehow more qualified to determine my father's cognitive state than the former navy admiral. President Obama promoted Dr. Jackson into his position, and he faithfully served our nation's last three presidents as an appointed physician for almost fourteen years. Not to mention the fact that Dr. Jackson actually spent hours overseeing a whole *cadre* of doctors testing DJT. "I had a cardiologist. I had a GI doctor. I had a dermatologist," Dr. Jackson explained. They had a representative of every specialty, all doing their part in a collaborative exam of about a dozen doctors. "These are military doctors that have been practicing medicine for decades that are [at] the very top—that are the chairmen of their departments," Dr. Jackson said of the team.

In other words, it's not just Dr. Jackson's word against that of some psychiatrist; Dr. Ronny Jackson presented an entire medical *team's* findings. Their overwhelmingly conclusive results? That my dad is in amazing physical and mental health.

Some of the media expressed genuine shock that my dad passed the cognitive test thirty for thirty. What, did they think my father built a globe-spanning business by being an idiot? Could an idiot get into politics in his late sixties and dismantle the entire establishment of both political parties, winning the highest office in the land? Could that same person then create the greatest economy and lowest unemployment in US history? It's not a fluke. Even today they continue to stupidly cling to the tired attack of Trump's mental acuity, despite all evidence that there's not one grain of truth in their narrative.

Now, what do you think the odds are that good old Joe Biden would take the Montreal Cognitive Assessment test? And what would his score be if he did? Because I think we would all really like to know—in fact, let me take that up a notch. America *needs* to know, preferably before the election, whether or not Joe Biden's history of aneurysms and other health issues have affected his ability to think and operate effectively.

I asked Dr. Jackson about Biden. He was quick to tell me, "There's such an incredible double standard with these people [in the media]. . . . To my knowledge, the president has never made one single flaw in anything he said that would ever lead anyone to believe that he has any cognitive issues whatsoever. . . . Vice President Biden does it every single day. So much so they won't even let him speak anymore! And nobody says a damn thing about it. It's crazy; it's hypocrisy at its highest."

If Trump made even *one* Joe Biden gaffe, they would never let it go—we would get a full telepsychiatrist diagnosis, ethics be damned. If Trump had suffered two brain aneurysms and had undergone brain surgeries, people would rightfully bring it up—they would be putting together cause and effect. And they would be right to question if he had a health history like Biden's! It would be a daily onslaught, but for Joe it's crickets.

Dr. Ronny Jackson is in a unique position as one of the few medical professionals who has spent time around both my father and Joe Biden. "I was not his doctor," Dr. Jackson explained to me, "but I saw him around a lot." The former admiral was quick to say that he's never seen Joe Biden's medical records and was not involved directly with his care and was not trying to diagnose Biden. "Speaking as someone who was in the White House, [I] saw him frequently around the West Wing and other places like that. I know he's always been prone to gaffes, but these aren't gaffes anymore. He can't form sentences. Sometimes he can't complete a thought. I mean, he gets stuck and he doesn't know how to get out of the situation that he's in. And he just finally has to give up."

He went on to say, "I won't make any particular diagnosis about dementia. . . . But what I will say is that something is not right."

Uncle Joe can't remember if he's running for president or

senator, but we are not supposed to talk about it. He has repeat-edly—day after day, even with a teleprompter—demonstrated he can't get it right. On May 25, 2020, Biden came out of his cave and had a two-point—*just two!* —response to my father's handling of the coronavirus, and he had two months locked in his basement to prepare it. He went on a live podcast to talk about it, and *he forgot both points!* I guess two points in two months was too much for Joe.

If it had been a forty-seven-point presentation and he had forgotten point twenty-nine, I could give him a pass. But two points to make? Two months to prepare. Presenting it, he was desperately waving his hands around, begging for help! It was just sad—or it would be, if it wasn't so serious. What's truly sad is ev-eryone pretending it's not an issue for America's future.

People, a rough day at the office for Uncle Joe is just going to be tying his shoes! How could we expect a man like this to be president of the United States? Is this man, with a history of gross incompetence, the person you want handling the launch codes for our nation's nuclear arms or responding to an immediate threat from a foreign power? It's kind of a big deal to be in charge of the free world—don't you think we should ask for proof that Biden is capable of handling it?

Dr. Jackson pointed out that this is not just an issue of age. People all across this country handle their age differently.

No, Biden's problems aren't an issue of age—they're an issue of *competence*. For multiple reasons, Joe Biden is simply no longer competent. Some people in their seventies seem pretty young, while others in their seventies are really, *really* old. Hell, as I get older, I see people my age who seem older than dirt. It's not about age. To pretend that Joe Biden, who's only a few years older than my father, is in the same real age category in terms of aptitude, competence, and energy as Donald Trump is just asinine. Just turn on the TV—you can see the evidence of it in a single press conference. When they questioned DJT, he offered himself up for an aptitude test—Joe's clearly not so willing to do the same. While Biden has claimed to have taken some tests multiple times, one might wonder why multiple tests are required to prove competence, unless one failed? I've yet to hear him say he took the Montreal Cognitive Assessment test, though.

Dr. Ronny Jackson commented on how age can affect our minds differently. "Some people can go all the way into their late nineties or live to be one hundred years old and still be sharp as a tack. Some people get into the early seventies and they start having cognitive disabilities and they start looking like they're old and they start sounding like they're old. They can't put thoughts together, and they forget things."

Dr. Jackson went on, "Some people age more gracefully than others, and I think [this is] the big difference between President Trump and Vice President Biden. President Trump is great—[he] is aging gracefully. He's still sharp as a tack. He's probably still as sharp as he was when he was in his fifties. And he may age to one hundred years old and be like that."

What about Biden? "Unfortunately, Vice President Biden is not like that. His age is showing, and it's showing aggressively at this point. Maybe there was a window for him to step out and be a candidate for president of the United States, but I'm a firm believer that that window has closed now. . . . His cognitive decline has got to a point where I'm not comfortable as a citizen of this country having him as my commander in chief. I'm not. So,

I think that . . . he's not aging gracefully, and he's a lot different than he was, say, eight years ago when he was around the White House. He always made those gaffes, like I said, but I never heard him where he got to a point where he didn't know where he was at or what he was running for. . . . The best way I can describe him every time I see him is that he's just lost."

I asked Dr. Jackson about Joe Biden's aneurysms. He spoke about the condition in general. An aneurysm "disrupts the blood supply to a certain part of your brain," he explained. "So, I think the long-term consequences are related to how big the aneurysm was, how extensive the bleed was." He went on to ask the important questions we should all want answered: How much brain tissue was affected? How long was it starved of oxygen? What part of the brain was affected—speech, memory?

"It all depends on where the aneurysm was located and how big the aneurysm was," he told me. Together we wondered what was "downstream" of the watershed—the aneurysm—in Joe Biden's brain. We may never know.

In modern history, can you think of a candidate who has more question marks around his health and ability to last a full term? Look at how much grayer Obama was after eight years under the stress of the office. Can you imagine how Joe will look—if he could even make it that long? Being president takes incredible stamina. My father routinely puts in grueling sixteen-hour days.

"The physical stress is incredible," Dr. Jackson explained of the job of president. "You never get a break." He said his stamina is one of the most impressive things about President Trump. "He can literally go for sixteen-hour days back to back, even overseas in another time zone on the other side of the planet, and he's still got the energy and the enthusiasm to finish the day. . . . So, the physical endurance that you have to have to do this job is pretty incredible."

I asked him about other presidents he served. He said President Bush rode his bike all the time and was in good shape. Dr. Jackson described President Obama as being in good physical shape as well, but obviously he was significantly younger. "He had the stamina. Bush had the stamina. Trump's got the stamina."

What about Joe Biden? Again, Dr. Jackson is not commenting on him as his doctor but as a person who has been around Biden personally. "Biden does not have that stamina—he's not going to have it," Dr. Jackson told me. "You can look at him now, and you can tell. There's no way. He's not going to have that kind of stamina, in my opinion. I'm not trying to make a medical diagnosis," Dr. Jackson affirmed. "I'm concerned."

As a citizen of this country and someone who has spent time around Biden, he's worried about Sleepy Uncle Joe sending the military into harm's way. He's worried about Biden's mental capacity and physical stamina to do the job. And he's very concerned about the double standard that would question Trump's abilities but not tolerate concerns about Biden's physical and mental ability to lead the free world. This is something we should all be able to agree on, but sadly, in 2020 it's a one-way street.

I don't think a reasonable human being can look at everything Joe Biden says—all the times he gets confused about major things like wife or sister, state, and office he's campaigning for—and not wonder if he's 100 percent there. That's a significant question to ask ourselves.

Biden can't even deliver a coherent speech to twenty or thirty supporters without a teleprompter. And, call me crazy, but I would think being able to talk to a handful of people for twenty minutes might be something he would have gotten good at after fifty years of practice. You know, it could come in handy for someone who wants to do this for a living. I mean, come on—can you imagine Biden doing daily coronavirus task force press briefings like my father did? Even with a press corps trying their hardest to help him manage, it would be a bloodbath.

Okay, so here's a scarier question: If you vote for Joe, who is really going to be in power? Many people feel like they're simply voting for whatever Democrat is on the ticket, but we need to be asking ourselves, "Why would the DNC want such a weak Joe Biden in office?" Scary thought—what if it's just because they know they can control him? Through him, whatever liberal has wrestled control behind the scenes could get their leftist wish list by pulling hapless Uncle Joe's strings. Is he really the best they've got, or is he just the easiest to control?

Do you really want conniving Nancy Pelosi, who shamelessly slipped billions of untold liberal pork into the stimulus packages, pulling Biden's strings? It could just as easily be imbecilic and incoherent babbler Alexandria Ocasio-Cortez (AOC) and her idiotic Green New Deal. What about Cryin' Chuck Schumer? Crazy Maxine Waters? How about Ilhan Omar and her reckless comments about wanting to "dismantle" our entire system? Dear God, no! Will it be whichever Democrat happens to be the thought leader and headline maker, like a Rashida Tlaib? Do you want any of these people manipulating the president?

Are you okay with electing a man whose health and capacity make him a likely straw man for whatever leftist extremist is calling the shots in the DNC at the moment? Don't for a moment think that it's going to be Obama's second coming. Consider about how long it took him to endorse his own VP—and even then, it was lackluster at best. Don't believe me, watch the virtual announcement yourself.[2]

Biden just isn't right—in the head or in his decisions. He's the only guy who didn't want to go kill the mass-murdering terrorist Osama bin Laden. In fact, documents released this year from the bin Laden raid showed that Osama bin Laden himself, America's most wanted terrorist, actually wanted *Biden* to be our president because he's so unprepared, he would be destructive to the USA.[3]

Think about this for a moment. A decade after bin Laden wished for Biden to get the top spot in the White House because he was so grossly unprepared for the job, the Democrats actually nominated Biden willingly! If Democrats have their way, Osama will get his wish in November. Endorsements are coveted in politics, but I'm pretty sure no one running for president wants that one—well, maybe just a few ladies in Congress.

Former Defense Secretary Robert Gates, a loyal Obama appointee, said in 2014 that Joe Biden "has been wrong on nearly every major foreign policy and national security issue over the past four decades."[4] This is Obama's guy lampooning Biden—someone from his own side! It's a big deal that Obama's own secretary of defense thinks Biden is a clown, never considering he would end up the nominee.

The Dems and their accomplices in the media trying to paint Biden as a moderate, but his positions will show he is not—far from it; he's a radical. Like on the Second Amendment: Biden said he would appoint as his gun czar—Beto "Hell, yes, we're gonna take your AR-15"[5] O'Rourke—something you don't do if you're a moderate on guns. Joe Biden has been confronted several times about his stance on the Second Amendment and his responses have tended to be quite hostile. For example, at a Fiat Chrysler Assembly plant visit, when asked if he would take guns away, Joe quickly lost his cool and started screaming at one of the workers, declaring: "You're full of shit. I did not—no, no, shush. Shush."[6] Sure, sounds like someone defensive to me. I have always been a supporter of the Second Amendment, a competitive shooter, a hunter, and a collector of firearms. I actually understand these issues. Joe Biden doesn't. I continue to be thankful to groups such as the NRA who protect us from loons such as Joe Biden, who preach one thing on the stump but practice another thing when elected to office. Make no mistake, the Obama-Biden administration was no friend to gun owners.

They're trying to make him seem like Blue-Collar Joe, but he absolutely is not. He is the definition of the leftist establishment elite. They're saying Biden is the man who can change things in DC, but if he was such a game changer, why hasn't he done anything about DC corruption over the last fifty years? What makes anyone think he can—or even wants to—change the system now? He is the epitome of the problem with DC. He hasn't changed a damn thing about the culture of entitlement and cronyism. He is a career politician who now can't even stitch together a complete two-point speech for a podcast.

Biden is a swamp creature to his core, as establishment as it gets.

We must honestly ask ourselves the tough questions. Is Biden fit to do the job? Is he able to do the job? And if he's not—if he has lost it and is just a puppet—who is pulling his strings? Do we really know who will be in charge? Do we really want that person who might be at odds with today's Joe Biden to be the shadow president?

And this is where it gets sticky. As I said earlier in this chapter, conservatives don't fight battles the way liberals do. We generally keep to certain rules, and for too long we've let the Democrats set the rules of the game—rules they then don't keep.

The Left is willing to do whatever it takes to win with no enduring code or moral compass. Their only guiding principle is to win so they can instill their socialist bullshit. And all this time, we real conservatives have been trying to play their game with one arm tied behind our backs because we don't stoop to their level. We're playing on an uneven battlefield, and the Left has been finding unscrupulous, unethical hacks—like every single doctor who signed off that they had diagnosed Trump without examining him, despite the Goldwater Rule—to further their narrative.

I'll admit, you may not always like what Donald Trump says—it's a personal style. Hell, we're from New York! It's been said like this: Obama lied to people very eloquently; Trump is brutal with the truth. I'm sorry if that offends people's delicate sensibilities, but the people it offends most are the ones who are willing to turn a blind eye to the double standard that threatens to destroy our country.

Donald Trump is the blunt person that America needs at this time. He's the guy who tells you what you *need* to hear, not necessarily what you want to hear. He's the disciplinarian parent we all required at some point in our lives. America has to have that disciplinarian now more than ever—there's too much at stake not to. He doesn't sugarcoat or bullshit you; he just gives you brutal honesty. Yeah, you may not always like the way he says things, but sometimes we all could use a kick in the ass from someone honest enough to say what needs to be said, even when it hurts.

But as long as we let them play their game—hardball with nails in their bats—while we line up with our plastic Wiffle balls, we're never going to get justice or fairness. We're always going to get a media that baselessly attacks conservatives and shamelessly covers for liberals.

Like him or not, my father is who he is. What you see is what you get—tough talk and decisive action that benefits all of America. The only president not elected by the establishment elite, he came in as the populist president and has proceeded to do what he said he would do. From achieving the lowest unemployment in history to nominating two conservative Supreme Court justices and over two hundred federal judges, to moving the US embassy to Jerusalem, Donald Trump has kept his promises.

Who will be pulling Biden's strings behind the curtain and become his puppet master in six months, a year, two years? Who will be creating the talking points for his speeches? Who will be setting his policy during a four-year term of office?

I'll tell you this: there is absolutely *no way of knowing* who will be in control of Joseph Robinette Biden Jr. tomorrow, in two years, or later.

I don't know about you, but I might be just a little bit more inclined to go with the hard-hitting guy with the track record that will save our economy than with the DC swamp creature who's lost his mind and could be easily manipulated by those who want to destroy this country.

Let me tell you why.

CHAPTER 4

The Wrong Side of History

Did you know that nearly two-thirds of all Americans living today were not even alive in 1972 when Joe Biden first entered politics?[1] I might think I feel old on some days, but in 1972, it would be another five years before I was even conceived.

Let me put into perspective exactly how long Biden has been entrenched in the Washington establishment, because we're talking *half a century*. When he first ran for office so many years ago, there were just 3.9 billion people in the world, today that number has nearly doubled. The average American made less than $13,000. A new car might run you $3,200, a house $32,500, and a gallon of gas $0.40. The highest-ranked TV programs included *All in the Family* (which could have never been made today), *M*A*S*H*, and *The Waltons*. If you went to the drive-in theater, you might take your girl to see *The Sting* or maybe *American Graffiti* while listening to "Tie a Yellow Ribbon" or maybe "Bad, Bad Leroy Brown" in your Ford Mustang Boss 302.

In short, half a century ago was a *completely different world*.

We were about to legalize abortion through *Roe v. Wade*, and the Islamic countries of the Middle East were ready to slash oil production and trigger a worldwide energy crisis that showed everyone they really had us where it hurt. Somewhat ironically, we finished building the World Trade Center right at this time, which Islamic extremists would knock down decades later. Watergate— the biggest political scandal until the attempted coup that tried but failed to unseat my father as duly-elected president of the United States—was about to blow up in Nixon's face.

Does all this set the stage for exactly how long Uncle Joe has been lurking in the hallways of the Senate? What were you doing in 1972? What were your *parents*—and *grandparents*—doing back then?

What if I told you that the same Joe Biden who was Barack Obama's vice president once ironically called state-mandated school integration "the most racist concept you can come up with"?[2] Integrating schools is *racist*? Wow! Another time Joe Biden actually said that the racial integration policies he opposed would cause his children to "grow up in a racial jungle."[3] Liberal privilege. Because let's be honest, if a conservative said anything remotely similar, their career would have been over long ago.

You see, when Biden's first campaign for Senate began in 1972, he set out in favor of desegregating American schools—only to flip-flop when he learned that his white Delaware constituency opposed integrating children of all races. That's right, when Joe first ran, we still had *segregated schools*—let that sink in—and he decided to roll with the white Delaware voters' pressure to keep it that way.[4] How has this guy not been canceled by woke liberals and BLM?

Biden actively opposed integrating schools across racial lines, betraying his so-called progressive values because his white Democrat Delaware voters didn't want their kids going to school with minority children.

That's kind of a big deal, especially when your party courts black voters by lying that you're the party who does more for minorities. These are the racially sensitive Democrats, advocates of all things that benefit minority voters, who would never ever do anything to screw them over and keep them in poverty, who would never vote to keep them in segregated schools, right?

Or at least that's the story they tell. But it's false.

You might be thinking, *That's fifty years ago, Don.* Well, how about we take a look at recent history? In a rare instance of the fake news tattling on one of its own, Biden is on record with the *New York Observer* showing his true colors regarding Obama (this is before he got offered the veep, of course). In 2007 Biden went par for the course and stuck his foot in his mouth, saying that Barack Obama was "the first mainstream African-American who is articulate and bright and clean and a nice-looking guy."[5] Imagine the utter fallout if DJT said that? He would be "canceled" so fast, your head would spin!

You may have heard of that one, but just go back and read it—*really* read it. The *first* mainstream *articulate, bright, clean* African American? There hadn't been any others, apparently, according to Biden. Sorry, Dr. King and Muhammad Ali, you weren't articulate and bright enough for Uncle Joe.

Just stop for a minute and think about this: Can you *even imagine* the hell my father or any Republican would catch, in 2007 or any other year, for making such a blatantly racist comment?

I think all the liberals in the media would simply explode with outrage—and they would actually have some fodder to use for that tired old trope that Republicans are all old, racist, white men. But no—this came from a supposedly enlightened Democrat, and while it's at least documented on CNN and other outlets (which often doesn't even happen these days), it's all now forgotten. All good—nothing to see here!

Why wasn't Biden crucified for his utterly unacceptable and tone-deaf characterization? How does he get a pass on this—and any of a dozen other gaffes he's made over the years—that show he is not an advocate of minorities but in fact is part of the liberal elite who have built themselves up, to the detriment of their constituents? Because the liberal media is nothing more than a propaganda machine and the talking points say that we can't confront Biden on his racist comments, we give him a pass.

Well, that's just unacceptable.

Biden opposed everything my father did that reduced African American unemployment to its lowest rate in history. An October 2019 report stated that "the jobless rate for Hispanics hit a record low of 3.9% in September, while African Americans maintained its lowest rate ever, 5.5%."[6] Biden would roll back the Tax Cuts and Jobs Act (TCJA) of 2017[7] and the thriving Opportunity Zones which brought hope along with hundreds of millions of dollars to low-income, economically depressed areas of nearly nine thousand neighborhoods.[8]

Biden didn't enact a sweeping prison reform bill—that was Trump. In fact, Biden crowed over his 1994 Violent Crime Control and Law Enforcement Act, which resulted in the mass incarcerations the Left blames for minority prison numbers. Biden

proudly said, "Lock the S.O.B.s up."[9] Don't just gloss over that—
he's saying to lock the sons of bitches up. So the guy who was
against busing, and for segregation, goes on to brag about being
tough on crime—but really was he tough on crime or just a racist? The reality shows that Joe Biden has bad judgment and his
legislation destroyed families and put its foot on the wealth of
African American communities.[10] Even the Center for American
Progress, no friend of conservatives, says this law exacerbates racial disparities in criminal justice and continues to undermine the
safety and well-being of communities of color.[11]

Yet, these days, he claims he's the one who can right injustices.
If Biden was going to fix any of these things, why didn't he do it
beside Obama for eight years? But now, after half a century, *now*
he's going to act? Give me a break! You can't escape the double
standard—either he's pro-minority by the Left's own standards,
or he's not.

He has proven time and again *he is not*.

Democrats didn't take the Hispanic unemployment to the
lowest it's ever been—that's Trump again. Biden certainly didn't
get more jobs to Asian Americans than ever before or empower
America's women with high-paying jobs thanks to his economic
policies. Under Obama, jobless rates *skyrocketed*.

How historic were job gains for minorities trying to change
generations of poverty under Donald J. Trump? The White
House released a statement that puts it into perspective: "Since
the President's 2016 election, the economy has added over 6.7
million jobs—more than the combined populations of Wyoming,
Vermont, Alaska, North Dakota, South Dakota, Delaware, Rhode
Island, and Montana in 2018. Additionally, this total is 4.8 million

more jobs than the Congressional Budget Office projected would have been created in its final forecast before the 2016 election. . . . Most notably, the unemployment rate for African Americans reached a new low of 5.4 percent, falling 2.6 percentage points since President Trump's election."[12] For anyone with a brain, that is a big deal.

Not only that, the labor force participation rate—a critical metric for measuring how many people are trying to work—saw steady gains under my father's pre–COVID-19 economy. Seemingly small percentage points of change in the labor force participation rate actually add up to major boosts for the economy. In the same White House statement, these changes to the labor force participation rate indicated that "2.1 million more prime-age adults were in the labor force in October compared to if the participation rate remained at November 2016 levels."

In short, *minorities* saw some of the greatest benefits in the Trump economy, and Donald Trump put more Americans to work than had existed in the workforce in decades. Democrats didn't do any of this! Biden had fifty years, and he has never done anything to help minorities that didn't make them more dependent on him and his fellow liberals. It took my father coming into office to shake things up and make America's economy great again after Obama had already read us its obituary. "What magic wand do you have?" Obama asked my father back in 2016. Well, I think we answered him—maybe there *was* a magic wand. Abracadabra! Obama just didn't have it, and Biden certainly doesn't!

You can argue with my father's tone of brutal honesty, but he's absolutely not a racist and has done more to get the vulnerable minority populations up onto their own two feet than Joe Biden could ever dream of doing. What would you rather have?

Someone who tells it like it is and has helped you off welfare, into a job, and participating in the American economy? Or someone who lies to you, saying they're sensitive to racial issues yet holds you down in poverty, and after half a century in DC is doing nothing to help you become proud and independent? Biden knowns that your dependence means you'll vote for him, so why would he really help you?

For far too long, Democrats such as Biden, Pelosi, and Schumer have taken minorities, immigrants, and many other constituents for granted. They don't even compete for their vote anymore because they assume it's automatically theirs. All the while the policies the Left supports have done very little, except to keep those citizens dependent upon government. That is the definition of liberal privilege.

I've seen what my father has done for minorities before and during politics, though I was pretty young when he received the Ellis Island Medal of Honor by the Statue of Liberty-Ellis Island Foundation in 1986, along with Rosa Parks, Muhammad Ali, and seventy-eight others.[13] In 1998, Jesse Jackson praised my father for his commitment to "under-served communities"—minorities.[14] Who? The very same people my father's policies helped get jobs and off their dependency on liberal Democrat handouts.

In my book *Triggered*, I talk about how when I was little we would have Michael Jackson over to play Nintendo all the time. We were neighbors in Trump Tower. And when I was only six I went on vacation to the Bronx Zoo and Disney World with Herschel Walker, the Heisman Trophy winner, and his family. Herschel's wife just about killed herself riding my dirt bike at our family's house in Connecticut one weekend. I recently joked with Herschel on my *Triggered* podcast, along with NFL legend Burgess

Owens, about the irony of the media trying to portray my father as a racist while ignoring all the positive things he's done and the lifelong friendships he's had with minorities. It's amazing that DJT only became a racist when he decided to run for office.

After all these decades of love from the establishment, they now declare my father a threat. He ran for president and his conservative Republican politics suddenly, magically made him a *racist overnight*. Only an idiot would accuse my father of being a racist—but that's pretty much the liberal establishment playbook, because it's one of the only attacks they know.

The Dems have been playing the racist card for as long as I can remember, and here's one of the problems with that strategy: it's like the boy who cried wolf. When you cry "racist" over the stupidest little things all the time, eventually people start to tune you out. Then one day when there is real, racially insensitive stuff coming out of someone's mouth—like Joe Biden's gaffes—either no one listens because they're burned out, or it goes unremarked because the speaker happens to be a liberal Democrat who gets a free pass. "Racist" has become the easy button of left-wing politics, but when you always overplay your hand and bring nothing new, it becomes ineffective and does a huge disservice to those actually affected, as real racism is then blown off and ignored.

Democrats who claim that things like racism are big issues for them are willing to ignore the fact that their nominee began his political career on the wrong side of virtually *all* racial issues and hasn't improved much since. Even decades later, Biden's clueless statements about Obama himself clearly show that he does not share progressives' values about race. So how do Biden's real voting record and the principles he has stood on for fifty years get shoved under the carpet?

The media will try to convince people that Joe Biden is a viable candidate, brilliant orator, wonderful politician, good all-around blue-collar American guy, and an advocate for minorities. But he is none of those things! He's a puppet moron DC swamp creature!

Let's look at what he's actually done. This is the guy who started out spinning the party line about enlightened liberal policies, dutifully calling Republicans racist bigots, but soon he subtly changed his tune. As he campaigned, he realized that his voters in the north didn't support desegregation—that was maybe for those people "down south" where racists had been in charge for years and made laws that needed fighting—but not up north in Delaware—no sir, no racists lived in Delaware, no kids there needed busing to integrate school districts.

Joe teetered back and forth in those early years, failing to adopt a hard line against desegregation and forced busing, but waffling instead—until he joined causes with like-minded individuals who also opposed integration and shared similar views on racial issues. This group, with Biden, *opposed* a federal movement to integrate schools all across the country by voting down a measure that would require schools to provide racial information on their student bodies.[15]

Fortunately for the advancement of civil rights in our country, Biden *failed*.

Joe sticks his foot in his mouth on racial issues every time he comments on them, yet the political pundits still expect him to carry the African American vote. If Donald Trump made even a single Joe Biden–style error, every mainstream media telepsychologist would be telling us that DJT has lost his mind and is in the later stages of dementia or Alzheimer's, or perhaps a combination of both. Joe says dumb things every single day, and no one says a word.

Biden went on *The Breakfast Club* radio show in May 2020 and spouted off, "Well I tell you what, if you have a problem figuring out whether you're for me or Trump, then you ain't black."[16] He reminded me of a poor imitation of when Hillary Clinton would hilariously channel her inner African American during a speech! On *The Breakfast Club*, she even said she carried hot sauce in her purse.[17] *You carry hot sauce in your purse?* Yeah, sure you do, Hillary! You're full of shit!

Few today discuss Biden's dozens of problematic bills which disproportionally targeted minorities or his countless wrong votes. Biden wasn't tough on crime; Biden enabled a broken system to go after disenfranchised communities, and unfairly. Add to this Biden's constant gaffes and soft spot for former segregationist politicians like James Eastland and Herman Talmadge,[18] and I can't understand why any reasonable person would think he's the candidate that will stand up for minorities.

When working with a teleprompter, Biden can talk the talk. Well, not really, but it's better than him trying to give a speech without one. But never mind his fluffy words—what is his *track record?* How can anyone confuse the impact of what Biden has done for minorities (empty words and destructive crime legislation) with what my father has done (record unemployment, prison reform, and Opportunity Zones)?

It can't possibly have anything to do with the incredible, multibillion-dollar advertising campaign the fake news media has done for free for Democrats for the last few decades, can it? Do you think that if every liberal news network says the same

Republicans-are-racists talking points long enough, people will believe it? Hell, they probably even believe it themselves, they've been telling the lie so long. Generations have grown up hearing that Biden—remember, he's been a fixture of the swamp for *half a century*—is this blue-collar, hardworking American who every minority should vote for, but every time he opens his mouth he reveals that's not the truth at all. Joe Biden was elected into the DC swamp in his late twenties; he never had any real, blue-collar job. He got to Washington as fast as he could, he created an aura of being a blue-collar Joe, yet reality is, he's the furthest thing from that.

Joe tells people that government has failed them, but he wants *more* of it! He claims he can fix it, but he's been part of the problem for five decades. He says he is for minorities, but from the get-go his voting record has shown that as an absolute lie.

I don't know if I would run with saying that big government has failed you, Mr. Biden, because people might just see through the smoke and mirrors and marketing hype to realize *you've* been part of the problem all along. If you knew how to fix the economy, why didn't you tell Barack Obama?

Have you taken a look at who runs the largest cities in America? New York, Washington, Los Angeles, Minneapolis, San Francisco, Houston—every single one of them is run by Democrats! And have been run by Democrats for decades! If there is any blame, look at the local officials for mismanaging those places into the ground. You would think that maybe my father's record unemployment numbers for minorities might speak for themselves, but aside from the handful of conservative outlets, you would be hard pressed to find good press about what has happened as a result of Trump's economic policies.

You may not remember, but during the 2019 Democratic debates, Kamala Harris absolutely destroyed Biden on his record. While she claimed she didn't think he was a racist, she then proceeded to rub his nose in his nostalgia for working with people like Jesse Helms. She was, after all, one of those little girls he fought to prevent from being bused into an integrated school. Harris's attack was effective and had bumbling Joe lying to cover up his record on busing.

Then after the debate, she suddenly stopped. Where once you had heard Joe attacked on his race and voting record, now you only hear crickets. That certainly wouldn't have anything to do with her wanting to be in the running to be his VP, would it? The minute Joe became the presumptive nominee, no longer were there any questions about whether he's a racist. Amazing. Now that Kamala Harris was running for VP and not for president, Joe magically became totally *not* a racist—despite a long record saying exactly the opposite.

On paper, this election should be a no-brainer, but a sly marketing gimmick worth billions perpetrated by the fake news media has positioned "Blue-Collar" Joe as the choice for minorities. You no longer hear him held accountable for how he's acted, voted, and spoken during his fifty years in office. None of that is even remotely relevant anymore!

You do not hear the truth from the liberal media propaganda machine, and you never will between now and November 3.

Fifty years is a long time to accomplish so little yet continue to do so much damage. If Joe were capable of telling the truth, he would say, "I accomplished nothing during my fifty years in Washington. Please give me a chance to continue to fail."

Put Biden's segregationist policies up against Trump's policies. We have Biden's failed methods as opposed to Trump's deliverables for every American. Donald J. Trump got it done, reversing decades of damage from Biden's community-destroying, education-killing 1994 bill. Trump introduced Opportunity Zones made possible thanks to his sweeping tax cuts, but Biden would cancel these tax breaks stopping new investments in some of our most poverty-stricken communities.

If Joe Biden actually *wanted* or had the ability to right any of these wrongs, he would have done it already. Donald J. Trump just did it all, but no one is willing to say it. So, who is on the wrong side of history, and who is on the right?

And who is someone you better keep your eye on around your loved ones?

CHAPTER 5

A Tale of Two Bidens

I could get into a lot of trouble for this, but all I can do is call it like I see it—Joe Biden is downright creepy. If you want to cringe a little, watch some of the video compilations of good old Uncle Joe sniffing hair and making women and kids feel uncomfortable.[1] I can't get over how he continues to do it, even when they flinch away. Just look at the expressions of dread and fear on children's faces as he paws at them, or on the faces of parents who pull their kids away. Look at the young teenage girls who stand still, frozen stiff, as he rearranges their hair. There is no self-respecting guy in America who would knowingly let someone touch his kids that way without wanting to take him out to the woodshed for a lesson on boundaries. Notice, no one pipes up to defend Joe and say this is all totally normal.

In pointing out this behavior, I have led the media outrage cycle. I admit, the joke I put up might have been in bad taste, but it also drew media attention to something they try to sweep under the rug. The joke was a meme of Joe Biden saying, "See you later, alligator," and a picture of a cartoon alligator saying, "In a while, pedophile." Oh, man, the *New York Times*, Anderson Cooper at CNN, and others exploded with outrage.

Why isn't that outrage directed toward actual video and photographic evidence of Biden hugging and sniffing and making people squirm? He's *earned* the nickname Creepy Joe because there's something to it. After their response, I posted a four-minute thirty-second video compilation of him touching and sniffing kids and doing some bizarre stuff. All commonly available video of actions Biden has displayed *on camera*, if anyone will look.

Think about this for a second: Joe does this creepy stuff on camera in front of big audiences. If he's okay with making women and kids so uncomfortable in public, what does he do in private? I'll tell you this—he won't be babysitting my kids anytime soon.

After I posted the meme, what really got me was no one denied Biden as creepy—they only complained that my joke was in bad taste. So, after they watched the video, I asked everyone if they would allow their kids to be around this guy, and guess what—their response was unanimous, even among the liberal-privileged crowd: *No!*

You grandfathers, do you kiss your granddaughters on the lips? Who does that? I'll tell you who: Joe Biden. This wasn't one of those situations where they went in for a kiss on the cheek and then missed or thought she was breaking right while he went left, and they ended up with a little accidental contact. This was just a totally normal kiss on the mouth.[2] Nobody does that with a daughter, let alone a granddaughter!

They try to cancel my father because Ivanka sat on his lap in a couple of family photos, and he's proudly bragged about her modeling career. But Joe Biden touches, sniffs, and kisses kids and doesn't understand how creepy he is—and no one calls him on it.

At least eight different women have come forward to allege that Joe Biden has made them uncomfortable, touched them, sniffed them, or done something else inappropriate. Former intern Vail Kohnert-Yount accused Biden of putting his hand on the back of her neck and pushing their foreheads together as they spoke. "I was so shocked that it was hard to focus on what he was saying," she reported. "I remember he told me I was a 'pretty girl.'"[3] Caitlyn Caruso felt uncomfortable when Biden held on to a hug for just too damn long and touched her thigh when she was just nineteen, ironically at a sexual assault awareness event at the University of Nevada at Las Vegas.[4] "It doesn't even really cross your mind that such a person would dare perpetuate harm like that," she explained to the *New York Times*. "These are supposed to be people you can trust."[5]

Lucy Flores wrote of Biden touching her inappropriately in 2014 by coming up behind her, putting his hands on her shoulders, smelling her hair (of course), and kissing the back of her head. "My brain couldn't process what was happening. I was embarrassed. I was shocked. I was confused," she wrote. "The vice-president of the United States of America had just touched me in an intimate way reserved for close friends, family, or romantic partners—and I felt powerless to do anything about it . . . Even if his behavior wasn't violent or sexual, it was demeaning and disrespectful."[6]

Tara Reade, a former Senate aide, has accused Biden of sexually assaulting her in 1993, twenty-seven years ago, as I write this book. She said he would repeatedly "put his hand on my shoulder and run his finger up my neck" during the months she worked in his Senate office.[7] Reade filed a complaint with the Senate personnel office regarding "sexual harassment and retaliation," but she didn't bring up the worst of it. In March 2020, Reade came forward and accused Biden of "pressing her against a wall in a Capitol Hill corridor, reaching under her skirt, and digitally penetrating her."[8] When she brought the complaint against Biden, her responsibilities were reduced, and then she was asked to leave.[9] Reade's story has more corroborating evidence than there ever was against Supreme Court Justice Brett Kavanaugh, with Reade's mother having called in to *Larry King Live* in 1993 about problems with a "prominent senator."[10] You can watch the episode from August 11, 1993, when her mother asked what someone could do if she weren't willing to go to the press.[11] Court records from 1996 show that Tara Reade also complained to her then-husband about being sexually harassed.[12] And she didn't just tell him and her mother; she told friends and her brother.[13]

If it were a conservative who did these horrible acts, it wouldn't be only a problem, it would be Headline News, Breaking News, News That's Fit to Print, 24-7. But because Tara Reade's complaint is against a prominent Democrat, those who ideologically should stand up for Reade are betraying their own values and exposing their biases. Welcome to liberal privilege.

Biden responded to these and other allegations by saying it never happened and an apology that wasn't an apology.[14] We've watched the media, who try to crucify people like Brett Kavanaugh with less evidence, try to sweep the Creepy Joe narratives under the carpet.

Now, I thought in this woke era, we were always supposed to believe it when women (*plural*) accuse men, *especially* creepy, old, white men, of sexual assault, without any question or hesitation. #MeToo was supposed to fight for the freedom of all women from sexual harassment, right? After all, a fraction of this evidence from Christine Blasey Ford was enough for the Left to nearly scuttle Kavanaugh's nomination. So where's the anger? Where are the bandwagons of infuriated, liberated women #Me-Too-ing the *eight* women who have been brave enough to come forward? Where's the National Women's Law Center, who tried to stop Kavanaugh's nomination?

Nowhere to be found, that's where—because Biden gets the full benefit of liberal privilege. They rushed to believe Ford; her testimony was treated as infallible and 100 percent accurate, even though nothing substantiated it, and she couldn't remember most of the details. In what year did it happen? She couldn't remember. But she didn't need *evidence*—she *felt* so strongly.

In an article comparing the accusations against Kavanaugh and Biden, *The Atlantic* sums up beautifully the problem for these lefty women who have betrayed Biden's accusers: "Condemning Biden carries a clear cost for these groups. They believe that four more years of President Donald Trump would be immensely damaging for their policy agendas and for women in general."[15] The Left hates Trump more than they love their "virtuous" beliefs. They're leaving these eight women and any others out in the cold because Biden is a liberal, and they hate Trump more than they want the perception of justice for all women accusing an attacker.

The entire left-wing media complex, the #MeToo movement, and everyone who claims to believe all women, revealed themselves to be a bunch of hypocritical liars. They can make all the right sounds about helping abused women and make sure their voices are heard—until it's a Democrat who is being accused. Believe all women—as long as they attack Republicans. Don't believe all women—if they attack Democrats. If they're going after Joe Biden, they've gotta be #fullofschiff.

In other words, liberals play by different rules.

If Biden were a conservative, he would be canceled for these accusations and forced to resign, but he gets the protection of the hypocrites on the Left because he's a liberal. When Senate staffer Tara Reade accuses Biden, the media is silent. Since Ford attacked a Trump-appointed judge, the media believed it must be true. They were willing to utterly destroy Kavanaugh—his career, his family, his reputation—on a rumor.

Yet it may go a level deeper. In his investigative book, *Search and Destroy: Inside the Campaign Against Brett Kavanaugh*, author Ryan Lovelace describes Debra Katz, Ford's lawyer, speaking on video about Ford's motivations. Katz indicates that Ford was motivated to prevent justices from altering *Roe v. Wade* by casting an asterisk on anything Kavanaugh might accomplish after being appointed. Problem number one, according to Lovelace, is that Katz's statements contradict Ford's testimony. Number two, the video of Katz ranting about Kavanaugh and her client, Ford, was available for months—with no comment from the media.[16] Had the senators and FBI agents in the Kavanaugh case known of these motivations, would it have changed the questions they asked? Was Ford's accusation a politically motivated hit attempt to destroy a Trump-appointed Supreme Court justice? We may never know, but investigative reporters with any integrity should consider the possibility and do their damn homework instead of acting as activists for every Never-Trump Leftist. Pro tip: They still won't!

Don't believe Joe Biden would sexually grope or fondle a woman? Despite the videos of him touching and sniffing like a weirdo, maybe you still think there's zero chance Uncle Joe would touch a woman inappropriately, let alone assault her? I would ask some of the female Secret Service agents how they feel when "COBRA COBRA COBRA" gets whispered through the radio.

The *Urban Dictionary* defines the phrase "COBRA COBRA COBRA" as the warning call male Secret Service agents give female agents when Creepy Joe is buck naked and on the move.[17] Now there's a mental picture for you! Given that I have a Secret Service detail, I may or may not have people I know with intimate knowledge of this problem, because "COBRA" alerts can happen at any time—you have to be on your toes.

Joe has a history of making female Secret Service agents uncomfortable by swimming in the nude. In Ronald Kessler's book *The First Family Detail*, he describes accounts from agents who saw more than they probably ever wanted to see of Joe Biden. Kessler writes, "Agents say that, whether at the vice president's residence or at his home in Delaware, Biden has a habit of swimming in his pool nude."[18]

Agents describe the Biden assignment as the second worst in the Secret Service.[19] The only one worse than Biden? "Agents consider being assigned to Hillary Clinton's detail a form of punishment and the worst assignment in the Secret Service because she is so nasty to them and the 'little people' she claims to champion," Kessler told *U.S. News & World Report*.[20] In contrast, Kessler says Secret Service agents speak glowingly of Obama and guess who—my father. Why? Because they treat them "with consideration and respect."[21]

I would never betray their trust; I have become friends with many Secret Service agents. But, man, I could write an entire book on stories I have heard about some of these politicians. Trust me, they are worse than you can imagine.

Biden's reputation is so bad, reports have been filed on Joe's nudity, but it's likely you won't hear a thing about them. The media isn't even trying to directly present facts without interpretation anymore; they're out to get political scalps by canceling as many people as they can who think differently than they do.

The political writers come after me regularly with multiple, thousand-word, fake news hit pieces their editors demand them to write. They don't want to burn their bridges with me and when I call them out, these whiny, little writers oftentimes can't seem to handle it. I do have a good working relationship with several major journalists to whom I've brought great scoops. They've known me for years and know I've never lied to them. Yet, they can't write the articles—not because the information is not good and truthful, but because these writers know what their editors will do to them and how it will fly at *their publications*.

A revealing example occurred in July 2020, when Bari Weiss, an opinion writer at the *New York Times* and self-described centrist, quit her job and then wrote a resignation letter exposing what we all knew was true. She said this about the *New York Times*:

> The lessons that ought to have followed the election—lessons about the importance of understanding other Americans, the necessity of resisting tribalism, and the centrality of the free exchange of ideas to a democratic society—have not been learned. Instead, a new consensus has emerged in the press, but perhaps especially at this paper: that truth isn't a process of collective discovery, but an orthodoxy already known to an enlightened few whose job is to inform everyone else.

Twitter is not on the masthead of *The New York Times*. But Twitter has become its ultimate editor. . . .

Showing up for work as a centrist at an American newspaper should not require bravery. . . .

But the truth is that intellectual curiosity—let alone risk-taking—is now a liability at *The Times*. . . .

The paper of record is, more and more, the record of those living in a distant galaxy, one whose concerns are profoundly removed from the lives of most people.[22]

I don't conform to the media narrative and won't comply with their desires. Why is it okay to lie about conservatives with no ramifications? They constantly try to lay perjury traps for Trump and his people—ask me about that sometime—and will exploit any small misstatement. Why aren't we similarly asking if Ford and others lied in their testimonies? Why isn't the shoe ever on the other foot? Where's the #MeToo movement for Tara Reade?

Where's the justice for every conservative the Left has tried to cancel, like Pastor Chris Hodges of Church of the Highlands, the biggest church in Alabama and one of the most diverse churches in the entire state. Some *fifty thousand* people come to Church of the Highlands at their numerous campuses to worship and listen to Hodge's practical talks every week. But after an out-of-control police officer killed George Floyd, an English teacher accused Hodges of being insensitive because he liked a couple of tweets from conservative Christian and one of my great friends, Charlie Kirk.[23] Can't have that, now, can we?

The result? The church's "Dream Team," consisting of hundreds of volunteers, were forced to stop mentoring kids and helping public housing communities.[24] How dare they try to help and love on kids and disadvantaged people! On June 8, 2020, the Birmingham Housing Authority voted to quit accepting the church's free help and also canceled Christ Health Center, which provided public health services for some of the poorest people in Birmingham.[25] In other words, Pastor Hodge's free speech not only got him "canceled," but the media backlash against him also canceled youth mentoring, help for poor people in public housing, and health services the church provided *for free*.

It's out in the open—the liberals hate conservatives more than they love helping disadvantaged Americans.

To the Left, freedom of speech is only free if you agree with them. Don't you dare try to exercise your right of freedom of expression if it's conservative. Or Christian. Or anything else they deem "socially insensitive" today. That's just outrageous, and you're likely to get canceled and all your horrible "good deeds" stopped.

Ask the thousands of people about it that Church of the Highlands *was* helping. I'm sure they're glad to no longer receive any mentoring for their kids, practical help, and medical care, all to teach that insensitive pastor a lesson! What a bunch of crap!

There is no one the Left will not try to destroy for saying or thinking anything different than they do, even kids or charitable nonprofits. The double standard strategy of the Left is obvious and sickening. It's antithetical to everything that made America great.

Everyone knows "Good ole Joe" isn't so good after all. By shining a blistering light on him and the duplicity of the media, we can agree with the *Washington Post* on at least one thing. Under their masthead, they declare "Democracy Dies in Darkness." We welcome, out in the open, the whole truth and nothing but the truth. I wonder if Joe does?

Can it get worse than this? How about unprecedented abuse of power?

CHAPTER 6

It Didn't Work

Nothing like this has ever happened before in the history of our country. Swamp dwellers, emboldened by the media and other players, feel like they can get away with anything because they believe they have all the power and are holding all the cards. What a crock.

It's a place where Hillary Clinton can pay foreign agents to dig up dirt on my father—and when they can't find anything true, they make up whatever they want. She can waltz that falsified dossier to the Democratic National Committee, who can send it to the FBI, who can leak it to the press. The marketing wing of the DNC—the fake news media—can make up insane, false stories that the FBI can use as a basis for an investigation into an active campaign for president of the United States.

President Barack Obama, Vice President Joe Biden, National Security Advisor Susan Rice, FBI Director James Comey, CIA Director John Brennan, and others can all be in on it and can remove some of our privacy protections by unmasking us just eight days before the inauguration. I was unmasked, along with my brother, sister, and numerous members of the incoming administration. What reason is there to unmask someone a week before the new team takes over? Imagine the outrage if George W. Bush had done this to Obama a week before he took office. The media would still be talking about it.

Respected and nationally recognized legal scholar, Jonathan Turley, said this in an article for *The Hill*:

> When candidate Donald Trump said the Obama administration placed his campaign officials under surveillance, the media universally mocked him. That statement was later proven to be true. The Obama administration used the secret Foreign Intelligence Surveillance Act court to conduct surveillance of Trump campaign officials. . . .
>
> The media portrayed both Obama and Biden as uninvolved. But now we know they both actively followed the investigation. According to former acting attorney general Sally Yates, she was surprised that Obama knew about the investigation and knew more than she did at the time. Obama called upon former FBI director James Comey to stay after a meeting to discuss the investigation. Comey had mentioned using the Logan Act to charge Flynn, even though the unconstitutional law has never been used successfully in a prosecution since the country was founded.
>
> Biden has repeatedly denied knowledge of the investigation. Just a day before the latest disclosure, George Stephanopoulos asked Biden in an interview what he knew of the Flynn investigation. Biden was adamant that he knew

nothing about "those moves" and he called it a diversion. But that is not true if he took the relatively uncommon action for a vice president of demanding the unmasking of Flynn information.[1]

And still, for all their lying and cheating, they weren't able to keep the American people from electing my father to the presidency. We won.

This whole fiasco fueled two years of an unprecedented witch hunt, the entire Mueller farce. Every day brings new truths revealing how empty their accusations were. But that doesn't matter, right? This was one of the biggest stories in the world for over two years, and the media covered it ad nauseam. It was only when it became clear that the Obama administration was doing exactly what they accused us of that magically no one had any further interest in the story. Two years of speculation and false stories, and now no one wanted any more information. When it became clear there was a smoking gun, when Rick Grenell revealed the names of those who had the information of the unmasked, it was a one-day story, at best. Plenty of media went out of the way to diminish, dismiss, or simply ignore.

The Democrats think they're above the very law that's supposed to ensure we are all treated equally. Try loading national secrets on a mom-and-pop server and see how nice they are to you—you can tell me how it went from *prison*. The leftist elites can get away with all these things because the liberal media is deep in their pockets and won't do anything to jeopardize the goose that lays the golden eggs. These elites believe they have enough power to put in the fix whenever they want, and if you've been watching they may be right. And though they keep trying, I'm not putting up with it anymore.

Did you hear the story about the three ministers, two retired judges, and two rabbis who walked into a bar—well, actually, they filed a complaint with the Alcohol Beverage Control Board to revoke Trump International Hotel's liquor license. Their grounds? That the president of the United States, one Donald J. Trump, lacked sufficient moral character to be granted a renewal to the liquor license.[2] Understand, the Board gives liquor licenses to strip clubs and bars where people are stabbed and murdered; somehow, they have the moral character to obtain liquor licenses. But Donald Trump, leader of the free world, who isn't involved in the day-to-day operations of Trump International Hotel, is morally bankrupt?

And it gets better. We hired a private investigator to check things out, and he discovered that one of the liberal clergymen filing the complaint had lied about his residence to make the claim. You have to be a DC resident to have the standing to complain, but most of the accusers didn't live in or own property in DC.

I just had to laugh, because they're saying my father lacks the moral character to have a liquor license while lying about their addresses! Moral character, eh? Pastor, don't you know that those who live in glass cathedrals (particularly outside the District) shouldn't throw stones?

There's an ugly double standard in our country, and it's time for it to stop. I'm finished with being a good, quiet conservative while they outrageously lie about my father, you, and me. I'm tired of putting up with the bull the fake news shovels daily and the pass they give the liberal elite of this country, no matter how corrupt the Democrats are.

Aren't you sick of it too—the constant stream of negative press, false narratives, and vicious witch hunts? Aren't you tired of your beliefs being belittled and mocked, while those like my father who speak up for hardworking Americans like you, face backlash for anything they try to do that gives conservative America a voice?

If you have a point of view or a political background the liberal elite doesn't like, you face everything from being de-platformed, demonetized, or worse on online to butthurt outrage on Twitter to organized violence by Antifa. Today, if you even question BLM, you're canceled. If you support anything Trump has done, you're canceled. Hell, if you try to be apolitical, you're canceled for not being vocal enough—for the liberal narrative only, of course.

A *New York Post* article says "no one is safe":

In the course of a week, three editors went down: James Bennet of the *Times* was canceled for publishing an opinion on the opinion page about Senator Tom Cotton's defense of the Insurrection Act, which permits the use of federal troops to quell riots; Claudia Eller was pushed out at *Variety* (suspended, formally, but not expected to return to her position) after penning a white-privilege mea culpa that was found to be unconvincing; and Adam Rapoport of *Bon Appétit* was canned for much the same reason, his offense aggravated by a turn-of-the-century photograph of him dressed as a stereotypical Puerto Rican at a Halloween party. [As someone with a Puerto Rican girlfriend, I will neither confirm nor deny if Kimberly makes me dress up in stereotypical outfits.] But faux claims of racism are far from the only thing that can cost someone a job in these

stupid times, and it isn't only public figures who are targeted. Fender, a guitar maker, exiled a master guitar-builder
after he tweeted an ugly joke (a blood-covered Jeep over
the caption "What protesters on the freeway?") at the expense of the recent demonstrations.[3]

Was it a tasteless tweet, sure? But when Kathy Griffin holds
up a decapitated bloody severed head of my father, some on the
Left find it acceptable. Better manners won't save you: A data
analyst and veteran of the Obama reelection campaign was fired
by Civis Analytics for tweeting a link to a paper written by a
well-regarded (and, worth noting, biracial) Princeton professor
of African American studies finding that riots are bad for black
communities. No criticism, however respectful or intelligent, is
to be permitted.

You can never be woke enough, the goal posts move daily.
What is woke today is alt-right tomorrow. It's impossible to keep
up.

The *New York Post* article went on to say,

These people were not fired for using racial slurs or
engaging in abuse. They were fired for giving voice to
views the mob wishes to see silenced. Of course, there is
rampant hypocrisy. The editor of *Bon Appétit* had to go, but
as recently as 2019 the Liberal prime minister of Canada
and the Democratic governor of Virginia both survived
blackface scandals resulting from some of those "youthful
indiscretions" the politicians are always going on about.[4]

But *they're* free to talk about anything they want, anyone they
want, in any way they want.

I wouldn't even bother to talk about it now, but I've been so relentlessly and ruthlessly attacked that I am just tired of quietly taking it. What do you think the media would do if I returned a rental car with a fresh crack pipe still warm in the back seat? (As some have alleged on Hunter Biden.)[5] They would have a smokin' field day!

You know, I'm almost tempted to do something Hunter has done, just to see the difference in the reaction—not because I want to go to Ukraine or develop a potential crack habit. I think I could solve the fake news media problem with one act because I'm pretty sure their heads would explode with outrage! There wouldn't be anyone left, and we could finally get on with our lives.

They spent over three years trying to manufacture evidence that I had committed treason—*treason*! But they don't bat an eye that Hillary Clinton can pay foreign agents to find dirt on my father. If a conservative politician had gotten caught in an abuse of power of this magnitude, it would be the story of the century. The media would never let it die. Instead, this is just another example of the unthinkable level of bias and the double standard affecting this country.

Imagine if George W. Bush had his FBI try to set up Obama? Since 1789, we've had a peaceful transition of power in America that has set us apart from most of the rest of the world—that's over two hundred years of peaceful transfers.[6] Never before has that been threatened like it was under the Obama-Biden transition with Hillary trying to cheat her way to victory. Never before has the Washington establishment tried to steal an election and, failing that, destroy a duly-elected president of the United States like they have desperately tried to do to Donald J. Trump.

Brave souls like Tucker Carlson, Peter Schweizer, Gregg Jarrett, and a handful of others fought the establishment. They followed this story, covering the unimaginable abuse of power that was happening right under our very noses. Breaking a story like this against a conservative would make a liberal journalist's career. It could irreparably damage a party, but what amounts to a coup attempt against a duly-elected president of the United States has gone unreported or derided as a wild conspiracy. Ignoring that they pushed their own wild conspiracy for three years.

Why? Because it goes against the leftist narrative. Corruption like this goes against the spin created around the Democrat leaders and the liberal media. As I've explained, the major media of this country has made the conscious decision to be the marketing wing of the DNC. But what a lousy product to sell! If anything, we should be looking into what this means for campaign finance abuse because they have given the DNC countless billions of free marketing for many years like they were handing out candy.

We conservatives have turned our heads and quietly taken the abuse for years, but that isn't how I work. During the Jim Comey testimony, I blew many people's minds by live tweeting during the process. My lawyers told me, "You can't do that; they will use it against you." Do you want to know what I said back?

I. Don't. Care.

And that's how I feel when confronting this double standard—I don't care what they think or how they'll respond to what I say. This is bullshit, and I won't be quiet anymore. I love our country too much. When you're not afraid to be canceled, it's very cathartic because you now have the freedom to fight like the Democrats.

You see, we've been making one critical mistake. We conservatives have thought that if we just curled up in the corner in a fetal position sucking our thumbs, they would go easy on us. Breaking news! They're not going to leave us alone or go away, just like any bully wouldn't, and the only way to deal with them is to stand up to them as my father has.

During the three-year Russia hoax "investigation," assclown Adam Schiff was on TV every day lying through his teeth and claiming he had actually seen the evidence that I had committed treason. Strange that to this day no one else has seen it! I wasn't going to sit back and let him have his way. Every time we took a bathroom break from the House "Intelligence" Committee, Schiff leaked his way to and from the men's room, disclosing to CNN what was happening in a closed hearing. When I saw my Twitter feed at seven o'clock at night, I would see live updates of the proceedings every hour on the hour, magically coinciding with the bathroom breaks. How did he get by with this, to say nothing of the constant stream of lies? Why would anyone ever again voluntary cooperate, as I did, with such committees in the future when they so flagrantly violate your privacy to further their political goals? The answer is you wouldn't, and you shouldn't.

It's time to push back. Some Republicans are finally starting to learn how to fight back from my father, because we've been putting up with the double standard for a long time. Why? Because we're afraid of a mean article? We're scared they might say something that's not nice about us?

My father has led the charge of conservatives standing up and fighting back against this double standard, and it's time to hold the Left accountable for what they've done. We've been open and honest, releasing emails and transcripts, and the American people have seen the difference between the way we do business and the way the Left does cover-ups.

I've faced a lot of critics who say I'm no different than Hunter, but this a false equivalency. First, no one has ever accused me of being a crackhead nor have I slept with my sister-in-law, nor did I spend multiple years trying to avoid paying child support for one of my children. Most importantly, I was an international businessman for fifteen years before my father was elected president, and he taught me free enterprise and honest leadership skills, which is far more than I can say for Hunter. We did it as businessmen and capitalists. I didn't do it under the guise of being a humble public servant while working for the US taxpayer, leveraging my dad's taxpayer-funded office like Hunter did. His dad hasn't even taught him to lie properly; he got up on stage and confessed to everyone he wouldn't have gotten the positions or millions he received if his father wasn't vice president. He magically became an "international businessman" overnight simply because his daddy held the checkbook for billions in international aid to corruption-ridden Ukraine. Fake news CNN fact-checked Joe Biden's response and pointed out that Joe and Hunter contradicted each other. Mark that down—CNN actually got one right for a change!

Here is something else the media won't cover. According to Judicial Watch, between June 2009 and May 2014, Hunter Biden took 411 flights to twenty-nine different nations, including five trips to China! On each of those trips, he was accompanied by the US Secret Service, at your expense, America. In comparison, in the last four years, I might have taken approximately a dozen international trips. You wouldn't know that by comparison, because my trips end up on front pages, while I never heard of a single trip that Hunter took. Unlike Hunter, people actually know me. I've been told by the Secret Service, I receive more threats than anyone but my father. I didn't even know what Hunter looked like until a few years ago. No one is coming after Hunter on his 411 flights. I wonder of those trips, how many was Hunter able to leverage money because of his father's office? If the media is going to scrutinize every single thing I do, it would be nice for them to look at the other side, but they won't. They run around screaming in outrage, yet they are deadly silent when it comes to the Left.

So, we're going to be looking at Hunter's business dealings and those of the whole Biden family, because we should be questioning everything this political machine has done during Biden's fifty years in office. Yes, you read that right—fifty years. He's been a swamp creature for half a century!

The double standard is despicable. I doubt most Americans know Hunter received $1.5 *billion* dollars to his fund, straight from the communist Chinese government on behalf of his client. If I had taken a buck fifty from China, you would never hear the end of it. Some don't even know that when Hunter was being investigated in Ukraine, his daddy, the great public servant Joe Biden, was recorded bragging that he would withhold a billion dollars in aid if Ukraine didn't fire the prosecutor investigating his boy wonder. This is just the tip of the iceberg, and we're going to dig into the details Joe and Hunter Biden don't want you to know.

Stop and look at the differences.

When Donald Trump took office, we, at the Trump Organization quit doing any new foreign deals after the 2016 election so there wouldn't even be a hint of any impropriety, which we had no legal obligation to do—but we did. We've been transparent and forthright, even though it's cost us, but it's never enough for these people—because they're not after truth.

I'm proud to be the son of the first president elected without the ruling class's approval. I'm also proud of the incredible successes we've had together in the free market. I have a great deal of personal experience with having a father who is larger than life. Still, we've done everything aboveboard while exposed to incredible scrutiny.

And right there is the difference. While I worked hard in business with my father in the free market, Hunter Biden sat on his ass in mahogany boardrooms, secretly reaping the rewards from his daddy's taxpayer-funded office, and magically becoming an international businessman overnight when his father became vice president. He had no experience, no track record—just access and the willingness to totally exploit it to the max.

But we're not supposed to talk about it. Not any of it. I recognize that I am the son of a wealthy and successful father, and I have greatly benefited from those open doors, but there is a difference between privately succeeding versus profiting greatly under the guise of public service over decades.

Isn't it just a little ironic the Biden family secrets are still secret? The same media outlets that say we should leave the kids out of it, have freely attacked me since my father was elected. They say fifty-year-old Hunter is off-limits, but Barron wasn't off-limits—the media started hitting him when he was just ten. My sister, Tiffany, who was still in law school, wasn't off-limits, and they've even stooped so low as to subpoena my youngest child, Chloe, from the time she was just *four years old*. Four? Really? But we're not supposed to talk about poor little fifty-year-old Hunter.

I certainly wasn't off-limits when they spent three-and-a-half years trying to accuse me of treason. When Democrats in the House and Senate tried to jail me, those same Democrats and a bunch of weak Republicans didn't even want to take a look into the Bidens, despite piles of obvious impropriety. As comedian George Carlin said, "It's a big club, and you ain't in it."

Had I done a tenth of what Hunter has done, it would be in every paper and on every news channel. They would try to tear my father to shreds and do their best to rip apart my privacy and reputation to expose every bit of dirt they could find. Can't you picture the glee on the face of Little Lord Fauntleroy Anderson Cooper (as he was known in high school)!

There's a sickening double standard when we can't talk about Hunter's shady double-dealings, but my younger siblings and even my children get hit left and right. Did you know Hunter landed a great job at MBNA Bank right out of school, the biggest bank and the largest employer in the state of Delaware, where his daddy was conveniently a senator and was busy promoting favorable banking legislation? But no one says anything about this. The same Hunter, who had a drug problem and was thrown out of the Navy Reserve after just *two weeks*, and magically rose through the ranks of MBNA.

And I'm sure it was just a complete coincidence that he later landed an even sweeter position at Amtrak at the age of thirty-six. Let's just give that some context, shall we? The average age of an individual on the board of directors is currently sixty-three at S&P 500 companies. Only 6 percent are fifty and younger, with most of them ages forty-five to fifty.[7] So why would Hunter find himself on the board of Amtrak, which serves millions of passengers and grosses billions in revenue?

It certainly wouldn't have anything to do with his dad sometimes being called "Amtrak Joe," as I mentioned earlier. Joe Biden rode Amtrak for thirty-six years—the equivalent of two million miles.[8] In fact, in 2016, Biden facilitated a loan for over $2 billion for railway improvements, so I think it's safe to say Daddy likes trains.

What was Hunter's experience or qualification for this job? Either he also really liked trains, or maybe Joe taking the train every day had something to do with it, because it certainly wasn't Hunter's business acumen or experience. Yet no one batted an eye. If Joe Biden becomes president, imagine the opportunities to freeload that will open up for Hunter. Maybe Pop will appoint his boy as ambassador to China because of his "foreign policy" experience, which includes continuing the Biden family desire for China to succeed at the expense of the United States, as they have done for decades.

When Joe Biden became the vice president of the United States, Hunter was magically transformed into an international businessman *overnight*. One minute he was just into domestic cronyism; now with Daddy Joe as the VP, the world was the limit. Within weeks of his father becoming Obama's running mate, Hunter Biden launched a consulting and lobbying firm called Seneca Global Advisors with the aim of helping companies expand within the US and into foreign markets.[9] Together with Christopher Heinz (of ketchup fame) who is Senator John Kerry's stepson, Hunter formed Rosemont Seneca Partners in 2009 together with Devon Archer, a buddy from Yale. The connection with Archer was about to bear a lot of crooked fruit.

A lucrative board position with a notorious and corruption-riddled Ukrainian top natural gas producer, Burisma, followed for a cool $83,000 monthly compensation.[10] That's the same corrupt Burisma that has repeatedly been embroiled in controversy—including a recently intercepted $6 million bribe trying to halt a criminal investigation into Mykola Zlochevsky, Burisma's crooked president.[11] Just a few minor details—Hunter didn't speak Ukrainian and had *zero* (as in no, none, zip) experience in energy. But apart from that, I'm sure he was immensely qualified. After all, he's a Biden. Never mind that Ukraine is the second most corrupt country in Europe after Russia according to the Corruption Perceptions Index.[12] That certainly didn't have anything to do with Biden's suddenly lucrative position and his father's influence, right?

How lucrative was Hunter's deal? Let's compare. Oracle's average compensation to a board member is $46,000 per month. Comcast is $35,000. IBM and Wells Fargo? $28,000. Ford averages $30,000[13]—that's nearly *one-third* of Hunter Biden's $83,000! The board members of S&P 500, the top five hundred companies in the country, average $25,000,[14] and Hunter was making $83,000—with no experience and without even knowing the language. Does that not seem off to anyone?

According to Peter Schweizer's revealing books *Secret Empires* and *Profiles in Corruption*, in 2014 Hunter Biden's buddy Devon Archer set up private meetings for Joe Biden. I'm sure the meeting had nothing to do with Burisma dropping over $112,000 into Hunter and Devon's company, Rosemont, marked "c/o Devon Archer." That, apparently, is the price of a meeting with the vice president of the United States if you are Joe Biden. Days later, Devon Archer landed on the board of directors for Burisma. Must have been a good meeting! Hunter joined his buddy on the board shortly, even though, like I said, both of them lacked experience in energy and probably couldn't locate Ukraine on a map to save their lives. They both received a cool million dollars a year from the sketchy Ukrainian energy company.[15]

Hunter's political connections aided Burisma with the corruption case that later entangled him. Cue Papa Joe Biden threatening said-Ukrainian prosecutor for looking into his son's questionable business dealings: "'I'm telling you, you're not getting the billion dollars. . . . I'm leaving in six hours. If the prosecutor is not fired, you're not getting the money.' Well, son of a bitch. He got fired."[16] What if anything like this was learned about a Trump? Can you imagine the scandal? Let's be honest, President Trump was wrongfully and immorally impeached for less! Yet this came straight out of Joe Biden's mouth! You would think that having the elder Biden's own voice incriminating himself *might* turn this into a constant news headline of rampant corruption and a reason for a detailed investigation—but you would be dead wrong.

Minor details—under Biden, the Obama administration had put roughly $3 billion into Ukraine's corrupt sieve of a government,[17] and the investigation into Burisma and its founder Yanukovich, who fled to Russia in 2014, ended with a whimper under Uncle Joe's attention.[18]

Are you ready for the best part? We don't really know how much Hunter may have made off Ukraine. Only Joe and Jill Biden had to disclose information on their finances. But Schweizer points out that court documents and financial records give us some clues. Here are some of the interesting bits, if the media cares to cover any of this:

A Morgan Stanley investment account from which Hunter regularly received funds shows money arriving from mysterious sources around the world. There is a $142,300 deposit in April 2014 from Kazakh oligarch controlled Novatus Holdings. Kenges Rakishev, whose father-in-law is the former vice prime minister of Kazakhstan and a close ally of Kazakh dictator Nursultan Nazarbayev, runs the offshore firm.[19] In August 2014, $1.2 million arrived into the account from an anonymous LLC via a small Swiss bank called BSI S.A. In 2016, BSI was one of several companies that were part of an embezzlement and money-laundering investigation spanning ten countries and at least $4.2 billion in irregular transactions.[20]

The financial documents also demonstrate that someone in the Biden family has other LLCs set up to receive payments. In August 2015, for example, $150,000 was transferred into an account controlled by something called MFTCG Holdings LLC Biden.[21] It is unclear what that account is or who controls it.[22]

Hunter's questionable dealings weren't limited to his Rosemont ventures but included other groups such as the Burnham Financial Group, with which buddy Devon Archer was also involved. "As they had with Rosemont, Hunter Biden and Devon Archer used Burnham to make foreign deals with governments and oligarchs, including Nurlan Abduov, an associate of Kazakh oligarch Kenges Rakishev."[23]

Do you think it might be worth the time of someone in the liberal press to look into these issues? But, of course, they won't touch it; remember, Hunter is off-limits. It's no longer their job to look at Democrats. They only look into the GOP.

You know what? America isn't going to tolerate it anymore. Even people in the middle see the insanity, and they see that the other side doesn't talk about issues or do anything to lift a finger for hardworking Americans. Prior to COVID-19, they saw what the economy could do under my father, with unprecedented unemployment numbers across every demographic. Americans watched my father get nearly seven million people off food stamps, which scares the crap out of the Left because these millions are no longer dependent on the government.

This is a real problem for the lying Democrats. They couldn't beat my father at the ballot box in 2016, so they were left with cheating in another way—impeachment. And guess what? They couldn't even get that right, either!

The American people have seen my father do an incredible job for them despite unprecedented attacks from every corner— and it hasn't even slowed him down. What the Left has done is disgusting, and it's a disgrace to our republic. It must come to light, and it must never, *ever*, be allowed to happen again to either party or to any duly-elected president.

You can fight back. You don't just have to lose because they want you to, and you don't have to give up because they say something bad about you.

We can do this—we can get this country on the right track again. We have real problems in our nation, but we can fix them together. The only cure for Trump Derangement Syndrome is four more years of fighting back against the double standard, which also means four more years of prosperity for the American people.

But some people are more interested in their own prosperity.

CHAPTER 7

Family First

Years of corrupt deals and unearned job positions in the United States turned into lucrative international deals when Joe Biden became the vice president. If the media has its way, he and Hunter will get away with it, but the full cover-up not only involves Hunter, but the whole Biden family. Trouble is, the rabbit hole goes deeper than the crooked Ukrainian government or Chinese government investments.

Let me put a thought in your mind that has troubled me. If your son's entire career depended on you, would the people paying him have influence over you? And let's say that you had used your power unethically—possibly illegally, or simply because you accepted it as the spoil of politics in the swamp—to get your son those positions. And what if some of those deals were with a country that's a clear and present threat to the national interest of the United States—a country you helped to make a trade juggernaut during your political career, while your son reaped the rewards. I don't know, perhaps a little country like *China*! Would that compromise you at all? Might you worry, just a little, some-day that country would pull a skeleton out of your closet and use it against you or your son? How do you think this would shape your actions regarding that country? Do you think some of the most corrupt countries really wouldn't try?

Maybe you can see where I'm going with this because it's exactly what Joe and Hunter Biden have done. Joe's influence has set Hunter up to make millions—and that means the people who paid those millions *own them both*. First MBNA, then Amtrak, then the Ukrainians and others, and later the communist Chinese government—and those are just the ones we know of—have bought and paid for Biden, Inc. They *own* Joe and Hunter Biden like their bitches. The sickening irony is that the Democrats tried to spin this around and pin it on my father with the whole Ukrainian sham—it's the epitome of the double standard. It's wrong and disgusting.

It's time to look at the most dangerous aspect of Joe and Hunter's crooked deals, because all this nepotism culminated when Hunter's company netted that cool $1.5 *billion* deal I told you about before from the *Chinese government* (not even a subsidiary) days after Hunter traveled there on Air Force Two with his father.

Total coincidence, I'm sure! The money and bribes Hunter received—including a 2.8-carat diamond that a Chinese energy tycoon gave him,[1] just to be nice, obviously (eye roll)—certainly would *never* influence Joe Biden on his China policy, right? It's not like handing someone bribes gives you influence over them—at least, not if you're a Dem.

But maybe you're like me and don't think it's a coincidence that Joe Biden has been historically weak on China, helping to make them the inequitable trade giant they are. We'll dig into that in the next chapter, but for those of you who might be concerned about the Chinese government's ties to the Bidens, let's first dig into how their dealings make Joe ripe for blackmail—and worse.

As far as we know, it all started as soon as Joe Biden was announced as VP. Hunter began capitalizing at a whole new level right away. The Ukraine deal is terrible enough, but there were deals in Romania and Kazakhstan too. In the words of another famous Kazakh, Borat Sagdiyev, it must be very *niceeee* to be a Biden!

The book *Secret Empires* by Peter Schweizer, which I mentioned in the previous chapter, describes all the backroom financial deals and shady players, so grab a copy to get the details while I hone in on the scary aspects pertaining to China.

With all that's happened after the Wuhan coronavirus pandemic, China is in the national spotlight. From covering up the severity of the infection, the virulence of the disease, to corrupt dealings with the WHO and worse, most Americans have finally become aware that the communists in China are *not* here to help us.

In December 2013, Hunter flew to Beijing, China, with his father. Joe was there to have some conversations with Chinese leaders. Frankly, the Bidens got a lot more from the trip than the American taxpayer did, whom Joe was supposed to represent. Hunter and his Rosemont Seneca firm landed a major deal, though we don't really know precisely all what Hunter was up to while in China. Hunter denies doing any kind of business on that trip, but we do know that Hunter introduced his father to his Chinese business partner, Jonathan Li.[2] According to an NBC article trying to say this was all no big deal, "The Chinese business license that brought [a] new fund into existence was issued by Shanghai authorities 10 days after the trip, with Hunter Biden a member of the board."[3]

It took my friend Steve Feinberg, one of the largest investors in America, many years to get his foot in the door for any investment from China. Sovereign funds in China are similar to other funds around the world. China does their due diligence and is meticulous before investing in any ventures. Steve told me without equivocation that the Chinese like substantial, known names with a proven return and track record that speaks for itself. They are careful, slow, cautious, and very good at what they do. They will have dozens of meetings before making any decision. I was blown away that Hunter did it in a week. Wow, what a fantastic international businessman he turned out to be! The only way that happens is if China is buying you or your access. *One week*—it's like magic! Rosemont Seneca landed a deal that grew to be worth $1.5 *billion* and may have totaled as much as $2 billion throughout the relationship—of the money we can find—in a joint partnership that included Bohai Harvest RST (BHR), a mash-up of the names of those companies involved.[4]

Schweizer points to the elephant in the room: "It is important to note that this deal was with the Chinese government—not with a Chinese company, which means that the Chinese government and the son of the vice president were now business partners."[5] Oh, but it's fine. There's no semblance of impropriety or conflict of interest with the son of the VP and a hostile nation being in bed together; nothing to report here.

It's all just a day in the life of a Biden.

This was no corrupt energy company deal like Ukraine; this was a deal with the Chinese government entities themselves. This is Hunter and Joe Biden getting down and dirty in bed with the biggest, most powerful and influential players in all of communist China.

At least some of these deals Hunter started as soon as his father became VP continue to this day. "Public records show that Hunter Biden still sits on the board of BHR Partners, a private investment fund backed by a number of Chinese state entities including Bank of China, China Postal Savings Bank and China Development Bank," according to the *Financial Times*.[6] Even though Hunter said he would get off the board on or by October 31, 2019, he still appears to be on the board as of April 2020.[7]

Hunter claims he only got his compensation after his dad was out of office—because *deferred* payment on an equity stake of billions makes it totally okay, right? Amazing—it wasn't that he wasn't getting paid, it's that he waited to cash the check. Known (poor) liar Joe Biden, with his history of crooked deals and crony-ism, tells us it's all good, so there must not be any corruption—or so the Bidens want us to think. And the media has dutifully played along, the faithful lapdog of the Left. Joe Biden has said questions about his son, are a "damn lie" or only a "smear" aimed at saving President Trump's job. I'm glad to "smear" the truth ev-erywhere I go.

Why haven't we investigated the hell out of this? Why aren't there national commissions to get to the truth and find out every sleazy detail? Wow, is the media simply missing in action? Hunter Biden has profited immensely from financial dealings that also benefit a hostile and adversarial nation. How are we okay with this?

Perhaps there is no better example of media bias than when the media, which conveniently chose to ignore Hunter Biden's multibillion-dollar dealings with the Chinese government, took issue with my sister Ivanka for simply trying to protect her name from being used by infringers, squatters, and outright criminals.

Over the years, Ivanka had spent a considerable amount of time and energy cultivating her own unique brand and image. Following the 2016 election, reports emerged of hundreds of trademark applications being filed all across mainland China for Ivanka's name on various products. From diet pills to underwear to beer to mattresses, there was no shortage of Chinese businesses trying to profit off her name on products Ivanka had absolutely nothing to do with. According to the *Washington Post*, "an astounding 258 trademark applications were lodged under variations of Ivanka, Ivanka Trump and similar-sounding Chinese characters between Nov. 10 [2016] and the end of last year [2016], records at the China Trademark Office show."[8] None have any connection to my sister. Sadly, this was not at all unusual as China has had a long history of stealing valuable American intellectual property. Though largely ignored by prior administrations, my father was the first president who chose to stand up to China for the systematic theft of American technology and intellectual property. Still, the media scrutiny on my sister for trying to stop people from stealing her name was intense. In contrast, Hunter Biden went to China with the goal of trying to profit off his name and received no media scrutiny. Based on the outrage about Ivanka you would think she was making millions, like Hunter, rather than spending hundreds of thousands of her own money to simply prevent others from trying to make money selling products using her name. Once again, the media let America down.

Oh, and what about that diamond? Turns out, while Hunter was on the board of something called the World Food Program

USA—qualifications be damned, I'm Joe Biden's son—Ye Jianming, a Chinese energy tycoon and head of CEFC China energy, kindly gave Hunter Biden a lovely 2.8-carat diamond worth almost a hundred thousand dollars.[9] Hunter claimed he tossed it—gave it to his business associates—but his ex-wife, Kathleen, claimed that the diamond was one of his "personal indulgences."[10] Wonder if he paid taxes on it . . . we all know he didn't.

Ye and Hunter continued to work together as they brokered a deal for CEFC to invest $40 million in Louisiana's liquefied natural gas—up until the Chinese detained Ye on corruption charges in 2018.[11] Sorry, Hunter—no more diamonds for you.

Then there's Patrick Ho, the assistant to Ye Jianming of the diamond bribe (I mean "gift"), who was arrested in New York on money laundering and Foreign Corrupt Practices Act charges.[12] Ho was convicted of bribery charges and jailed. But I'll tease you with one little detail. Ho's first phone call when he got in trouble? He tried to get ahold of a certain Hunter Biden by calling Jim, Joe's brother, who helpfully gave him Hunter's number.[13] We'll get to Jim here in a minute.

The crooked deals are just the tip of the iceberg. If it was just Hunter, it wouldn't be (quite) so bad, but it gets so much worse when you think it through. Biden has taken a soft position on China, and the more business Hunter was doing with China, the more Joe downplayed any problems with China.[14] That nearly brings us to the present, when Biden said China—which he helped make the world's second-largest economy—was "not competition" to the US.[15]

Not competition? What planet does Joe live on? Is this gross incompetence talking or something more nefarious? He helped make China the IP-stealing, forced-labor powerhouse it is today! Interestingly, Biden's statement drew criticism from both sides of the political aisle. Even Crazy Bernie didn't agree with him! I don't know about him running for the president of the United States, but Joe Biden is certainly China's MVP—perhaps he should run there.

Does it scare you that China could have such compromising ties with a political candidate, yet no one talks about it? But, honestly, I'm not sure which is worse—that he has these numerous points of potential blackmail or that the media would refuse to report on it. Do I have to pick which one makes me angrier?

We're not supposed to talk about Hunter. We're not supposed to talk about the alcohol, the drugs, the divorce, the strippers, the failure to pay child support, and dating his late brother Beau's widow shortly after he died, then cheating on her and fathering a child, confirmed by DNA tests.[16] Again, not the characteristics the Chinese government meticulously seeks out when looking to invest billions of dollars. We're not supposed to talk about how these business deals could put Joe over a barrel with the Chinese if he were ever elected president.

If the media abdicates their previously hallowed role, someone has to fill the void and do their damn jobs for them. Like a true believer in the free markets, I'm happy to take up the reins on this.

The double standard and the implications of all this are just sickening. Had my father and I done the smallest fraction of these things, we would be crucified. I did thirty hours of congressional testimony for a twenty-minute meeting, paid for by the DNC, where everyone's recollection was the same. If China had this much dirt on my father, it would be bigger than the next Russia probe. But when we try to raise questions about how Hunter's crooked business deals could compromise Joe Biden as a potential president, we're met with ridicule, scorn, rejection, and backlash.

My father has rightly called for investigations into the Bidens, but I doubt China will ever do it. They would lose their leverage against the Bidens, and then what would they have to show for their money? Oh, wait—they, too, made a ton on these dealings, inserting their communist fingers deep into commercial real estate, energy, and more in the United States! Yet we're told there's no corruption and we should move along.

I could go on and on, but I can't spare any more time for Hunter—not when questionable dealings are such a family affair for the Bidens.

These business deals are definitely a family staple. For instance, how did Patrick Ho have Jim Biden's phone number? We may never know, but this just points out that the Bidens make profiting from politics a family affair.

The family business has lined the Bidens up with "sketchy companies, violent convicted felons, foreign oligarchs, and other people who typically expect favors in return."[17] From foreign corrupt governments like Ukraine, China, and Romania to smaller players like Kazakhstan, Costa Rica, and others, the Bidens have played big—sometimes even using taxpayer dollars for chips. And the deals keep coming as Joe Biden rises in the ranks of a broken DC political system.

At least four members have raked in the rewards of the Biden clan: Hunter, of course; Joe's brothers, James (a.k.a. Jim) and Frank;

and Joe's sister, Valerie (the one he sometimes now confuses for his wife).[18] They've been in politics together forever, with James and Frank, having helped organize supporters from the beginning, and sister Valerie leading his campaigns for decades.

Joe plainly admitted he attempted to "prostitute" himself to raise money in the course of his first run for the US Senate.[19] Some things never change, right, Joe? From those humble beginnings, Joe's influence expanded globally—and so, too, did the family's opportunities for profit.

Joe and Jim have a special bond, with Jim often traveling with his big brother on official trips to Jim's island home near Naples, Florida, acting as a de facto family resort—the so-called "Biden Bungalow."[20] Jim isn't a business guy or an insurance guy or a real estate guy—but he has been whatever he needed to make himself out to be so he could profit from his brother's taxpayer-funded office. Everything Jim has ever been involved with has been aided by his brother Joe—whether Joe's position or legislation. Jim has conveniently gotten 100 percent, seemingly legal, financing for various deals and never risked anything himself—it was always about leveraging what he could get out of his brother Joe. This is the worst of what DC stands for and what people are so sick of, yet this is what the Bidens have been doing from the start. Do you think that's going to change now? Hell, if Joe wins despite all this, it will only embolden the DC corruption so much more!

After Jim and Hunter bought Paradigm Global Advisors, they showed up together with Beau—and some muscle—to order the firing of the fund's president. Jim proudly proclaimed, "We've got investors lined up in a line of 747s filled with cash ready to invest in this company."[21] That was in 2006, and Joe was about to become chairman of the Senate Foreign Relations Committee, opening up whole new vistas for the Biden clan. One Paradigm Global Advisors executive recounts Jim explaining, "Don't worry about investors. We've got people all around the world who want to invest in Joe Biden."[22] China, you're going to have to take a number.

Jim was well positioned to come through on his brag, including when Biden became VP and Jim became a frequent visitor at the White House. While he was sometimes caught in photos when he wasn't on the official visitor logs, Jim attended meetings that benefited his business dealings, including one with construction firm HillStone International, a subsidiary of Hill International.[23]

Though Jim had *no* prior experience in housing construction, naturally he became an executive VP with HillStone—just in time to help the firm land a contract to build 100,000 homes in Iraq as part of a $35 billion project that would build 500,000 homes overall. Think about this for a minute: the vice president's *brother* gets a job with a firm, astonishingly just in time to help them land a contract that would make $1.5 billion over three years—triple what they normally made[24]—not to mention a State Department construction job, and we're all just supposed to be okay with this? Where was the media during this time? What happened to the Republicans during this time? How come no one investigated this at all? We're not supposed to ask questions about inappropriate connections or conflict of interest? Jim's take? He split about $735 million with some minority business partners.[25] Mere pocket change. This is a huge deal, and it tells us volumes about what it means to be a Biden. What would another stint in the White House do for Jim while his brother is in office?

And what was HillStone's admitted reason for their success? The son of founder Irv Richter's Hill International shared his thoughts with investors at a private meeting about how much it helped "to have the brother of the vice president as a partner," according to someone who was there.[26] He went on to explain how having Jim on the payroll meant they had a connection who knew how to "deal with government officials," Jim's brother Joe.[27] Continuing an honored family tradition, Jim needed little or no understanding of residential construction to be executive VP of Hill International's housing interests.

Though the Iraq deal was set, HillStone couldn't honor it, partly because of a lack of experience (no shit?!), but Jim stayed on with Hill International as it continued to land government and international contracts.[28] Jim, of course, wouldn't comment on any of this when Fox reporter Charlie Gasparino asked repeatedly, and neither would Sugar Daddy Joe.

Shakespeare famously asked, "What's in a name?" Apparently, if you're a Biden, quite a bit. Many other questionable deals have linked the Bidens with suspect business partners, including Paradigm's links to Allen Stanford, convicted of his role in an $8 billion Ponzi scheme—yes, that's right, $8 *billion* with a "B."[29] Stanford was instrumental in selling Paradigm funds and is serving 110 years (for perspective, Bernie Madoff got 150). Of course, the Bidens deny any knowledge of Stanford's dealings.

Then there's Valerie, Joe's campaign manager, including his 1988 and 2008 run for president, who is either a really great political strategist or just hitched to the right pony. She has had some lucrative political consulting gigs, using her Biden name effectively as a marketing tool. To top it off, Valerie miraculously commands $40,000 a speech, but the media doesn't question a thing because Joe and Valerie are Democrats.

Together with Joe Slade White, Valerie was also the senior partner for Joe Slade White & Company (the Bidens would be the "company" part, I suppose), where she made considerable consulting fees from the Biden campaigns she was running for nearly twenty years as a nice way to get those campaign donations into the family coffers. From the 2008 presidential campaign alone, she made $2.5 million.[30]

Let's talk about Joe's little brother, Frank, for a minute. Carrying on the family tradition, Frank has known little or nothing about the businesses he gets involved in. But he knew everything about leveraging the Biden name. With no background in education, Frank became involved in managing and promoting charter schools the same year his brother became vice president. He became president and director of development for Mavericks in Education Florida LLC. His company charged management fees to the schools, and a related company, School Property Development LLC, owned the school buildings, and charged rent to numerous charter schools around Florida. No matter how a school performed, they didn't own the building. Whenever the company, Mavericks, was promoted, Frank's bio as the vice president's brother was always front and center.

The performance of the schools was awful. Teachers taught only a couple hours a day, while the remainder of the students' schooltime was spent looking into a computer monitor for instruction. No surprise that the best graduation rate was only 43 percent, and two schools came in at 7.2 and 4.5 percent. In 2013 and 2014, the state Auditor General's office discovered Mavericks wasn't meeting the minimum teaching hours and had inflated their student numbers. Do you think they did that because the higher the student count, the more you receive from the state?

So why did Frank stay in the charter school business? He knew the money wasn't coming from teaching but from the value of the buildings. By charging as high a rent as possible, he could pay off mortgages quicker, sometimes in only five years. All the while using taxpayer money and government grants to help pay for the properties.

By 2014, the two companies had received nearly $80 million in state funds. As Joe's brother, Frank had private access to Barack Obama on several occasions, including a private meeting with him and ten others at the White House to discuss charter schools. His companies received millions of dollars in "discretionary grants" averaging $250,000 per school while his brother was vice president.

Frequently name-dropping his brother to school boards and other politicians from whom he sought approval, he maximized his last name to gain an advantage in having his charter schools approved.[31]

In 2009, Joe helped Frank land a deal in Costa Rica to develop real estate because of VP Joe's involvement in Latin America under the Obama administration.[32]

Frank has received the same kind of corrupt opportunities in the Caribbean, thanks to Joe's "Caribbean Energy Security Initiative (CESI),"[33] again with taxpayer-funded loans made possible because of the Overseas Private Investment Corporation (OPIC), which is now the Development Finance Corporation.

Joe's cover for Frank didn't just involve cushy overseas business deals where Joe had influence. Frank and buddy Jason Turton were partying like it was 1999 (because it was) in a rented Jaguar convertible. With Jason driving (Frank's license was suspended), they piled three people in the back seat and headed to a concert, doing "between 70 and 80 mph in a 35-mph zone,"[34] before the car slammed into Michael Albano as he crossed the street. The impact flipped Michael, a single father of two young daughters, over the vehicle and into a back seat passenger's face before he came to rest on the road where he later died of his injuries.[35]

According to Peter Schweizer, "In depositions two of the witnesses sitting in the back seat recall Frank Biden telling Turton to 'keep driving' after Albano hit the ground."[36] While the driver pled guilty, the family sued Frank Biden for wrongful death. Frank did not show for the proceedings, and he never responded to court correspondence regarding the case, including the ruling that Frank Biden "owed each of the girls [Albano's daughters] $275,000 for his role in the tragedy."[37] A private investigator was hired to track him down. He reported that Frank appeared to stay with Joe Biden occasionally, but all attempts to locate Frank— including an appeal to Joe, who should know how it feels to lose loved ones in an accident because his first wife and daughter died that way—failed.[38] Those girls still haven't received their damages, which, as I write this, would now total roughly a million dollars with interest.[39] Not only did the Albano girls grow up without a father, but the man who helped put him in the grave has so far successfully avoided justice.

Schweizer writes, "Conveniently, any assets Frank might hold in Costa Rica would be out of reach of U.S. courts and the Albano family."[40] Despite serving as senior advisor to brother Joe's 2020 political action committee, there is little sign that Frank will ever pay reparations to the two girls, all thanks to liberal privilege and the last name Biden.[41]

Again, just think of the headlines if the Trumps did any of these things. To eliminate any cries of impropriety, we—who were already very successful in international business—quit signing new deals and have been completely transparent in our dealings. We didn't have to. It wasn't required, it was just the right thing to do to avoid the notion of impropriety. But that hasn't stopped countless media investigations. I wonder why they never bothered to look into Joe and Co?

The Left puts everything we do under a microscope and then makes stuff up when they can't find anything, but just between Hunter and Jim, there's enough to keep teams of investigative reporters busy for months. Except that there are precious few reporters on the Left. They're all activists hiding behind press credentials, and they're not interested in anything if it doesn't hurt Trump.

Hunter didn't even speak Ukrainian when he started working with Burisma. I wonder, how much did he contribute in those meetings? Like Hunter, Jim had no background in anything useful when he started matching his Biden name up with big deals that lined his pockets and when he probably bought that Biden Bungalow off the coast of Naples. Corrupt companies and nations have paid for access to Joe Biden throughout his political career, benefiting his family and making them wealthy. In the cases of Hunter raking in cash from Ukraine or Jim building with HillStone in Iraq, that's solely an issue of corruption. But China is a whole different story. They have their hands so deep into Hunter's pockets, they can feel Joe's car keys jiggling, and we all now know beyond any shadow of a doubt that China absolutely *is* a competitor, no matter what Joe says.

The fact is, Beijing Biden helped make China what it is today—a dangerous giant of trade that was nearly immune under previous administrations to the consequence of stealing our intellectual property, including state-directed acquisition of sensitive United States technology for strategic purposes, outright cyber theft, currency manipulation, and unfair trade practices. The list could go on and on.

In his half-century in office, Biden has not once stood up to China. Why would he, when Hunter was making so much money from them? They own him, and while China is on America's radar after COVID-19, the Left hasn't stood up to China or called them on their bullshit. Democrats aren't the ones who got the China trade deal done. Once again, it was Donald J. Trump who got blasted for standing up for American workers, who won a huge victory in the ongoing trade war, and who is righting wrongs of the past.

One thing is certain: if Biden is elected, his actions or inactions will help Make China Great Again.

CHAPTER 8
Beijing Biden

66 China is going to eat our lunch? Come on, man. They're not bad folks, folks. But guess what? They're not competition for us," said Joe Biden in May 2019,[1] and eight months later a lethal virus originating in the most densely populated city in Central China invaded us.

We quickly learned how dependent we are on China and how many of our critical pharmaceuticals come from them, along with unimportant little things like respirators and personal protective equipment (PPE), such as face shields, masks, gloves, gowns, and hazmat suits. As more information got out, it became increasingly obvious that China and the World Health Organization (WHO) had been part of a cover-up to keep details of the virus from getting out. Seems that the WHO, like the Bidens, is on China's payroll. And when confronted about the pandemic cover-up, the "not bad folks" in Beijing literally threatened to stop sending us the antibiotics we invented but they manufacture![2]

Guess you're wrong again, Joe.

We live in a new era where Americans finally understand the dangers of the Chinese trade injustices my father has been righting and the national security threat some of these inequities pose that no one bothered to address for decades. Nearly three out of four Americans believe that China was responsible for the level of COVID-19 deaths in our country[3] because of their lies and cover-ups, and that's not even counting the outcry when China threatened to cut off supplies. Roughly two-thirds of Americans have a negative view of China, with 62 percent (a number that doesn't include Joe Biden) seeing China's power and influence as a major threat to the US.[4] While the media has run with "Russia, Russia, Russia," China has been the real threat all along.

In the post–COVID-19 world, Donald Trump's MAGA agenda was more correct than anyone knew. All along, he had been saying we need to control our supply chain, recover American manufacturing, and bring jobs here—and now we've had the audacious Chinese government threaten to withhold needed antibiotics to sick and dying Americans. Guess DJT knew what he was talking about after all, and the pretend "experts" were wrong, as usual!

Approximately 80 percent of the active pharmaceutical ingredients (APIs) needed to make drugs in the United States come from China and other countries like India. And a Department of Commerce study revealed that 97 percent of all antibiotics in the United States come from China.[5] Ninety-seven percent!

If China cut us off, as they threatened to do in March 2020,[6] we would have months—if that—before our shelves would be bare and our hospitals and entire medical system would grind to a halt.

Last year, data from the Department of Commerce indicated that "China accounted for 95 percent of U.S. imports of ibuprofen,

91 percent of U.S. imports of hydrocortisone, 70 percent of U.S. imports of acetaminophen, 40 to 45 percent of U.S. imports of penicillin and 40 percent of U.S. imports of heparin."[7]

And they know it. An economics professor at Tsinghua University named Li Daokui pointed out, "We are at the mercy of others when it comes to computer chips, but we are the world's largest exporter of raw materials for vitamins and antibiotics. Should we reduce the exports, the medical systems of some western countries will not run well."[8]

This was no accident. China had carefully planned and played the long game while politicians like Joe Biden were sleeping—or even in bed with China. Senator Dianne Feinstein even had a Chinese spy on her staff for about twenty years as an office director and driver.[9]

China knew what was going on as the Wuhan flu spread—and *lied* about it. They lied to the World Health Organization, cutting off travel to Beijing and Shanghai—but not to Italy or New York or Los Angeles. Because they lied, the world didn't understand the gravity of a growing global pandemic. They also lied about the number of deaths, suppressed reports, and ordered doctors not to release findings, and refused to let in the best epidemiologists from the CDC to help.[10] Wonder why! Some of their own doctors are missing.[11] Maybe they're in some Chinese prison (I mean "re-education camp") somewhere?

White House Director of the Office of Trade and Manufacturing Policy Peter Navarro explained, "China has managed to dominate all aspects of the supply chain using the same unfair trade practices that it has used to dominate other sectors—cheap sweatshop labor, lax environmental regulations and massive government subsidies."[12] It's time to bring home the jobs they've stolen, and it's time to eliminate China's ability to hold us hostage.

Thank God we have Donald Trump instead of Joe Biden!

Earlier, we spoke how Joe Biden and his son, Hunter, are compromised on China, a major world power. Joe helped make China what it is, and Hunter lined his pockets with profits from his father's public office, including that $1.5 billion deal he received just days after visiting China with his father. Does anyone believe that China doesn't own the Bidens? They're bought and paid for.

No, Joe—China is more than a mere economic competitor to the US, the COVID-19 pandemic has shown us that China is a threat, and you're historically soft on them.

While some like Senator Chuck Grassley have called for an investigation into the conflict of interest in Joe and Hunter's China dealings, any accountability is yet to be seen. Grassley wants to see Hunter's travel record[13] and has raised concerns over how the Obama-era Committee on Foreign Investment in the United States (CFIUS) reviewed Chinese entities acquiring American assets that could prove to be national security issues,[14] but the media has been largely quiet on this potentially massive conflict of interest. CFIUS is supposed to look at strategic concerns and prevent foreign powers from buying US companies that could give them an advantage or compromise our national security. Anything from telecommunication to aviation to automotive to weapons must go through a CFIUS review, and Trump administration officials have noticed that some of these Biden-era reviews look questionable.

But wait, it gets better. Before, I wrote that the 2009 deal that created Rosemont Seneca—featuring Hunter Biden and John

Kerry's stepson, Christopher Heinz, among others—paved the way for a merger with Chinese private equity firm Bohai Capital. Well, that in turn led to creating BHR Partners, which acquired a company called Henniges, together with the Aviation Industry Corporation of China (AVIC). What does Henniges do? Anti-vibration technology that obviously has aviation technology potential. Not only is this another "overwhelming risk of conflicts" of interest, to Senator Grassley it also may pose "national security concerns."[15] The deal got held up in CFIUS—and then magically cleared. Grassley told Congress, "There is cause for concern that potential conflicts of interest could have influenced CFIUS approval of the Henniges transaction."[16]

If the media heard that one of the companies involved in the Henniges transaction was a billion-dollar private investment fund founded by Donald Trump Jr. and a Chinese government-linked firm, through a company formed with a prominent conservative's kid, there would be blood in the water. They would go into a feeding frenzy. But what do we hear about this? Nothing. Not one damn word!

How much did Joe grease the wheels to get deals for his family and other high-ranking Obama administration officials' families? We may never know. Frighteningly little—and the media likes to keep it that way. This is yet another lead that any traditional journalist would track to the fullest, but alas, there are no more true journalists, only liberal activists. We don't even know what else may have gone on—hardly anyone else is asking about what Hunter Biden did while his dad was VP.

How is there no coverage of this? Why aren't others crying for United States Secretary of the Treasury Steven Mnuchin to look into whether this Obama-era deal was properly vetted for our national security, not to mention conflicts of interest for the Bidens?

Personally, I think President Xi Jinping of China would *love* for Joe to get elected. Joe's so compromised and weak on his policies, China will push him around like a baby. He can't even speak to a crowd of twenty fans without a teleprompter. How do you think he will hold up against Xi or Putin? I know, it's scary!

Could it be that Osama bin Laden had it right? Do other countries want Joe Biden to be president for the same reason the most wanted terrorist in the world did—because "Biden is totally unprepared for that post, which will lead the U.S. into a crisis"?[17] Those were bin Laden's own words for why he wanted to assassinate Obama.

Though sometimes Joe tries to talk tough on China now that my father has stood up to them and hammered out a trade agreement, Biden's record shows why China President Xi Jinping would want Joe in power. Biden was one of the establishment swamp creatures in 2000 that helped establish China's permanent normal trade status, paving the way for its entry into the World Trade Organization (WTO), and status as permanent Most Favored Nation in 2001.

Biden said, "I would like to point out that my support for permanent normal trade relations with China is based not just on an assessment of the economic benefits to the U.S., not just on the prospects for political reform in China, but also on the impact on our national security."[18] After a decade of getting to see the results of his vote, Joe refused to see the cost to American workers and wrote, "I remain convinced that a successful China can make our country more prosperous, not less."[19]

Economic benefits to the United States? We've lost 2.4 million manufacturing jobs, hundreds of billions of dollars a year, and sixty thousand factories. We were losing them when Joe reiterated his support of the communist Chinese leadership, nearly ten years after he pushed for the vote. Joe's decades in politics have presided over China's rise and use of unfair trade policies—all under the belief of the failed liberal globalist policymakers that Chinese growth at our expense would make us all friends.[20] He created the trade imbalance with China and set the stage for the theft of trillions of dollars in intellectual property.

It didn't bother him—it was your money, not his. He idly sat by while they stole all our inventions and creations that we spent billions to discover—and made it theirs for free. FBI Director Christopher Wray on Tuesday, July 7, 2020, warned Americans that the Chinese government's theft of American information is taking place on so large a scale, suspected incidents make up nearly half of his bureau's counterintelligence cases.[21]

Political reform in China? They're still a communist country exploiting their workers for sweatshop labor and using that as an unfair trade advantage. Joe was flat-out wrong when he said that China has been forced to acknowledge the failure of communism to participate in the open-market economy.[22] They're still good little communists, and they leverage the advantages it gives them on the world stage, to the detriment of their people *and* ours. They imprison over a million Muslim Uighurs and other minorities in Soviet-style camps,[23] jailing some journalists and causing others to disappear, and repressing doctors and the truth during a worldwide pandemic.

Impact on our national security? People in universities and think tanks around the country engaging in classified research for the United States government are literally on the payroll of the Chinese government. Chinese agents infest universities like Harvard with spies, where the chairman of Harvard's Chemistry and Chemical Biology Department was arrested by the FBI and charged with lying about his Chinese connections and receiving hundreds of thousands of dollars from China.[24] Then there's Boston University, where a former student was part of the Chinese Liberation Army and accused of visa fraud and conspiracy against our government.[25] The communist Chinese have infiltrated soft targets—college research labs—in order to steal from us and exploit our national interests.[26] Most of this infiltration goes unnoticed, but according to an NBC News article, in a short period of time a Chinese Harvard-affiliated cancer researcher was caught stealing cells from a lab in Boston; a Chinese professor doing sensitive research at the University of Kansas was indicted; a Chinese student at the University of California, Los Angeles, was convicted of shipping banned missile technology to China; and a Chinese student at the Illinois Institute of Technology in Chicago was charged with recruiting spies for China's version of the CIA.[27] And that's just some of the ones we know about! "No country poses a greater, more severe or long-term threat to our national security and economic prosperity than China," said Boston's top FBI agent, Joseph Bonavolonta. "China's communist government's goal, simply put, is to replace the U.S. as the world superpower, and they are breaking the law to get there."[28] And it all happened on Joe's fifty-year watch.

Joe's establishment policies gave birth to the Chinese trade giant we know today. He made China's success on the world trade scene possible by setting up a system that did not punish their unfair trade practices.

Wrong, *wrong*, and *WRONG* again, Joe!

We looked at Joe Biden's record on race, but let's look at some of his other stupid and dangerous foreign policy decisions. Biden was for ousting the Shah of Iran in 1979—that worked out well, so well that it started the Iranian Revolution and led to the overtaking of the American embassy for 444 days. If he would have had his way, we would have lost the Cold War to the Russians, because he fought Reagan's military expansion that made us the dominant superpower on the planet. He didn't agree with George H.W. Bush taking us into the successful Gulf War, but he voted to take us into the unsuccessful Iraq War.[29] He's been wrong on all these policy issues, wrong on every bit of foreign policy he's ever supported, and he's been catastrophically wrong on China.

In August 2011, Biden said, "I believed in 1979 and said so and I believe now that a rising China is a positive development, not only for the people of China but for the United States and the world as a whole."[30] Biden went on to say, "When President Obama and I took office in January of 2009, we made our relationship with China a top priority. We were determined to set it on a stable and sustainable course that would benefit the citizens of both our countries."[31] It definitively benefited *one* (not us), because Joe was shortsighted and has no understanding of business. He showed his ignorance when he said, "Nor do I see the collapse of the American manufacturing economy, as China, a nation with the impact on the world economy about the size of the Netherlands', suddenly becomes our major economic competitor."[32] He was utterly, totally wrong again, just like when Obama's former Secretary of Defense Robert Gates said Biden, in the last four decades, was wrong on the most important national security issues and foreign policies.[33] (Even Crazy Bernie Sanders knew Biden was off and said that it's "wrong to pretend" that China isn't a major economic competitor.)[34]

China went from an economy the size of the Netherlands to the second largest in the world under Joe's tenure in DC—and he pushed for it, like the leader of the pack. Joe is China's MVP! They should build statues honoring him, because he *made* them.

And this is the guy to lead us into the future?

It's so important, let me say that again—is this the guy to lead the United States of America (not China) into the future?

Donald Trump did more than just *talk* tough on trade, something he's been doing for years. When he was my age, my father said, "I think a lot of other people are tired of watching other people ripping off the United States. This is a great country. They laugh at us. Behind our backs, they laugh at us because of our own stupidity." He railed against trade injustice to Oprah in an interview all the way back in 1988, and all these years later, he did it—he made good on a campaign promise that no one thought possible. Finally, in January 2020, we signed a Chinese trade deal that will put an end to their manipulative practices and stealing our IP and technology.

Donald Trump did the opposite of Biden. He's determined to regain America's trade success and dominance. No one has been harder on China than Trump. As a true leader, he realized it caused some Americans who voted for him some short-term pain when he hammered the trade agreement through with China. It was hard—the tariffs temporarily hurt our farmers, but they understood that they were feeling short-term pain for long-term gain. Yet DJT didn't lose any of that vote, because they recognized that he was the first guy who ever put China in their place. His base understood that if we didn't do it now, it was never going to happen. They all fully understood what Biden could never comprehend. It certainly never happened under half a century of Biden! If we didn't do it, no leftist bureaucrat would have the balls to stand up to China—they would just go on letting them steal our IP, technology, and jobs. The Left will give up America's position at the head of the pack—two hundred years of hegemony gone because morons were making decisions they couldn't begin to comprehend.

American firms are sick and tired of China leapfrogging them, stealing their hard-earned IP and technology that cost them billions to create. How much are we talking? The United States Trade Representative says it's anywhere from $225–$600 billion *annually*.[35] That's not just an insane amount of lost revenue, it's jobs, too. A study published by the US International Trade Commission in the same year Biden praised China's progress on the issue of IP theft[36] "estimated that if IP protection in just China were improved to a level comparable to that in the United States, the U.S. economy would obtain an estimated $107 billion in additional annual sales and net U.S. employment could increase by 2.1-million jobs."[37]

Biden claimed China's trade status would benefit the United States, but we now know that it has cost us *millions* of jobs. "The U.S. has lost 3.7 million jobs since 2001 due to its trade imbalance with China, with most of the damage done to manufacturing,"[38] according to one report from January 2020. The Chinese Communist Party has stolen from American businesses while Joe Biden has praised them, giving China a pass while they take our ideas, technology, and jobs.

China has been getting by with it, thanks to Joe Biden making them a permanent part of the World Trade Organization (WTO), which was created to destroy America's dominance in fair trade and has countless times voted down anything that could possibly be good for us. China's puppet is the WTO, and they're not going to let anything come out that may hurt China.

This trade imbalance was the foundation for their rise to prominence, paid for their military buildup, and cost us unimaginable amounts of money and countless jobs—and it was all made possible thanks to none other than Joe Biden. While we abide by the Foreign Corrupt Practices Act, do you think the Chinese lets the FCPA stop them from showing up in rogue countries around the world with a briefcase of cash, off the record, when they want a strategic or rare earth mineral contract? Getting ripped off and playing at a disadvantage has been the price of admission for doing business in China. Morons, like Joe Biden who have never been in business, created a situation where it's virtually impossible for America to compete with Chinese forced labor and unfair trade practices. Everyone knows they're bribing their way into these contracts; no one believes China is playing fairly. Yet liberals and many weak-kneed Republicans don't do anything about it.

But not anymore. Someone has finally called China out and held them accountable. In January 2020 the United States and China signed Phase One of a trade deal. This agreement covered intellectual property, criminal enforcement against trade-secret theft, corporate espionage, distribution of counterfeit goods, a ban on forced technology transfer, agriculture trade including pledges from China to purchase $200 billion in US goods and services, financial services, currency manipulation issues, dispute resolution, and expanding Chinese imports.[39]

My father asked his base to put up with temporary pain to get this trade deal pushed through—something politicians don't typically do—because Donald Trump is not a typical politician. He made the trade deal happen because it was the right thing to do for America and our workers. He knew that, in this game of chicken, China still needs us more than we need them. But that won't be the case much longer if we acquiesce under weak leadership. In a world of instant gratification Donald Trump is a businessman, and he knew that business doesn't work that way. You don't invest in something and receive instant gratification, (unless you're Hunter Biden). If you want to reap the rewards, you have to put in the time and effort. Joe Biden and the DC swamp creatures like him will never understand that.

It just makes you wonder. What if China spent a little more time attempting to feed their 1.6 billion people rather than trying to be a dominant world military power by illegal means? What if their people didn't have to eat bats because they actually fed them—maybe China would have more productive people and wouldn't *need* to steal the ideas and technology. Just a thought: instead of paying off the WHO, use the money to take care of your people.

Coming out of the coronavirus pandemic, there are some who want to make China pay for their lies and deceit. Who is going to do that? Joe Biden? Or the guy who actually did the unthinkable and got a trade deal done that everyone said could never happen? It was easy for Biden to give China the trade status at the expense of Americans to the tune of trillions of dollars and millions of jobs. It wasn't his money! He's never earned real money and signed paychecks (or layoff papers for those he's forced to let go because China stole decades of work).

Who do you think will hold China accountable? The guy who helped make China great, or the first guy to put them in their place? Biden had all his years in the Senate and then as vice president to do something about China, but he didn't. He doesn't want to. He doesn't really care about American workers, and he doesn't understand trade. He's going to fix things now? I don't think so.

Joe Biden doesn't know how to rebuild the American economy in the aftermath of COVID-19. If he had the answer and the skill set, why did he help China instead of America during his fifty years? On any one of his numerous trips to China, Joe could have told President Xi to stop stealing our shit, but he didn't. He had his chance to effect change, and he didn't. It's obvious he can't; he doesn't know how. The Chinese have leverage over him through Hunter, and who knows what else? Even if he wanted to, I doubt he would have the strength to stand up to them.

In 2016 Donald Trump made promises, just like any other politician. Yet the inescapable difference is that while DC swamp creatures like Biden talk tough, they can't perform.

Donald Trump delivered on his promises.

Biden made China great again. Trump made America great again. Only one puts the American people first, here at home and around the world.

PART II

"There's never been a time when two candidates were so different."

DONALD J. TRUMP, JULY 14, 2020

CHAPTER 9

A Suicide Note for America

When UK Parliament member Gerald Kaufman saw his Labour Party's socialist manifesto for an upcoming 1983 election in England, he coined the term "the longest suicide note in history."[1]

Only four days after Independence Day, team Biden-Sanders left their suicide note for America in their Unity Task Force Recommendations—a leftist manifesto wish list. Remember July 8, 2020, because it's their Declaration of Dependence Day.

Their proclamation should scare the hell out of you—if you love America and what has made it great. These ideas are dangerous, costly, and have proven ineffective time and time again. Socialism does not work. It didn't work for the USSR, it didn't work for Europe, it doesn't work in Latin America or Cuba, and it won't work for America. *It will destroy our country as we know it.*

Joe Biden has revealed himself as an extremist, dancing on Bernie's strings. Any chance Biden could disguise himself as a moderate just went out the window. Bernie and Biden joining forces to create a "compromise" is the latest proof that Biden isn't his own man but is in fact a sock puppet for whoever is the most vocal on the Left. Having tried to convince us that he is a moderate, the statements in this manifesto, many of which are lifted straight from Bernie's ultra-Left agenda, prove beyond a doubt that Democrats have abandoned any semblance of playing to the center.

Under this agenda, America will cease to be the land of opportunity for the hardworking middle class and will transform into a country that treats its illegal immigrants better than its tax-paying citizens. It's vital that we send a message to Uncle Joe and Crazy Bernie that America rejects this plan. Their blueprint for destruction would be laughable if it wasn't so dangerous. Here's some of what they want to do and why it matters to you.

They want free health care for illegals. Have you tried to get good care in a crowded city? The system is already overworked, so let's add a bunch of people who don't pay anything. Our schools are already failing, so let's add a bunch of kids who don't speak English, and then let's cater to them so they don't have to immerse themselves in English—which has been proven the most effective language-learning technique.

They will outlaw any charter schools that earn a profit and place the surviving charter schools under the control of the swamp in DC so the Left can continue to indoctrinate your children. Turning charter schools into national schools will remove school options for parents and eliminate educational competition. They'll close any remaining charter schools in financially stressed districts while simultaneously making our schools more dangerous by ending immigration enforcement near schools or school commutes, shielding the criminal gang MS-13 in prime recruiting areas. The only time Immigration and Customs Enforcement (ICE) is in or near a school is for the safety of the children because of criminal activity going on, so this would make all our schools less safe.

Biden and Bernie want to end ICE entirely, and they'll investigate ICE and border agents as preparation for this. Their list includes asylum for illegals. Hundreds of millions of people around the world would be eligible for asylum. We will see an end to denaturalization of criminal aliens who defrauded US authorities, meaning we'll no longer be able to deport them, and they'll allow previous deportees to return. So then, what's the point of kicking them out?

What about Biden's two favorite "constituents"—illegal aliens and criminals.

The want to end cash bail. Cash bail is set in place to prevent criminals from fleeing justice. Not having it releases criminals to go out and commit more crimes. In 2019 New York passed a progressive bail reform law, resulting in repeatedly catching and releasing a serial criminal named Gerod Woodberry and charging him with stealing or attempting to steal from *five* New York-area banks. The last time, he had been released from custody only four hours earlier. "I can't believe they let me out," Woodberry said in disbelief.[2] Even career criminals are incredulous at the stupidity of the idea.

A December 2019 report more fully explains the adverse effects of bail reform: "Under New York's bail reform law, 90 percent of criminal cases will have cash bail eliminated. That means defendants will be released from court, in 400-plus crime categories, to await trial at home."[3] And "if you go to court," said New York Special Narcotics Prosecutor Bridget Brennan, "you'll hear that the judges are very anguished about this. They're very concerned the defendants not only will not return to court—but that the defendants pose a public safety risk."[4]

So, of course, if it's failing in New York, let's try it all over the country. I mean, what could go wrong? Fox News contributor Tammy Bruce provides a brief rundown: "Among those who've been released so far: An alleged serial bank robber, an alleged serial slugger [with a history of slugging women and who was released from custody only a few hours before police brought him in again for aggressive panhandling] . . . and a woman who allegedly physically attacked multiple Jewish women while screaming Jew-hating insults at them."[5] That last one is the "whirlwind Brooklyn case of Tiffany Harris, who was twice released without bail despite getting arrested three times in five days on assault charges. She's accused of attacking multiple Jewish women."[6]

Don't these Jewish women have rights? If it's falling apart and failing in New York, magnify those failures across an entire country. How many law-abiding Americans must pay the price while liberals experiment with a revolving door for criminals? Will you? Your kids?

This isn't reform, it's stupidity. If Biden and Bernie get their way, I guarantee this will happen all across the country.

Eliminating cash bail and other examples of restorative justice that these irresponsible progressives want to implement are all about nonprison rehabilitation, and they are *failed experiments* from the 1970s. Biden and Bernie's manifesto will throw away decades of learning about how to reduce violent crime in this country, and will return America's cities to failed models that absolutely do not keep our citizens safe. This is what I mean when I say Biden and the liberal extremists are "lawbreaker first, America last."

Biden and Sander's manifesto will end the cooperation between local law enforcement and federal officers, turning our entire country into a sanctuary nation for illegal alien criminals, criminals who can continue to steal, rape, and murder.

Biden also wants to end solitary confinement in prisons. Solitary confinement cells hold some of the most dangerous criminals in the world, including terrorists. These are criminals who will try to kill guards and radicalize other inmates. To Biden and Bernie, keeping our country, inmates, and prison workers safe is unimportant. To them, isolation is too harsh a treatment for murderers and terrorists. On top of eliminating that safety measure, the duo want to abolish the death penalty.

They can't wait to expand welfare for new immigrants. Remember, they believe in helping illegals first and American citizens last. Within the day they arrive on US soil, they can sign up for any welfare program they can. This is yet another Biden flop; in the nineties, Biden voted for a law enacted by Bill Clinton hindering immigrants from obtaining welfare.[7]

Where they will get the money for this? You can be sure they want to reach in your back pocket to get it. And, to add as many potentially troubling new residents as possible, they're determined to increase refugee admissions by 700 percent.

Meanwhile, illegals who don't show up for their court date with an immigration judge two years after they were caught and released are taking jobs, for cash under the table, from our African American and Hispanic youth who are trying to stand on their own two feet instead of on welfare. Biden and Sanders are all for blanket, unconditional amnesty for all illegals, full stop.

While they're at it, they'll give free public housing to all former inmates. How many *law-abiding* Americans could use free housing? Well, screw them—we'll give it to criminals getting out of jail. While transitional housing is a great idea to help people integrate after they've been inside, this would create a reverse incentive. Need somewhere to live? Great, just commit a felony crime and do the time. When you get out, boom! Free housing. Thanks, American taxpayer, for working so hard for me!

Biden would appoint social justice prosecutors, a danger many may not appreciate, because "social justice" sounds so inclusive and delightful! But this is just neo-Marxist ideology that would install prosecutors who don't uphold the law but are directed to make politically driven decisions about who goes to jail and who does not. Instead of justice that is neutral and impartially equal for all, this would promote "justice" that's as randomly unfair as the next activist judge. San Francisco already faces problems with this, where prosecutors are now worrying about so-called "quality of life" crimes.

Tucker Carlson has done a five-part series called "American Dystopia," and in one part of the series SFPD Lieutenant Tracy McCray describes the legal process that occurs when a police citation is handed over to a prosecutor: "Right then and there, they will make the decision whether it will get charged or not. And the most times, it's like nope, not charged."[8] This politically motivated abuse of justice has many criminals never entering a courtroom, according to Carlson. Among America's twenty largest cities, San Francisco "has the highest rate of property crime."[9] San Francisco-based writer Erica Sandberg said, "Crime is really out of control . . . whether it's property crime or even violent crime. It is scary."[10]

So, since it's failing so spectacularly in San Francisco, let's do it all over the country. Right, Joe? Biden will hand our cities over to the neo-Marxist wackos with no consideration of our safety, but that's not enough—he plans on annexing our suburbs, too, so nowhere will be safe from this liberal lunacy.[11]

Treacherously going beyond the Affirmatively Furthering Fair Housing (AFFH) regulation, Biden and Bernie's plan includes an outright attack on the single-family dwelling—what many consider the American dream. Following Cory Booker's strategy, Biden wants to create "little downtowns" of government-funded affordable housing outside of the cities and the end of single-family zoning in the suburbs.[12] Their destination of choice? *Your* neighborhood.

Author Stanley Kurtz writes, "Combine the Obama-Biden administration's radical AFFH regulation with Booker's new strategy, and I don't see how the suburbs can retain their ability to govern themselves. It will mean the end of local control, the end of a style of living that many people prefer to the city, and therefore the end of meaningful choice in how Americans can live. Shouldn't voters know that this is what's at stake in the election?"[13]

A vote for Joe Biden is a choice for the destruction of the suburbs as we know it. This destructive idea will decrease your home's value and increase nearby crime. Anyone still under the delusion that Biden is a moderate needs to know this is a war to abolish a long-held American dream.

President Trump withdrew from the Paris Climate Accord, which obligated America to spend trillions trying to reduce emissions while allowing China and India to do nothing for a decade to reduce theirs, but Joe and Bernie want back in. They love the idea of destroying the middle class to help the Left's globalist ambitions, further damaging America and hurting its people, while other countries get off scot-free and prosper at our expense. If you live somewhere like Pennsylvania, Ohio, Oklahoma, Texas, or any other state that produces energy, kiss your job goodbye. Ironically, Joe Biden tries to claim that Pennsylvania is his home state, when he's actively trying to destroy it, running off jobs, and killing the economy while simultaneously raising the tax burden. What other politician tries to ruin the state they came from?

Eliminating carbon emissions by 2030 is one of the dumbest things on the Biden-Bernie list. How do they expect to make electricity by 2030? Do they have any idea how long it takes to construct plants? And what will power them? They hate coal and dislike nuclear energy, so what are we going to use, hamsters in wheels? Their zero-emissions goal would completely destroy the auto and air travel industries. It's the ridiculous and failed Green New Deal by another name.

Biden will remake the Federal Reserve, one of the most apolitical parts of government, into a political one. The Reserve is charged to hold up the stability of our nation's economy, but Biden's manifesto requires them to end racial inequality. This is inserting identity politics where they don't belong. The Federal Reserve should continue to make economic decisions that are best for America, period, not woke social justice pipe dreams. The Reserve has a fiduciary responsibility, the same as any investment advisor, to make the best decisions for your money, and this policy would betray that principle.

Whether Crazy Bernie is calling the shots or another one of Joe Biden's puppet masters, Biden is the radical left-winger we've all feared he would be, even if by default. Bernie and Biden's manifesto spell out the socialist liberal agenda of the Democrat Party. They're showing their true colors, and if Joe Biden gets elected and implements this socialist wish list, it will be death by suicide for America. It will affect you, your children, and your grandchildren more profoundly than anything else in American history. The America we know and love will die on arrival, lost to future generations.

Bernie's deceased BFF and former Premier of the Soviet Union, Nitkita Khrushchev, predicted, "We will take America without firing a shot. We do not have to invade the U.S. We will destroy you from within." If he were still alive, he would be applauding Bernie and Biden.

I've only covered a handful of their forty-plus disastrous ideas, but think about it: the list of Bernie and Biden's Unity Task Force Recommendations is only what they're willing to disclose for now. Consider how much more they would love to do. They have come out into the open, admitting they will transform our country into a twisted parody of a once-great republic. If this is the content Joe Biden is willing to present on his website for the world to see, imagine how much worse his plans really are.

This is just the tip of the iceberg. On July 14, 2020, President Donald Trump defined the Biden-Sanders agenda as "the most extreme platform of any major party nominee, by far, in American history."

We need to send a message *now* that this is unacceptable, and that America is not ready—will *never* be ready—to lose what has made us great.

CHAPTER 10

Cheering on the Crisis

Tell me if you've heard this one before. A new virus emerges. Some groups have little or no immunity to it because it's a novel virus. Millions become ill, hundreds of thousands are hospitalized, and thousands die. It's a pandemic sweeping the globe, with the CDC estimating the worldwide death toll in the hundreds of thousands.

Sound familiar? It should—it happened in 2009 when the influenza A (H1N1)pdm09 virus swept across the globe. Differences appeared, of course, between the H1N1 pandemic of 2009 and the COVID-19 pandemic that hit in early 2020. For one, people in their sixties seemed to have some immunity to the H1N1, therefore many of those who died of the so-called swine flu were young.[1]

Another big difference? Over a thousand people died of H1N1 before the Obama-Biden administration announced a national emergency declaration. In April 2009, Homeland Security Advisor John Brennan warned Obama and Biden about the spread of swine flu.[2] In October 2009, CDC Director Thomas Frieden reported that more than one thousand people had died in the US, and finally Obama declared a national emergency.[3]

Contrast that with Donald Trump's response to COVID-19. While Obama and Biden took far longer to respond to the threat, my father quickly shut down travel from the epicenter of the outbreak, under great criticism and the tired old cries of racism. They now also cried "xenophobia,"[4] which I'm pretty sure they had to look up in a thesaurus. Donald Trump responded to the virus before a single American had even died. On January 31, 2020, he declared a travel ban on flights to the US from China,[5] and the first death from the disease occurred on February 6.[6] Of course hardly anyone in America is even aware of this, and the media will go out of their way to omit this fact and remain silent.

Biden, who helped lead the response for the Obama administration, bungled his response to H1N1, nearly causing a nationwide panic and muddling the national message so royally, the Obama administration had to walk it back.[7] Right away, Trump acted swiftly to restrict individuals coming here from the hardest-hit areas. Not that they'll give him any credit; only two months after they criticized him for moving too quickly, they railed against him, alleging that he had moved too slowly.[8] So which is it, people? No matter what Trump does, the liberals think it must be wrong.

Biden said it was too aggressive to shut down travel to China because of the coronavirus, but then again, his son had 1.5 billion reasons to avoid pissing off the Chinese. In any other point in history, going back to the bubonic plague, it would make sense to shut down travel from the epicenter of a viral outbreak. It's no different than schools telling you to not send your sick kids during flu season—it's just common sense. But things like common sense are far from common when dealing with the mentality of the Left.

Furthermore, Biden said, "Banning all travel from Europe or any other part of the world may slow it, but, as we've seen, it will not stop it. All travel restrictions based on favoritism and politics rather than risk will be counterproductive,"[9] insinuating that my father was restricting travel based on politics. Apparently, stopping travel from the origin of a virus amounts to "fanning the flames" of "hate, fear and xenophobia," according to Biden.[10] Seems like the logical thing to do to most people. The leftist bullshit never ends.

I guess Biden lucked out by "only" getting the H1N1 situation. The funny thing is, his own chief of staff, Ron Klain, from the swine-flu era agrees. Ron gives us the most honest assessment of what happened during the swine flu: "It is purely a fortuity that this isn't one of the great mass casualty events in American history. It had nothing to do with us doing anything right. It just had to do with luck."[11] Obama and Biden had another term in office to fix America's preparedness for another pandemic but failed miserably, passing on their responsibilities for someone else to handle. If Biden and Obama had faced the COVID-19 pandemic, it would have flooded and overwhelmed our hospitals like the health experts feared it would, because they did nothing to flatten the curve like Trump did. If Trump had waited for months to respond to COVID-19 like Biden and Obama did, it would have had disastrous consequences, far greater than we feared. Lucky for the American people, that didn't happen.

Unlucky for America was the depleted stock of PPE and res-pirators my father inherited from the Obama-Biden administra-tion. Not only did they go through a pandemic with a sluggish, muddled response, they didn't learn anything: Obama did not en-sure the supply was replenished. The H1N1 outbreak left N95 masks at about a one-quarter capacity.[12] Once containing over

100 million respirator masks, our national stockpile was down to 12 million N95 and 30 million surgical masks.[13] Instead of choosing to restock them, the Obama administration decided to use the national emergency stockpile's $600 million budget in other ways.[14] When the coronavirus hit, we realized we needed to come up with some five hundred million masks[15]—and fast. America responded. Ford, GE, and 3M, to name a few, shifted their production to building PPE to quickly supply our country's need.[16]

But of course no one criticized the Obama White House for their response to the H1N1 flu or even noted that the supplies were not replenished. Most people didn't hear anything about it at all. It was business as usual—protect the Democrats!

Even as our country has pulled together to fight the disease, liberals haven't ceased complaining and criticizing, though they freely talk out of both sides of their mouths. Only in 2020, only under Democrat reasoning, was it rational to fight Trump's travel ban and still promote gatherings in the face of the growing pandemic. In late February, Nancy Pelosi was still encouraging people to tour businesses in Chinatown. "You should come to Chinatown," Pelosi told reporters February 24, claiming the city had taken "precautions."[17] My father tweeted, "Crazy Nancy Pelosi deleted this from her Twitter account. She wanted everyone to pack into Chinatown long after I closed the BORDER TO CHINA. Based on her statement, she is responsible for many deaths. She's an incompetent, third-rate politician!"[18] I couldn't have said it better.

My father has faced down China before and won a trade victory many said was impossible. But another fight is shaping up over the way China handled the coronavirus outbreak in Wuhan that later spread into a worldwide pandemic that has killed hundreds of thousands at the time I write this. Seventy-seven percent of Americans hold China responsible, and 54 percent think China owes the rest of the world a monetary debt for the lies and attempted cover-up that made the outbreak harder on us all.[19] Given Joe Biden's soft and compromising record on China, that kind of showdown would not go well for him. He would roll over and show them his soft underbelly, and no one would hold China accountable. They would get away with one of the greatest mass casualty events in modern history. Let's not let that happen.

I'm so glad Joe Biden wasn't in charge when the virus came to the United States! The Wuhan flu hit us when our economy was at historical highs and is the only thing that put a dent in the Trump economy. Can you imagine what would have happened if the virus had attacked when we were in the stagnant economic growth Biden and Obama presided over? It wouldn't be pretty, I can tell you that.

The Democrats want to change history. And of course, because of liberal privilege, they can have their cake and eat it too. Because you don't have to be consistent when you're a liberal; you just have to be emotional and say and do whatever the hell you want. The media will take care of the rest, revising history in favor of Democrats every step of the way.

Take ventilators for instance. At one point, everyone was crying and saying there wouldn't be enough ventilators. People were going to die in the millions. The media mob was outraged when Trump questioned New York's desire for thirty or forty thousand ventilators.[20] It was quite the topic of the outrage cycle, and the sense of impending doom hung heavy—with a heartless Trump administration to blame, of course. We were expected to need one hundred thirty thousand ventilators and had about sixteen thousand in the stockpile, with maybe a few thousand more from some other government agencies, with largely unknown numbers in medical facilities.[21] But the supply would be nowhere near enough to stem the tide. Or so we were told.

Then suddenly, nothing. Why is that? Maybe because there was no ventilator crisis to begin with. All the projected ventilator numbers, all the resulting deaths, all the shortages—none of it happened.

The Left ridiculed the coronavirus task force for putting the ventilator issue in the hands of Jared Kushner's team of seasoned, private-sector businesspeople. They thought it should be in the hands of DC swamp creatures—bureaucrats who couldn't imagine thinking outside the box even once in their lives. Kushner's task force, sharpened by the free market instead of dulled by the Washington establishment, quickly realized that too much guessing was going on by panicked liberal governors who didn't actually know how many ventilators their states had or needed. They also saw that they could ship the ventilators as the need arose, à la Amazon's supply strategy that has worked so well and changed the supply tide forever.[22] All the country's ventilator supplies weren't utilized, so the Dynamic Ventilator Reserve quickly asked US health systems with extra ventilators to ship them to others needing them most, adding a promise to replace them within forty-eight hours if needed. The Defense Production Act ensured that American-made ventilators went to Americans first, not to patients in other countries. We proceeded to increase ventilator production by more than six times, from around thirty thousand to around two hundred thousand.[23] The Trump administration did the unprecedented by mobilizing an unheard-of number of people and companies, many that didn't even previously make ventilators, like Tesla, which embodied the American spirit in the face of crisis by creating an innovative new design.[24]

At a coronavirus task force briefing in April 2020, US International Development Finance Corporation CEO Adam Boehler confirmed, "There's been no American that has needed a ventilator that has not received one."[25] Think about it, not one American died because they lacked access to a ventilator. You would never know that by watching the hysteria on the news. In fact, you would believe thousands of people died because they couldn't get ventilators, because that's what they made it seem was happening.

After all the screaming and hollering in the media and from the liberals about ventilators, did you hear this good news anywhere? No way—that would help Trump. Think maybe they were disappointed it turned out so well? Good news for the country is bad news to them.

The DNC's marketing arm tried to crucify Trump and his task force over ventilators, but, by any standard, his response to this crisis was a resounding success. When he delivered, they shifted their focus to complaining about something else.

New York Governor Andrew Cuomo whined that the president of the United States shouldn't get to have national press briefings for an hour every day, yet no one had any problem giving unfettered access to the press for Cuomo's briefings as governor of just one state out of fifty.[26] But he thinks the president of the United States and the crisis task force, comprised of ranking members of the CDC and the federal government, shouldn't get the airtime? Sure, that makes total sense. Never mind that Trump did an amazing job day after day. Nobody said a word about the New York governor being puffed on national TV, groomed to sweep in and take over for Biden, because no one believes Joe is a viable candidate. But you know what, I would like to see Biden talk without a teleprompter like Trump was doing daily! If he had tried, the election would be over, I can tell you that. Biden would stumble and bumble himself right out of the White House. But the media will spend the equivalent of billions of dollars hiding him from America.

At the time of these briefings, we were being told that up to two million Americans were possibly going to die from COVID-19. One person dying from this disease is too many, but, as I write this, the death toll is around one-twentieth of the projections. Explain to me why this isn't in the headlines. Either their projections were ridiculously inaccurate, or the Trump response was just that brilliant. Why didn't the insightful way the ventilators got to the people who needed them make the news cycle? If they didn't give Trump the recognition for so expertly handling this national crisis, could they at least have rejoiced that only a fraction of the projected number of people actually died? That would be asking too much of the liberal media. We couldn't possibly give the Trump administration and those who worked so hard any credit for saving so many American lives.

According to a recent study by the Henry Ford Health System, those who were prescribed hydroxychloroquine early upon their diagnosis were less likely to die by 50 percent.[27] When Kimberly Guilfoyle was diagnosed with COVID-19, my father called to check in on us during our two-week quarantine. He immediately recommended hydroxychloroquine for all of us. Kimberly started taking the drug a day later, and thankfully continued to be asymptomatic, with a quick recovery. Chief of Staff to the Trump Victory Finance Committee, Sergio Gor, was also in quarantine with us during this time and took it as a preventive measure. How many lives could have been saved, had the media not gone out of its way telling Americans that hydroxychloroquine, a drug that has been FDA approved and on the market for decades, was ineffective? How much blood is on their hands for haphazardly attacking a drug, simply because Donald Trump had hoped it would work? Turns out he was right. We'll never know how many tens of thousands of sick individuals avoided trying the drug because of the deranged media. Of course, none of them will ever reflect on the damage they did to this nation and the globe.

Then when the Trump team solved the ventilator problem, the media shifted over to talking about testing. They talked about the rising death toll in New York, but they didn't talk about how Florida, with a larger population, outperformed New York in every conceivable way. They didn't talk about the fact that death rates in blue states were *triple* those in red states.[28] It certainly wouldn't have something to do with competent leadership and more reasonable responses to the pandemic, would it?

The mainstream media certainly didn't want to discuss how many of the deaths in New York were among the vulnerable elderly population forced back into nursing homes, when literally the one thing everyone actually knew was that the Wuhan flu grossly hit a disproportionate number of the elderly. New York didn't take that into account. Andrew Cuomo signed that nursing home order on March 25, 2020, in the middle of the pandemic. By some estimates, that order sent more than 4,500 recovering coronavirus patients into the very place Cuomo labeled "the optimum feeding ground for this virus."[29] We now know there have been more than 6,300 deaths in New York nursing homes.

I couldn't put this any better, so let me quote a New York resident, Daniel Arbeeny, who called it like he saw it: "It was the single dumbest decision anyone could make if they wanted to kill people. This isn't rocket science. We knew the most vulnerable—the elderly and compromised—are in nursing homes and rehab centers." Arbeeny lost his eighty-eight-year-old father to COVID-19, the victim of an idiotic, duplicitous decision.[30] This was nothing short of willful neglect of the elderly. But because the news media still give Cuomo the benefit of the doubt, his approval numbers remain high.

As horrific as Cuomo's decision was for those who died, he defended his decision to ridiculous heights in June 2020. He dared to blame his act of malfeasance on Donald Trump and the federal government, saying to Stephanie Ruhle, on MSNBC, "The federal government missed the boat and never told us that this virus was coming from Europe and not from China."[31] What kind of bullshit reason is that? Of course, there was no response or follow-up to the governor's ridiculous alibi from Ruhle. No wonder the Democrats say whatever they want to their fellow liberal, privileged conspirators. They know they'll be told they're right, and if not, we know you meant well. Most importantly, no matter what, it's Donald Trump's fault.

The stupidity of the decision didn't stop Cuomo, nor did it hinder Dr. Rachel Levine, the health secretary for Pennsylvania, who sent elderly coronavirus patients back into nursing homes where two-thirds of the state's deaths occurred—but pulled her own aged mother from a care home.[32] You didn't hear the mainstream media calling for her to be "canceled," did you? One state senator, Doug Mastriano, did call for her resignation and said, "Our secretary of health, Dr. Levine, decided that it would be good to allow COVID-positive patients to be returned to elder-care facilities. And as a result of that, it broke out like fire."[33]

I guarantee that if Dr. Levine was an old, white, Republican man, the rage mob would have tried to destroy her over this. But like I mentioned in *Triggered*, there are certain people you can't question. Though she was born a man, as a transgender woman, Dr. Levine is fully protected! You risk getting canceled if you say anything about her order sending COVID-19 patients back to nursing homes yet removing her mother. After all, we can't call a trans woman to account for her actions—that's reserved for conservatives! Mind you, this is the same person who had a meltdown when the wrong pronoun was used—"sir"—when discussing reopening businesses in Pennsylvania during a press briefing.[34] Obviously, the pronouns were much more important than the health of Pennsylvania's elderly or reopening businesses. Give me a break, ma'am!

Liberal. Privilege.

Let's come back to some really interesting numbers I touched on a moment ago. Mortality rates in states that voted for Hillary in 2016 are *three times* higher than in those that voted for Trump, as I write this.[35] Is the virus political? Absolutely not—viruses can't vote. But *incompetence* can be very political, and we can clearly see the negative consequences on average people in states overrun by liberal stupidity. The impact on workers is also significant. Unemployment rose to 12.7 percent by early April in states Trump carried but spiked to 16 percent in those that went Democrat.[36] The difference? Conservative policies work for Americans; liberal policies don't. Democrat leadership put more people out of work during COVID-19, and didn't save more lives.

But the difference is even starker than this. Not only did liberal policies betray workers and fail to reduce loss of life, the overreach among liberal governors was sickening. Across the country, these petty tyrants locked down on their control, went all-in for big government, and treated their citizens like prisoners.

I like to pick on Andrew Cuomo because he makes it so easy, but Governor Gretchen Whitmer of Michigan was especially eager in overstepping her bounds. Slapping restrictions on gatherings of people outside of single households, travel to second homes in Michigan, and gardening and home-improvement purchases,[37] she put an iron fist around Michigan.

She was also slow to declare an emergency, making it hard for small businesses to be able to apply for federal stimulus checks.[38] After she kept the rigid restrictions in place far longer than other tyrannical Democrat governors, armed protestors legally gathered at the capitol in Lansing. Michigan allows firearms inside the capitol, but it couldn't have been a good feeling for lefty lawmakers to keep frustrated constituents in the Senate gallery exercising their Second Amendment rights.[39] The media, which describes looting and rioting by the Left as peaceful protesting, now described peaceful citizens exercising their Second Amendment rights as violent anarchists. Given what we have actually seen take place in early summer, there is one thing for certain: the Left's argument for gun control is dead. Finished. When leftist lawyers want to defund the police and encourage anarchy, Americans must be able to defend themselves! Thank goodness for organizations like the National Rifle Association! Whitmer extended the stay-at-home order *four* times, justifying the fears of people who wondered if there was anything stopping governors who overreach from "temporarily" taking away their rights—and then extending that temporary violation over and over.

If you're a Democrat, you don't even want to mention the difference between Cuomo's results and Ron DeSantis's in Florida. I'm not saying that things couldn't change, but it sure seems that the initial wave was handled much better by DeSantis. With populations in the millions close to the same number—Florida has around two million more people[40] and is an obvious retirement place for the elderly—Census Bureau estimates show New York with roughly 26 percent fewer vulnerable elderly people over sixty-five than Florida.[41] Yet, as of this writing, New York has had 32,092 deaths[42] as opposed to Florida's 4,408.[43]

The liberal Left mocked DeSantis's measures, yet the economic results and low death toll speak for themselves—under Cuomo, the people in New York lost, and under DeSantis, the people in Florida won. Maybe I should trade the Manhattan apartment for sunglasses and boardshorts. There really aren't many reasons to stay anymore.

Draconian Democrat restrictions, stealing civil liberties in the name of health and the greater good, fined people for taking a drive alone; this happened to a woman in Pennsylvania.[44] In Kentucky, Democrat Governor Andy Beshear tracked license plates of "Easter worshipers,"[45] and Greg Fischer, the Democrat mayor of Louisville, banned drive-in Easter church services.[46] This latest attack on Christianity highlights the extreme, domineering measures to which the Left will stoop to control people under the disguise of their enlightened ideals. You can't gather for church, even sitting in your own car, but mass protests and riots—loot away!

I'm no medical expert, and it makes some sense to be afraid if you live in the middle of New York City or another major metropolitan area during a massive pandemic, but does that mean you shut down every rural town five hours outside a city center? Does it mean you continue to keep things shut down when numbers in those areas are nothing like they are in the metros? It takes some common sense to navigate these changing circumstances—something that's in short supply on the Left.

Across the country, Republican states took my father's lead and reacted more conservatively to the coronavirus than Democrat-led states.[47] Red states like Georgia posed fewer restrictions yet experienced lower death tolls than blue states like Michigan where the governor dramatically overreached her authority. And what about their state economies? Along with higher death tolls, blue states hurt their economies more. Surely they wouldn't hurt their economies and put millions out of work just so they could get a federal bailout? And if it made Trump look bad in the process, well, that was just icing on the cake, because we certainly couldn't have a thriving America that owes its record-breaking economy to one Donald J. Trump, now could we?

Over decades and sometimes centuries, incompetent Democrat leaders and failed policies have dug massive financial holes in their states and major cities.

Nancy Pelosi, Andrew Cuomo, and others saw COVID-19 as the perfect opportunity to bail out these failed liberal governments. As my father put it in April 2020, "Why should the people and taxpayers of America be bailing out poorly run states (like Illinois, as example) and cities, in all cases Democrat run and managed, when most of the other states are not looking for bailout help?"[48]

For instance, as I mentioned, Florida's population is pretty close to New York's and actually larger, but Florida is more than ten thousand square miles larger.[49] Florida has no income tax and New York has one of the highest tax rates in the nation, yet Florida's budget for 2021 of $93 billion is balanced, while New York's of $177 billion was already $6 billion in the red from *before* COVID-19.[50] Let's add New York City Mayor Bill de Blasio and wife Chirlane McCray's lost $900 million to that tab, while we're at it. This isn't "lost" like they spent it foolishly; this is that they don't have receipts and don't know where almost a billion dollars went.[51]

An article appearing in *The Blaze* amplified the situation: "New York City Mayor Bill de Blasio's wife, Chirlane McCray, was given $900 million to start a mental health initiative focusing on helping the homeless in the city. Four years later, no one seems to know what that money was actually used for, according to the *New York Post*."[52] In the name of helping New York's mentally ill population, Chirlane McCray's Thrive initiative will cost a billion dollars every four years.[53] Benefits to the city? Queens Councilman Robert Holden said about crime in the subways, "The situation is not improving. It's actually getting worse."[54]

You don't see Florida doing the same things bailout states are doing. They don't have an income tax, yet they have a balanced budget. It's almost hard to believe! It's almost like maybe this conservatism thing works! But you'll never hear that in New York.

All these blue states, which have been mismanaged for decades and have run up numerous bills, looked at COVID-19 and said to themselves, "We can solve twenty-five years or so of mismanagement with this disease. Let's get the government to bail us out for all of it." Why should Florida, which is managing its finances well, bail out failing New York or Illinois? Why should you, the taxpayer, bail out failing states or cities you don't even live in?

The Mercatus Center at George Mason University has calculated the numbers for the states with the best and worst financial records, and it consistently shows that of the top ten best, all but one are solidly red states like South Dakota and Florida. Of the bottom ten, all but one are blue, like Illinois and New York.[55] Liberal taxing and spending policies and general pandering to every special interest group have failed; their states have more debt, and they have hamstrung their own economies far worse than conservative-led states, yet now they expect taxpayers across the country to pay for their mistakes—so they can make more.[56]

The coronavirus hit, and it seemed Democrats everywhere rejoiced at shutting hardworking Americans down and making them dependent on big government to save them. Are they *trying* to hurt their state economies? People can exercise caution and wash their freaking hands without being micromanaged in every little detail by the government. I was used to washing my hands and using hand sanitizer before the coronavirus. How hard is this, and how dumb do Democrats think Americans are?

They haven't learned; they'll just keep doing what they've always done. In the face of crisis, they'll try to take away liberties and spend their way out.

Until someone calls them on it.

I admit, I was somewhat amused watching the blatant hypocrisy from the media and the Left as they shamed everyone about wearing masks. They're quick to destroy anyone for not wearing one, but the second the press conference is over and they think the cameras are no longer running, they're ripping their own masks off and standing and talking close to each other.[57] In one funny scene, an MSNBC reporter live on the air was saying nobody was wearing masks, when Andy Olson, a bystander with a phone, exclaimed, "Including the cameraman!"[58] Some other members of the MSNBC crew weren't wearing them, either, giving a funny example of just how self-righteous these media activists can be. When I retweeted the clip, it quickly racked up 3.9 million views as of this writing.

While the message from the Left has consistently slammed Donald Trump and shamed people all across the country for doing anything they don't approve of at any given moment, which is subject to change without notice, the messages have gotten pretty mixed up from liberal leaders as well. "Occasional contact, glancing contact, temporary contact does not, from everything we know about coronavirus, lead to transmission," Mayor Bill de Blasio said at the beginning of March before encouraging major gatherings about a week later: "It's not people in the stadium, it's not people in the big open area or a conference and all" that have to worry.[59] Of course, none of this was in line with CDC recommendations.

Faced with his own comments from the past, de Blasio responded, "We should not be focusing, in my view, on anything looking back on any level of government right now."[60]

Does that mean my father gets a pass from liberals as well? You know the answer to that question.

As awful and indiscriminate as this virus is, you would think that maybe, just once, the fake news and liberals would set politics aside and work together with our president to help their fellow Americans. No way. As Democrats love to say, "Never waste a crisis." If this hurts Trump, they're all for it.

There's another crisis at our border, and Donald Trump has the best answer for it.

CHAPTER 11

Ta Damos La Bienvenida Legalmente
(We Welcome You Legally)

Right now, 158 million people want to come live with you and me here in the United States—if they could.[1] Currently, over 328 million people live here, so if that deluge of 158 million more moved here, the total would be as much as the nine most populous states put together. We can't possibly take that many people all at once—we have to set rules. But some don't want any, like Joe Biden and his liberal privileged, open-borders crowd.

I don't blame anyone for wanting to move to the best country on earth! I understand this firsthand. I come from a family of immigrants, including my mother, who was fleeing communism and seeking freedom in the United States. I spent summers in communist Czechoslovakia with my grandparents, learning firsthand the very real dangers of socialism taken to its next step (and why people would do anything to leave that oppression for America, the land of opportunity).

My grandparents longed for the freedom I was experiencing in the States. They had to live in a simple, plain house that looked like everyone else's, with the same kitchen appliances, thanks to the demands of the government. The government decided what their people needed to live and doled out the bare minimum. People worked but were only allowed to make about the same as everyone else, outside of government connections, which killed their dreams to improve their lifestyles. The government even controlled when people received their food. It controlled what they could watch on TV from the two channels that were available, what style and color of clothes they could wear, and what drab color new buildings could resemble.[2]

Having endured these evils and failures, my grandmother still can't comprehend why Westerners would ever consider socialism. "They don't know how bad it can be," she told me. "Please do something. Don't they know this is all lies?"[3] At ninety-three, having endured communist tyranny for over forty years, she appreciates our freedoms more than most Americans can ever understand.

Mary Anne MacLeod Trump, my father's mother, came over from Scotland during the Great Depression, and my great-grandfather, Frederick Trump, came over from Germany in 1885 with a single suitcase and a boundless work ethic. Like so many others, they were chasing the American dream. When they did it, there was no safety net. It was sink or swim! Their dream wasn't one of entitlement, like the Left is trying to make it out to be, but a dream without restrictions where they could take hold of their future.

But one and all, my family immigrated the *right* way, and yes, there is a right and wrong way to immigrate. Every single country on the face of the planet has set up a system for immigration, rules and laws designed around that country's interests and its people's needs. That's why our laws should be created from the ground up with Americans in mind—"America first" should always be our top priority. Even über-liberal Canada has a merit-based immigration system. Why on earth wouldn't we, other than Democrats hoping to grow their voter files?

On the campaign trail in 2016, I met an amazing woman in Colorado who, together with her husband, had recently come here from Ethiopia. When she first asked if she could tell me something, I wasn't sure if we were going to have a good conversation or a bad one. She told me my father was right and "people who think they can just come into America and get whatever they want makes it so much harder for people like me."[4] They had worked very hard to become American citizens, and she put a face to the *right way* to immigrate to America.

And if there's a right way, there's also a wrong way. Every month, sixty thousand people cross our borders illegally.[5] The US has an established legal path to immigration, but these illegal immigrants choose to break the law instead. Many bring drugs, violence, sickness, and more into our country, trying to avoid law enforcement. Joe Biden said so himself, because he was *for* the wall before he was against it. "Why I believe the fence is needed does not have anything to do with immigration as much as drugs," Biden said. "And let me tell you something, folks, people are driving across that border with tons, tons, hear me, tons of everything from byproducts for methamphetamine to cocaine to heroin and it's all coming up through corrupt Mexico."[6]

This was the first time Joe Biden had made sense in years, but of course he had to change his tune. Illegal immigrants take the jobs that our most needy citizens need, and often refuse to integrate into our society, pay taxes, and contribute to the common welfare of their new homeland. According to the latest data from Pew Research Center, 7.6 million illegal immigrants were in our workforce in 2017, representing 4.6 percent of our workforce.[7] The 10.5 million illegal immigrants in the US in 2017 equaled 3.2 percent of the population[8]—3.2 percent who are consuming social services without paying taxes back in and who were part of immigrants in the US collectively sending more than $148 billion back to their home countries.[9]

Who is hurt most by this? According to the United States Commission on Civil Rights, it is young black men who are "disproportionately employed in the low-skilled labor market in likely competition with immigrants."[10]

Every nation has the right and responsibility to regulate who enters it, and Article I Section 8 of the US Constitution[11] stipulates that the federal government is responsible to establish a uniform Rule of Naturalization, the process by which US citizenship is granted to a foreign citizen or to a national after he or she fulfills the requirements established by federal law.[12]

In an open letter to Congress, my father wrote,

It is the sovereign right of every nation to establish an immigration program in its national interest—lawfully admitting those who have followed the rules, while denying entry to those who break the rules or fail to meet the requirements established in law.

A nation that fails to control its borders cannot fulfill its most basic obligations to its citizens—physical safety, economic security, essential public services, and the uniform protection of our laws.[13]

Here really is the crux of the immigration issue: immigrants founded America, immigrants who played by the rules and worked to make their new home *better* by contributing to it. They weren't coming only to take; they wanted to make a positive impact in a place big enough for their dreams. When we don't hold future immigrants to that same standard—the standards of our laws—we are jeopardizing our citizens.

Consider this: How about I show up at your place, sneak in, and expect to stay with you. I expect you to find me somewhere to sleep, to feed me, clothe me, and otherwise take care of me. Oh, and it comes at the expense of your kids. I get their beds, wear their clothes, and eat their food. And I like to listen to my own music, speak my own language, and generally want to do things my way rather than the way you do them in your home. You might put up with that for immediate family members for a while, but even then, eventually, you're going to get tired of having a freeloader around. And if money is tight and your children are going without, so that I can have it, well, you're going to tell me to take a hike.

And you should. But Democrats want to shame us into thinking it's okay for millions of people to slip into our country who don't obey our laws or integrate into our population while consuming our resources at the expense of the citizens.

Rule-abiding citizens don't have any right to be safe or to get first dibs on the resources in their community, right? Strangers slipping over the border should get the top priority, true? It sounds crazy, but this is the thinking of the Left. People breaking the law get more favorable treatment than those who live lawfully.

Citizens have played by the rules, paid taxes, and given their abilities and resources to contribute to the system. Illegal immigrants take from that system—claiming resources the citizens need—without giving back. When times are good, a big country can handle some of that, but in the end it's unsustainable. Now more than ever, post–COVID-19, Americans need their resources for themselves.

Take a look at the strain illegal immigration puts on California. If you speak out against illegal immigration in California, you're obviously a racist, and you get canceled. But from social services to medical care to its supply of fresh water, California is straining under the burden of "sanctuary state" status. And it continues to worsen. To me, it looks like their immigration policies have contributed to putting them on the verge of bankruptcy, with their hand stretched out to the federal government for help (from you and me)! Their Senate Bill 54 (SB 54) became a state law in 2017 and made California a sanctuary state, making it much more difficult for state law enforcement to work with federal law enforcement agencies. But this doesn't only apply to keeping track of people who enter the country.

This law hampers the ability of law enforcement to keep citizens safe from criminal illegal aliens, and the citizens are paying the price.[14] SB 54 releases illegal criminals back into the population rather than letting ICE prosecute and deport them. ICE reported that hundreds of Orange County illegal immigrants who were released under the SB 54 law were rearrested over the last two years because they raped people, assaulted others with deadly weapons, or sexually abused children, just to name a few examples.[15] That is simply indefensible.

We do have a crisis on our southern border. Donald Trump is no racist, and we're not anti-immigrant, but our country definitely has a problem. Ignoring it won't make it go away. Calling us names won't help. And, if left to the Left, disaster is a certainty. In fact, *anything* left to the Left is trouble.

Let's look at some of the numbers my father shared in his open letter to Congress:

- In fiscal year (FY) 2018, 17,000 adults at the border with existing criminal records were arrested by Customs and Border Protection (CBP) and border agents.

- In FY2017 and FY2018, ICE officers arrested approximately 235,000 aliens on various criminal charges or convictions within the interior of the United States—including roughly 100,000 for assault, 30,000 for sex crimes, and 4,000 for homicides.

- We are now averaging 60,000 illegal and inadmissible aliens a month on our Southern Border.

- Last month alone [December 2018], more than 20,000 minors were smuggled into the United States.

- The immigration court backlog is nearly 800,000 cases.

- There has been a 2,000 percent increase in asylum claims over the last five years, with the largest growth coming from Central America. While around 9 in 10 claims from Central American migrants are ultimately rejected by the immigration courts, applicants have long since been released into the interior of the United States.

- 300 Americans are killed every week from heroin—90 percent of which floods across our Southern Border.

- Illegal immigration is a humanitarian crisis: 1 in 3 migrant women is sexually assaulted on the journey nortward to the U.S. border; 50 illegal migrants a day are referred for emergency medical care; and CBP rescues 4,300 people a year who are in danger and distress.[16]

On top of these statistics, now migrants have been coached to immediately claim asylum, when there is no merit whatsoever to their claim. Methamphetamine seizures have increased dramatically as Mexican cartels ramp up production to meet an increased US demand.[17]

In chapter 17, "Promises Kept," I'll share positive steps my father's administration has taken and accomplished in response to these statistics.

The media doesn't want to cover immigration reform because it's a pillar of Trump's administration. Still, every day American citizens are being hurt or killed by convicted offenders who can't get into our country legally, so they do so illegally. Take Marvin Oswaldo Escobar-Orellana, a Guatemalan man accused of killing an Iowa woman and her two children. He's been deported *twice* and was back in the US again for the third time. He now faces three charges of first-degree murder.[18]

Or maybe we should let in guys like Esdras Marroquin Gomez, convicted of bludgeoning an eighty-three-year-old woman to death in her home and sentenced to twenty-two years. He was looking for her husband but found this gardening grandmother instead.[19]

He would probably get along well with Reeaz Khan, an illegal immigrant from Guyana, who is accused of sexually assaulting ninety-two-year-old Maria Fuertes, captured on video near her home in New York. She died of her injuries.[20]

How about Ramon Hector Martine Ontiveros, who has been deported five times, and confessed to killing Paige Gomer, a young mother in Oklahoma? We tried to get rid of this guy *five times*, and that fifth time he should have served jail time—but didn't. That meant he was roaming free on an American street in Canadian County, Oklahoma, where he could kill a twenty-eight-year-old woman.[21] I want the people who promote sanctuary cities and states to look at her face or that of her young daughter and tell me that they're just fine with aiding and abetting criminal illegal aliens and resisting the ICE officers who try to keep us safe. The relatives of victims of illegal immigrants called Angel Families, like Paige's daughter, have been denied interviews by the liberal media.

What about rapists? We should just let them all in, right? The so-called Rideshare Rapist, Orlando Vilchez Lazo, is accused of a *series*—as in more than one—of *violent* rapes in San Francisco while driving for Lyft. He faces charges of rape by force or violence, sexual penetration by a foreign object, kidnapping, and kidnapping to commit another crime.[22] You seriously want to protect this guy and give him sanctuary in California? Federal officials ripped the city's sanctuary policies over this case, but a criticism isn't enough. How about this guy? Frederick Amfo, an Uber driver, skipped to Ghana despite being *caught and charged* with raping a passenger. Why was he set free? "Officials failed to notify immigration agents about his arrest." His victim was at a loss for words over her rapist's release from police custody. "I was angry, I'm still angry. I'm confused."[23] But of course, it makes total sense that his rights as an illegal alien come before protecting citizens or seeing justice served to a liberal. I would say, "Only in San Francisco," but this kind of insanity is happening all around our country, particularly in those liberal sanctuary cities.[24]

Of course, Amfo's victim is confused—*it doesn't make sense*. We can and must require that these people abide by our laws, and one of the first is that we don't need to let convicted murderers and rapists cross our borders, and if they do come in, we don't give them the chance to hurt anyone; we see them brought to justice. I guess according to the Left, she's not woke enough to get it. Remember, a Leftist went on CNN to say that calling the police on a home intruder is from "a place of privilege,"[25] so you can only imagine how little they care about this victim.

These are some extreme examples, but the idea behind immigration is that you want people to come in who are going to obey the rules and be a productive part of society. They're going to work hard. They're going to learn. They're going to integrate. They're going to share America's values. They're going to make us all richer in culture and ideas and in every other way through hard work—and we in turn will do the same for them. That is the system. A great system that has served us well, until now.

Name a professional sports team that doesn't at least *try* to get the best player available to fill their needs. For that matter, name a business that doesn't want to hire the best people. If I gave you the binary choice of someone who brings more to the table or someone who brings less, which would you choose? Whether intelligence, business acumen, youth, energy, medical skills, or any other asset, it's natural that every country would want to bring in people who contribute. Again, even super-liberal Canada has an immigration system based on merit.

Yet the system the Democrats want has nothing to do with what people can contribute to their country; instead it focuses on causing people to become dependent on big government taking care of them—on your tax dollar. This doesn't make any more sense for a country than it does a sports team or a business. For our society's sake, we want to invite those who will contribute to it.

Contrary to the propaganda from the Left, the Trump administration is not against immigration. Rather, we are pro-American worker, which would include merit-based legal immigrants. We recognize the difference between the right kind of immigration, where a country chooses who comes in on a merit-based system, and the wrong type, where we welcome in anyone, anytime. We want the best to come to America.

Loopholes like asylum have become a popular way to game the immigration system. Someone can just say, "Help! I'm seeking asylum," and get in, but the vast majority of them don't qualify. Yet, we release them into the system, where they disappear and begin draining resources that should go to American taxpayers first. If you pay taxes, you're supposed to be the first to get the benefit that comes from those dollars.

As I write this, in the immediate aftermath of the coronavirus pandemic, America faces high unemployment. All across the country, people are out of work. We're spending trillions to revive the economy, and, again, the American taxpayers' dollars should go to help American taxpayers first. Certainly, ahead of anyone here illegally.

According to the Pew Research Center, a rising percentage of illegal immigrants (about 66 percent) who come to our country are staying here for over a decade.[26] The same report states that adult illegal immigrants have lived in the US for an average of fifteen years—that's fifteen years without becoming a citizen and contributing to the system. And that number is rising.[27] Why would they put in the effort to become a citizen, when they're already getting the best of both worlds? They've been receiving better treatment than most citizens, and they've made a home here.

I'm all for preserving your unique culture, especially if it involves good food. But there's an element of immigration that accepts becoming part of the place where you live, rather than bringing your old country with you and recreating it in your new home. When you legally immigrate to a new country, you're accepting that this place has values and ways of doing things—and you're going to be part of that. It's sort of like the way all the woke, full-of-shit liberals always say they're going to move to Canada but never leave, because America is the best country in the world. We have to fight to save her! By the way, have you noticed that those same liberals never say they're going to move to Mexico? Obviously, they're all racists! Just playing by their own rules, folks!

Illegal immigrants who are not becoming productive members of society are draining it. It's hard to believe, but illegals want a sort of preferential treatment; they don't want to play by the rules, but they want all the benefits. You can't put the economic burden of supporting unproductive illegals onto citizens who contribute to society, amounting to a transfer of wealth (the liberals favorite thing to do with your money and mine). There is simply too much, and it overburdens the system. You can't just leave the doors open, welcome in everyone all the time, and give them all the benefits of a citizen, including free education and health care. *Nothing* is free. Someone always has to pay for it.

Led by Joe Biden, every single Democrat candidate for president promised just about everything for free, all trying to beat one another to give away *your* tax dollars. Think about it. Every Democrat on the debate stage wants to give *free* health care to illegals,[28] while hardworking, tax-paying American citizens are struggling to pay thousands of dollars a year for their health-care coverage—these days even more, thanks to Obamacare. This is their platform, people—giving away other people's money. *Your* money! Don't believe? When asked at a Democratic debate, all candidates raised their hands when asked if they would fund free health care for illegals!

We already have a stressed health-care system and an over-loaded education system, but I don't think Democrats notice or care. The US invests more than many other countries, spending 24 percent of our GDP on health care[29] and 6.2 percent on education.[30] The consequence of increased health-care spending is higher taxes or decreased spending on other vital government areas, such as infrastructure and public safety.[31] Who wants that? For education, the cost is already $12,800 per student in elementary and secondary school (35 percent more than the average in other nations) and $30,000 per student on postsecondary education (93 percent higher than average).[32] We spend almost twice as much, yet we rank 38th in math and 24th in science.[33] We're not even competitive with other developed nations. It's sad! Hell, we are behind a bunch of second- and third-world countries like Vietnam, Macao, and Estonia.[34] Democrats want to take this stressed system that's already overwhelmed and underachieving for our citizens and add *millions* more people who will do nothing but take from the system without giving back. And the hard truth is that these illegal immigrants are often coming from a disadvantaged place—they may not speak English, or they may not have received an adequate education or health care in their country of origin. So now our overburdened system is supposed to overcome that, as well? Why do they want to give everything away for "free" when your children are already getting subpar education? Why do they want to give illegal immigrants free care when our veterans, who have sacrificed body and soul for the country they love, get subpar care? Fortunately, this is a problem my father is addressing,[35] (which I'll cover later within these pages).

Meanwhile, the children of real-citizen taxpayers, doing their best to learn to become successful individuals, are learning in yet more-crowded schools. More overworked medical professionals treat them. And their parents are going to pay for these degraded services while others get it all for free. Why would anyone here disadvantage our own kids this way?

In what world does that make sense? The whole concept is mind-blowing to me, yet if you question it, you're labeled a racist. Again.

If we had a system where everyone did their best to bring a net benefit to the table, it would be fantastic. But that's not what we have, and it's not what Democrats want. They want dependents and even more so, voters! They want someone who is totally reliant on big government, because as dependents, they will vote Democrat. People who are trying to make their own way aren't going to be Democrat voters, so Dems are not interested in them. They prefer those who owe their livelihood to their "government allowance" and who will indefinitely depend on handouts.

I pay a crazy amount of taxes, and realistically, I can't even send my kids to public school, given their last name and the disparity in educational options versus New York private schools— sorry, but it's true. They would be endlessly harassed and bullied, so I'm missing out on that benefit for my tax dollar for my five kids. I probably pay six figures a year just in New York state taxes, and what can I show for it? I use the crap roads to get out of the city to go hunt and fish whenever I can. Few people know that we've spent over $2 trillion in taxpayer money in Afghanistan,[36] while the total spending on domestic infrastructure in our own country fell by $9.9 billion from 2007 to 2017.[37] Are the roads in Afghanistan better than those in New York? I don't know for sure, but before you decide, check out 57th Street—can't be too far off.

Only a limited number of people in our country even pay taxes. The top 50 percent of taxpayers pay 97 percent of the country's individual income tax revenue, and the top 1 percent pay more than the bottom 90 percent combined (about 40 percent). That means that people who are making less than $40,000 pay roughly 3 percent of the income tax burden in our country.[38] Mitt Romney got in trouble in 2012 for saying that 47 percent of people who filed their income tax didn't actually pay any tax,[39] because they got refunds. He wasn't wrong, and he got slammed for saying it, but he was too afraid to stand by the facts. You don't have to like them, but these are the facts.

When Rand Paul shared these facts on *The View*, he got booed down. The man was quoting IRS statistics—real, hard data—but cohost Sunny Hostin heard the negative response in the audience and proclaimed, "Our audience says that's not true."[40] The mob claims another trophy.

Liberal privilege: if it doesn't *feel* true, it's not true. After all, why should a silly thing like the facts get in the way?

When Rand Paul rightly explained the tax information, they tried to shut him down, and this is the kind of thing that is happening all across our country regarding immigration. The facts tell us our country cannot support the additional burden of millions of illegal immigrants already within our borders, not to mention the millions more who want to enter. Our immigration laws have deteriorated from laws that focused on uniting immigrant families and attracting skilled immigrants to the United States into a lottery system that allows random selections of people who do not always represent the best needs of America.

Other countries, even ones that are far more socialistic than we've become, don't do it this way. It's time for us to stop letting in anyone who wants to enter, especially those who bogusly claim asylum or slip across our border illegally. America needs immigration reform, and *fast*.

CHAPTER 12
Buying Votes with Your Money

I love stories of hardworking, legal immigrants who come to this country to make something of themselves and give back to the place that gives them the best opportunities in the world. One story I heard was of a young Afghan woman.

Young and well-educated, Fatima (not her real name) reluctantly flees her home in Afghanistan to come to the US under death threats for trying to give a voice to abused women. She doesn't intend to move here permanently, but it's unsafe at home, and her parents tell her it's better to stay in America. Years pass, and this smart young woman earns her master's degree and integrates into her new country, succeeding through hard work after emigrating from a country full of oppression. She has made a place for herself in her new home, America.

When asked if she would ever go back, Fatima says, "I left because I didn't feel safe anywhere. Afghanistan doesn't need another dead body or another dead woman."[1]

I love this story. I'm definitely not anti-immigrant, and neither is my father. However, as a sovereign nation, we have the right to pick who is the best fit to move to our country, and people like this intelligent, hardworking woman are prime examples of those we want to see coming to our shores.

It's time to replace the lottery system that lets random people into our country with a merit-based system that rewards people like this young woman. Regarding the issue of immigration and his proposed merit-based changes, my father said, "Only 12% of legal immigrants are selected based on skill or merit. In countries like Canada, Australia, and New Zealand, and others, that number is closer to 60%."[2] The 12 percent refers to the employment-category numbers, like businesspeople, skilled workers, educators, and their families. In Canada—which no one is going to confuse for a right-wing country—they use a point-based system. Canada draws 56 percent of their immigrants from the "economic class." Australia came in at 68 percent in their "skill stream" class of immigrants, and in New Zealand, about 60 percent were "skilled or business."[3] If you take away the numbers from the family and dependents category, some of these countries are being incredibly strategic by mostly bringing in skilled workers and contributors, while in the US we're merely letting people play the diversity lottery.

Canada began its point-based immigration system in 1967, and my father believes this is the guide to a twenty-first-century merit-based immigration system for the United States.[4] For our purposes, let's define merit simply—we want to encourage people to come to America who are good for America. Instead of only meeting a quota for bringing in people of diverse backgrounds, let's see what our country needs and then encourage people to come who fill those needs. If we need doctors, find doctors. Skilled laborers? Bring in more of them.

You say, "Oh, but Don, that's not progressive thinking!" Yet this is the policy of countries like Canada and Australia, both of which are pretty left of center. If it's okay in a liberal bastion like Canada and for Australia's Labor Party government, why should this be a right-wing or left-wing issue here? Around the world, it's the Left that has initiated merit-based immigration. It's just common sense, yet heaven forbid we do it here because then we're "racists"! The only reason they fight it here is Trump Derangement Syndrome. Liberals here are not interested in what's best for America; they're only interested in opposing whatever Donald Trump wants and expanding their own power over a population increasingly dependent on their handouts—a population in the Democrats' best interest to permanently keep down.

They're buying votes with your money.

Merit-based immigration policies encourage competition. And despite what they've tried to preach to youth sports teams where everyone gets a trophy just for participating, competition is actually a *good* thing. It drives us to do our best, to strive to do it better, faster, cheaper. The free market thrives on competition, and without it, governments, companies, and individuals become lazy and corrupt—just look at the DC swamp and its creatures like Joe Biden, Chuck Schumer, Nancy Pelosi, and creepy-crawly Adam Schiff.

Healthy competition is a net benefit to our country. When we bring smart, creative, innovative, and determined people, they raise the bar. They're not going to be dependent on government; they're going to pay into and build up the system so that there's money in it to help Americans who need it most. When we bring in nothing but those dependent on a government handout, we lower the bar and increase the burden on taxpayers.

Too many people benefit from the current system, so reform won't be easy. Cheap labor from illegal immigrants means
that some people profit from paying lower wages to illegals than
American workers will work for. If there's a ready supply of cheap
labor, why pay Americans who have financial obligations to dumb
things like taxes when you could pay less in cash to someone who
slipped over the border?

We're finding that this has turned around to bite us when it
comes to China. For years we've been sending our manufacturing
over to China's dirt-cheap, communist sweatshops. We allowed
them to do this and turned a blind eye to their cheating in hopes
that with prosperity they would become like us. Now we discover
they make most of our medicines and could threaten to cut off
our supply. From gloves to masks to sanitizer to antibiotics, we
have outsourced some of our most necessary products to Asia,
and it has left us exposed. In the face of a global pandemic, countries are keeping their goods for their citizens first, including in
India, where the virus hit hard. They cut exports of vital drugs
so they can get them to their citizens first—and honestly, that's
the way it should be.[5] A country takes care of its own people first,
then others. We're America first, and they get to be India first.

It's a harsh but necessary wake-up call, and Donald Trump
was right: we need to reclaim American manufacturing, especially
from China. Just as surely, we need to recover the most economically vulnerable Americans' jobs from illegal immigrants. We've
been taking jobs from our lowest income earners, such as minorities like African American youth, and putting them on welfare so
we can save a buck on cheap, illegal labor.

The benefits of smart immigration outweigh the benefits of
cheap, illegal workers. We're never going to be able to "out-cheap"

China or India or illegal labor, but we can make sure that we put American workers first with smart immigration laws.

Just look at the unemployment numbers we talked about previously. Under my father, the most vulnerable income groups, which include minorities, saw the most significant increases they've experienced in decades.[6] African American unemployment has never been as low in American history as it was under my father before the worldwide COVID-19 pandemic. It was at 5.5 percent, and Hispanic unemployment was at 3.9 percent, just to name a few.[7] These are incredible accomplishments that would be the talk of the town for any president not named Donald Trump.

A White House release shows the fantastic benefits to vulnerable low-income workers under the Trump economy:

> With incomes rising for Americans, the poverty rate fell to its lowest level since 2001. The poverty rate fell by 0.5 percentage points to 11.8 percent in 2018, following a 0.4 percentage point decline in 2017—or almost a full point drop over the first two years of the Administration. Since 2017, 1.4 million Americans have been lifted out of poverty. . . . [And] 4.2 million people were lifted off of food stamps during the year [2018].

> Disadvantaged groups experienced the largest poverty reductions in 2018. The poverty rate fell by 0.9 percentage points for black Americans and by 0.8 percentage points for Hispanic Americans, with both groups reaching historic lows . . . The poverty rates for black and Hispanic Americans in 2018 have never been closer to the overall poverty rate in the United States. Children fared especially well in 2018, with a 1.2 percentage point decrease in

poverty for those under 18. Poverty among single mothers with children fell by 2.5 percentage points.[8]

But don't Republicans just make the rich wealthier? That's all we hear from our activist journalist friends. Apparently not—the same release data shows:

> As incomes rose, inequality fell. The share of income held by the top 20 percent fell by the largest amount in over a decade, as did the Gini index (an overall measure of inequality in the population). In fact, households between the 20th and 40th percentile of the distribution experienced the largest increase in average household income among all quintiles in 2018, with a gain of 2.5 percent.[9]

The lowest-income workers, who benefited so much from the pre–COVID Trump economy, are the very people from whom unchecked illegal immigrants *take* jobs. And who is hit the hardest? Black and Hispanic youth trying to get started in the job force. When we aren't smart about immigration, the American worker gets undercut, put out of work, and ends up on unemployment or welfare. The immigrants taking their jobs also then drain from the system, and now suddenly you've got two groups drawing benefits without contributing instead of one. Can you see how this is a slippery slope? If you do that enough, the burden on the taxpayers becomes untenable, and you become a failed state, or you cripple your citizens under taxes like many countries in Europe.

Did you know that until a global pandemic came along, under President Trump's administration, 7 million citizens have come off food stamps, and 10 million people have been lifted off welfare?

These statistics would have been the holy grail of political accomplishments, prior to COVID-19. The guy that did it once, can do it again. Believe me!

Do you think Joe Biden knows how to get America back on her feet again? He can barely get up on his own. He would repeal the policies my father put in place that raised our jobs and incomes to their historic levels, and raise your taxes, resulting in significantly less take-home pay for you and more benefits for millions-more illegal immigrants; in other words, he will take care of them and not you to buy future Democrat voters with your hardearned money. That's not a solution; that's an obituary for our economy. The fact is, no society can sustain a mass influx of people who only drain the system and don't contribute. We can see the results of mass immigration in Europe from 2015 when a rise of immigration swept over European countries. They went from open and idealistic about immigration to being led by parties that have anti-migrant sentiments.[10] Why would they do that? It certainly wouldn't be that these enlightened, Left-leaning countries realized that unchecked immigration isn't sustainable, would it? Some of these nations have declining populations and need migrants, but they're quickly realizing that unrestricted immigration is not the solution.[11]

The "four freedoms" of the European Union (EU)—free movement of goods, people, services, and capital across borders—made those from backward, historically communist nations eager to move to the countries of the EU. People flooded into Paris and London. Eastern Europeans, accustomed to universal price points for everything, saw an opportunity in the west and moved there in droves. Hard workers, these Eastern Europeans were filling many of the jobs in their new countries and cities but often sent their money back home instead of spending it in the country they now live in. It created a lot of imbalances between the east and west.

My grandparents lived under the very worst of communism in Czechoslovakia. Later, in the Czech Republic, what I saw when I visited was an improvement but nothing like the countries in western Europe and the UK. If you've never seen a country like the Czech Republic, outside of the incredible and historic capital of Prague, it's definitely no England, France, or Italy. Look at their gross domestic product numbers (GDPs), their minimum wage, and their living conditions; it's no wonder people who know the real face of communism or its best friend, socialism, left those places in droves! But at some point, what does a little village in England do when they're being flooded with cheap Romanian labor? They do what they can to stop it. This was one of the main reasons for Brexit.

The EU borders are now open like those between states in the US, and you can cross freely. Technically, each of the countries is still sovereign, but what defines sovereignty? It's what you do and do not allow to happen in your nation. But all the EU countries gave their sovereignty cards to Brussels, the de facto capital, so they no longer have the final say over their own country!

The unforgivable sin of the United States against the globalist Left is that we have refused to give up our sovereignty. And we will continue to refuse to under President Trump. That would be all over with a Biden, Pelosi, Schumer US government. We believe our borders define our sovereignty. This used to be the norm all around the world, but the Left has a problem with that—it stands in the way of their one-world agenda. The EU may have started with a noble idea of getting rid of trade restrictions and preventing future wars, but the disparity between former-communist Eastern Europe and free, capitalist Western Europe is stark and very real. Just think of the two sides of the Berlin Wall. Socialism and communism failed Eastern Europe, and it will take them decades to catch up, if they ever can. You can choose to deny reality, but that doesn't make it any less a fact. So why would we want to adopt their ideas as our own? Yet that's exactly what the Left wants. We need to learn from history and others' mistakes and avoid making them ourselves.

Only the political elite at the very top of the power structure benefit from a genuinely socialist system. They sell it by claiming that socialism will make everything fair and equal, which appeals to a certain idealism. They're willing to surrender the good of everyone on whose backs they stand and don't care how many they must push down into the mud to get what they want. If you could ask my grandmother, she would tell you how the political elite at the top benefit from socialist policies while the rest suffer. It's equality in name only.

If you doubt me, look at Nancy Pelosi's district in California, which includes San Francisco. Strewn with used needles, homeless individuals, and human feces, the streets of San Francisco have devolved quickly in recent years, thanks to complete liberal control since the 1950s. Nancy cannot possibly miss the poverty, even if she doesn't have to smell the poop while being driven to and from her redbrick home in Pacific Heights. I wonder if she would let her grandkids play on the playground equipment, with its used needles scattered around? This isn't a bad area—it's a systemic problem with liberal policies that have made drugs, homelessness, and human waste on the street "normal." Don't just believe the statistic; I was there last year with Kimberly Guilfoyle for a fundraising swing, and we saw it with our eyes. Kimberly's hometown isn't what it used to be. We came out from one of the tallest financial buildings in San Francisco, only to witness three people simultaneously defecating across the street. This is what Democrats want to bring to your hometown. The closer you look at Pelosi's San Francisco, the uglier it is:

> The median rent for a one-bedroom apartment in San Francisco recently hit $3690 per month, 30 percent greater than in New York City. [It is a one-party city touting a civic philosophy, with its back up against the wall.] From afar city Democrats pay lip service to helping the poor. But up close the facts tell a different story. None of their policies in the last half-century have done much to rescue the poor from poverty. Inflexible limits on the housing supply push marginalized groups even further to the margins. The stratospheric cost of housing has flung minority families to the outer edges of the Bay Area, reinforcing segregation. A UC Berkeley study found that a 30 percent increase in the median rent led to a 28 percent decrease in the number of minority households in a neighborhood.[12]

If she gets her way, between immigration and socialist policies, the streets of all our cities will look just like this. And she won't care; Nancy is worth $120 million.[13]

The alternative for those in leadership is to use their influence to create circumstances where people can better themselves through smart economic policy and changes like immigration reform. We can encourage companies to create better jobs and higher wages so that instead of getting a handout, employees are pulling themselves up through hard work. This is what the Trump administration has done by putting the lowest wage earners in America back to work.

Our number-one priority should be employing Americans—now more than ever! We've never seen a pandemic like COVID-19 in world history, and while we've always been for America first, now is the time to step up and help the American taxpayer. We need to take care of our own people first—after all, it's *their* money!—so that our country can be stable enough to help others.

Has there ever been a successful civilization that put another one first at their own expense? Of course not. You put your own people first. It's asinine not to. Putting others first is a big part of the leftist globalist platform. It simply doesn't make sense.

Think about the last time you flew. I know, it's been a while because of COVID-19, but you can remember. They give you that little speech about what to do if the cabin depressurizes—that you're supposed to put *your* mask on *first*. Isn't that unkind to your children? Shouldn't you take care of the disadvantaged first? No, if you don't get your mask on, you'll pass out before you can be of assistance to others.

Before we can help anyone else, we've got to take care of ourselves. We've got to get Americans back to work *first*. We need to get Americans the health care they need *first*. We need to get our children the education they deserve and will need to succeed *first*. Before we spend money on anything else for illegal immigrants or any of the ridiculous pork that Nancy Pelosi and the rest put into the stimulus bills, we need to take care of essentials so our country is healthy enough to survive and then to thrive. Then we can turn to those around us who need us.

To do this, we need stronger border security. We need to end chain migration, and we need to cancel the visa lottery.[14]

At a recent speech on Mount Rushmore, my father said, "We recognize the solemn right and moral duty of every nation to secure its borders. And we are building the wall. We remember that governments exist to protect the safety and happiness of their own people. A nation must care for its own citizens first. We must take care of America first. It's time."[15]

For years, Mexico looked at the immigration issue as a net positive for themselves—many of the people crossing the border illegally are their least educated and most impoverished. Sure, let them go to America! We've been solving Mexico's problems for them. But when COVID-19 hit, we saw them shut down the border so fast, it would make your head spin. It's an issue of motivation, and my father has finally given them incentives to stop unchecked migration. He threatened to add tariffs on Mexican goods coming into the US, hitting them where it hurt: the pocketbook.[16]

The liberals in our country want American citizens to be second place, at best. If you look at their policies and the people they're supporting, it's clear that Democrats would rather fight for those who aren't Americans at the expense of their constituency. They've tried to create a dependent who will go along with their nonsense and keep them in power, creating a permanently reliant class of people. As our country recovers from the coronavirus pandemic, Americans must come first in America. Other countries should put their people first, and here we should put our people first—first with benefits, first back to work. Joe Biden and the Democrats' "America Last" policies put us in a hole. Trump dug us out. We need him to keep going!

As we try to recover from COVID-19, Nancy Pelosi wants billions for illegal immigrants and sanctuary cities that defy our laws. The Left wants to weaponize the crisis to push liberal talking points and legislation. The coronavirus knocked our country and the world on its ass, and we're mortgaging ourselves and our future just to try to get everyday Americans back to work and feed their families. Now she wants to give billions to people who will never pay it back into the system and are here in violation of our laws? No thanks, Nancy. If you want that so badly, why don't *you* write a check to every illegal in *your* district.

Nancy Pelosi acts like it's her money, but it's not; it's yours, and it's mine. It's taxpayer money, and it should go to benefit taxpayers first—especially in a time of crisis. That money needs to go to Americans. It's *our* taxpayer dollars. There is no such thing as a "government-funded institution." Everything is *taxpayer funded*.

Pelosi's HEROES Act, which contains ridiculous BS and pork, shows she has no understanding that this is *your* money. She's allocating over $1 *trillion*—a third of the bill—that failed, mismanaged state and local governments can use to bail themselves out. She's earmarked another $3.6 billion to mandate new voting rules and registration and to remove safeguards meant to stop fraudulent voting. Don't believe voting shenanigans? Just last month, Cody, a cat in Atlanta, received a voter registration form by mail. If that wasn't bad enough, Cody has been dead for twelve years! He wasn't even around for Obama's presidency, let alone Trump's. You can't make this shit up. I can only imagine how many other dead animals will be registered come November! Another $50 million in specific grants not only creates a slush fund for states' liberal wish lists but hurts residents in low-income neighborhoods by stopping economic opportunities. Pelosi added a $25 million fund for the arts, including the Kennedy Center, even though a previous Democrat designation of the same amount didn't prevent the Kennedy Center from laying off hundreds of employees on unpaid furlough.[17] So did Nancy learn to put some safeguards on that money? Of course not—she doesn't feel the pain—it's your money she's spending.

Countless millions of Americans genuinely need help right now and are in dire straits after losing their jobs and dealing with the difficulties of the pandemic and quarantine. The Democrats would love to turn them into permanent dependents, and Democrat voters. They would love to print more money for all their pet projects that have nothing to do with getting Americans back to work. That must be our top priority—returning America to work, to school, and to church.

Illegal immigrants may offer cheap labor, but especially right now we need jobs to go to Americans first. Taxpayer-funded programs should benefit Americans first. We can't give away "free" health care and other programs to illegal immigrants when our own people are hurting. *Nothing is free!* Just like the oxygen mask analogy, we need to take care of America first, and then we'll be strong enough to help others in need. That starts with smart immigration reform, and my father is exactly the one to do it right.

In Olympic diving, you don't want to flop. Let me introduce you to a man who not only flops, but flips and flops again and again.

CHAPTER 13

Will the Real Joe Biden Please Stand Up?

Let's play a little game. Who said this—a Republican or a Democrat? (You can even guess which individual said it, if you're feeling lucky.)

> Illegal immigration is wrong, plain and simple. Until the American people are convinced that we will stop future flows of illegal immigration, we will make no progress on dealing with the millions of illegal immigrants who are here now, and on rationalizing our system of legal immigration. That's plain and simple and unavoidable.[1]

Here's another:

> Folks, I voted for a fence . . . some of you won't like it—I voted for 700 miles of fence . . . unless you change the dynamic in Mexico and—and you will not like this, and—punish American employers who knowingly violate the law when, in fact, they hire illegals. Unless you do those two things, all the rest is window dressing.[2]

If you read these in your best Trump impression, you're wrong. It might surprise you to learn that the first was Chuck Schumer, in 2009, who for once was saying something that makes sense.

The second was none other than Joe Biden in 2006 when he supported the Secure Fence Act.[3] He firmly opposed giving drivers' licenses to illegal immigrants in 2007 and 2008 (so did Hillary, for what it's worth).[4]

On September 12, 2019, during the debate, Joe Biden said the Obama administration didn't lock people up in cages and separate families.[5] We're currently using detention facilities Biden and Obama *built*, which did indeed house those children Biden lied about or forgot.[6] In a rare case of them getting it right, the news outlets fact-checked Biden, and his statement was utterly false. (Now, if he had been debating Trump, I'm not sure we would have gotten the same result.) Laughably, opponents of my father's immigration policy tweeted photos showing children sleeping facedown on the floor—never mind that at least half the pictures were actually taken under the Obama administration.[7] The photo with the kids on the floor? Taken in 2014, under Biden and Obama.[8] The pictures from 2014 probably happened right around the time when Jeh Johnson, the United States Secretary of Homeland Security, was explaining the "surge in unaccompanied children" along the southern border.[9] By May 2014, forty-seven thousand unaccompanied children had crossed the border[10] because their families had figured out how to game the system. Trump didn't start separating kids from parents; he inherited the unresolved immigration problem from Obama. But of course, the DNC marketers in the media would never criticize Obama's immigration policy, even if he did lock up more kids than Trump.[11]

In a great example of the media's double standard, they pounced on Manfred Nowak of the U.N. Global Study on Children Deprived of Liberty (now there's a title for you!). Manfred said, and liberals happily repeated, the Trump administration detained one hundred thousand kids.[12] One little problem, Manfred—a small fact you left out. That number of detained children was from *2015*, under *Obama*, not Trump. Some of the many news agencies that ran the piece issued corrections because of Manfred's significant error. Hey, we all make mistakes—you just got the wrong administration, is all. Here is the fake news in all its glory.

Let me tell you a liberal bedtime story. Once upon a time, then-Senator Barack Obama, Hillary Clinton, Chuck Schumer, other Democrats—and, yes, Joe Biden—did some *very naughty* things. Things you would never believe a good little progressive would do if you've ever known their hatred for Trump's immigration policies. All of them voted for the Secure Fence Act in 2006.[13] More than that, Obama and Biden deported more than five million illegal immigrants—which is a higher number than under Trump.[14]

And guess what? Their progressive Democrat buddies didn't say a thing. There was no outrage. There was no bullying or shaming or calls of racism. Charles E. Schumer and Richard J. Durbin helped draft the 2006 law establishing border-fencing security. Good old Joe Biden not only voted for the barrier, he threatened jail time for employers who hire illegals, complained about sanctuary cities, and called for a fence to stop the flood of drugs into our country.[15]

In fact, they all got together again in 2013 and almost unanimously voted for a fence, a seven-hundred-mile physical barrier to address the problem of illegal immigration along the US-Mexico border.[16] Nancy Pelosi, who now calls a wall "an immorality," was one of them who voted for those seven hundred miles of border fencing, and together, they even agreed they wouldn't allow a path to citizenship for illegal immigrants until the fence was completed.[17]

I hope you hear this loud and clear: When Obama and Biden detain immigrants and separate families, it's okay. But when Trump does it, he's "putting kids in cages." And of course, he's a racist.

Now, I know that liberals want to treat illegal immigrants and criminals better than United States citizens—it's kind of their thing, it's what they do—but when you think about it, the immigration actions that both the Trump and Obama administrations took are consistent with our laws. If both parents of kids were arrested, the kids wouldn't be allowed to stay in jail with their parents or stay in the house by themselves. They would go someplace where they could be taken care of while everything got sorted out. That's no different than the treatment these parents and their children receive when we catch them trying to cross our border, and Obama and Biden saw it that way, too.

Until now. Today, Biden says something totally different. The media turned a blind eye to these kids under Obama, but it was one of the biggest outrage cycles of 2019, even though Trump inherited these policies from Obama and Biden.

Liberal privilege.

I'm curious, which Biden will you get if he's elected president? The pre-Trump Biden, who was more moderate and mainstream and voted for the fence? Or the more radical Left, controlled-by-the-squad Biden, who now opposes Trump's immigration policies, which are so similar to his own under Obama? I can't look into my crystal ball and tell you, because it could change week to week. Who's he going to be today? Like the DC swamp creature he is, Biden will tell you what he thinks you want to hear to try and get your vote, and he'll switch his position when it suits him because he has no resolve. None of them do.

They relentlessly slam my father's immigration policies, but the *Washington Post* points out that every Democrat senator, including over thirty of them still in office today, voted for the Gang of Eight Bill, which called for seven hundred miles of border wall with Mexico. Obama praised it, as well, calling the Senate bill "consistent with the key principles for commonsense reform that I—and many others—have repeatedly laid out."[18]

Former Attorney General Jeff Sessions pointed out that these same "lunatic fringe"[19] liberals who once voted for better border security live in gated communities; they have fences, walls, and security guards.[20] They have doors with locks on their houses. They used to support more careful—dare I say *conservative*—immigration policies. Why? Because it keeps them safe. "They like a little security around themselves," Sessions said, "And if you try to scale the fence, believe me, they'll be even too happy to have you arrested and separated from your children."[21]

Makes sense, right? They want to feel safe. So why don't they want to have a wall to keep the "tons" of drugs (Biden's words), deadly gangs, and convicted criminals out of our backyards now that Trump is in office? The question answers itself—Donald Trump is in office.

And if President Donald J. Trump supports it, they are against it, regardless of who gets hurt. It doesn't make sense, but then that's never been a requirement for the Left.

Democrats now say they want open immigration, but are they going to take the doors off their houses and invite these illegals to stay in their homes, or go without their security? No way! But they want *you* to go without the protection they voted for under Obama, simply to spite Donald Trump. How petty and stupid and duplicitous is that? And, worse yet, the media doesn't call them on this hypocrisy. Liberal privilege indeed.

Do you remember perpetually retiring pop star Cher? Cher had at one point tweeted that she would take a dreamer into her home and protect them. She further claimed others in her business would do the same; that was in 2017. In 2019 Cher tweeted, "I understand helping struggling immigrants, but MY CITY (Los Angeles) isn't taking care of its own. What about the 50,000+ US citizens who live on the streets. People who live below the poverty line, & hungry? If my state can't take of its own, (many are Vets) how can it take care of more."[22] If this isn't liberal privilege, I don't know what is. I would bet that Cher wished she could "Turn Back Time" and delete her first tweet.

People were outraged when my father said to release the illegal immigrants into sanctuary cities if they want them so much. The protests came pretty fast; they want them, but not in their backyards. Just ask Cher.

Democrats don't care if you're safe, as long as they are. They don't give a damn if their immigration policies hurt the job prospects of the Americans who need it most; they care if you're contributing to their power, which illegal immigrants who are totally dependent on them are giving to them. Schumer Democrats filibustered Grassley's Secure and Succeed Act, a compromise bill meant to cross the aisle, with Schumer leading the charge for the anti-Trump-at-any-cost Left.[23] This is the same guy who helped draft immigration laws under Obama. Democrats didn't care about getting it right and solving this critical problem. To them, it's all a gotcha game, even when it makes no sense and liberals flip-flop on policies they once supported, like the wall.

Joe Biden is the leading example of this, not just because of his flip-flop on the border wall and immigration policy, but because he's switched his position so many times on so many important policies. Consider how dangerous it is to have an unprincipled president like this.

This has got to be a new record for flip-flops. Around the same time he was changing his tune on China, Biden flipped on his position on the Hyde Amendment, which limits the use of federal taxpayer dollars for killing babies—I mean abortion—except in certain situations such as rape and incest. This amendment, which came three years after *Roe v. Wade*, put some limits on abortion. Even moderates on abortion had often been able to agree that since all taxpayers don't agree with abortion, we shouldn't use tax dollars to fund it. Repeatedly, Biden cast pro-life votes and was even against exceptions for rape and incest, such as his votes in 1977 and 1981.[24] Biden once bragged to his constituents in 1994 that he voted against taxpayer-funded abortions "on no fewer than 50 occasions."[25] While I'm personally glad for these votes, Biden's recent change from his longtime stance on abortion precisely displays that he's for sale to the radical Left—so much so that his campaign confirmed that he still supported the Hyde Amendment to NBC just *a day* before he flipped his position.[26]

Apparently, Biden changed his tune after coming under fire from his liberal buddies and such policy experts as Alyssa Milano from *Who's the Boss?*[27] His sudden flip on the Hyde Amendment reversed forty years of his voting record in less than twenty-four hours, as this liberal Catholic caved to the pressure. This had to be a new record, even for Biden. The flip-flop may make him more popular amongst his leftist supporters, but it's sure to make him less appealing to unborn future voters who could have died alone on a cold, abortion-clinic floor, instead of being adopted by a loving family who wants them.

David Axelrod, who was one of Obama's chief strategists, criticized the move. "So that was a flip, flop, flip, which is never a good thing in politics, and it raises questions about his own performance and his own steadiness and his campaign's performance. So this was not a good—you know, beyond the issue itself, this was not a reassuring episode for the Biden campaign."[28] That's a pretty damning statement from someone supposedly on your side.

Think about this for a moment. We have no way of knowing what Biden's real positions are or how he would vote in the future. Just because he's voted one direction for more than forty years doesn't mean he'll stick with it. He was bullied into this change and other changes. I doubt this guy has the character or resolve to make a tough decision that's the right call. If Biden reversed forty years of voting record because he got pushed around by actress Alyssa Milano, what's he going to do if he faces off with the radical Mullahs in Iran or Assad in unpredictable Syria? Does anyone think Biden, who is now betraying his Catholic ideals, is an authentic man of conviction? Or is he just caving to the pressure of the Left and doing whatever it takes to win? This further illustrates my point that we don't know who will be pulling Biden's puppet strings. It may be Elizabeth Warren and Alyssa Milano one minute, or some unknown Green New Deal anarchist the next. These power-seeking crazies are licking their chops and planning their takeover of Joe Biden as you read this book.

Since his Violent Crime Control and Law Enforcement Act of 1994, Biden has supported capital punishment—up until June of 2019.[29] Biden now says he regrets his signature crime law he hoped would "lock the S.O.B.s up." Still, the fact remains that a generation of minorities have been disproportionately affected under Joe Biden's legislation, whatever he claims to believe now.[30] His crime legislation destroyed African American families and their communities,[31] and now he simply flips on it because it's no longer trendy to be tough on crime? Seems to me, Biden never believed in anything. He just did what was politically expedient and beneficial to advance his sham of a career.

We've already seen how Biden has flipped on racial issues from his early days of opposing school busing to now saying that you "ain't black" if you don't vote for him. What total bullshit! Start with his crime legislation and just run through every racially charged "microaggression" and gaffe he's bumbled through over the last fifty years of fondly working with racists and anti-civil-rights politicians. Biden has proven he's no enlightened progressive on race. He's a good-old-boy swamp creature, through and through, no matter what he's flipped to saying today.

Biden has resisted opening his Senate papers that span from 1973 to 2009 or his documents from his time as vice president from 2009 to 2016. These aren't personal notes; these are documents from his time on the taxpayer's payroll as a swamp monster—I mean "public servant." We were supposed to receive these documents from the University of Delaware back in 2017, and they have yet to release them.[32] What's he afraid of? What do you think is in there? I sure would like to know.

David Harsanyi of the *National Review* offers some speculation on what we might find, and I couldn't put it better myself:

Perhaps his papers would shed light on why Biden voted for welfare reform and the Defense of Marriage Act and an "immoral" border wall? Maybe it will give voters some context as to why he voted to repeal Glass–Steagall, the supposed root of the 2007 great recession? Or why he advocated against green-lighting the raid that killed Osama bin Laden?[33]

The problem isn't just Biden's flip-flops; the problem is the duplicity, the lying, and the liberal privilege. Why wasn't the media all over this? This is a massive corruption case that should shake the foundation of our country. Biden's vote is available to the highest bidder or loudest argument. He has changed his opinion on nearly every major piece of policy, and we have no idea who he really is—except a liar.

While some of you might be familiar with Joe Biden's exaggerations, lies, and blatant plagiarism which effectively ended his 1988 presidential campaign, few of you might have heard of his false narrative of getting arrested while visiting South Africa. At the height of Apartheid, on his way to visit Nelson Mandela, Joe Biden falsely claimed that he was arrested while trying to enter the prison where Mandela was being held. Never one to pass up a good photo op, Biden figured why not lie and get a good story while he was at it.

Biden had initially claimed that he was arrested with former United Nations Ambassador Andrew Young. The only problem being, when the *New York Times* reached out to former Ambassador Young to inquire about the arrest, he responded with: "No, I was never arrested and I don't think he was, either."[34] When confronted with the discrepancy, Biden clarified by saying: "When

I said arrested, I meant I was not able to move."[35] Forget Jussie Smollett making things up in 2019, Joe Biden was ahead of him by decades!

If Biden is so weak of mind, if he has such little resolve, if he doesn't have any principles that he has stood by during his half-century in office, how does any voter know who he'll be in office? He's been conservative on some things, like immigration, but the Left faces incredible pressure to be "woke" today, so then he sounds like a radical. But the Democrats know they need center voters, so then they try to paint him as a moderate, blue-collar Joe.

The problem with the swamp is its creatures lack principles. They lack the conviction of their actions or positions. They will do and say whatever it takes to stay in office and in power.

Political correctness and identity politics are raising their ugly heads. Fake news and liberal radicals are trying to rewrite history to fit their narrative.

Something stinks . . .

CHAPTER 14
No Clue, No Resolve

Bullshit is everywhere you turn in DC. It's almost as prevalent as human shit in San Francisco. Competence, meanwhile, is hard to find, especially on the Democrat side of the aisle. There is also very little common sense, which is a hallmark of the American dream and our hardworking middle class.

The big problem with the DC swamp creatures is they love to pontificate at great lengths about important subjects they don't comprehend. Even more frightening is that we have people in positions of power, making trillion-dollar decisions, who don't understand even the basic, essential elements of business. Can you say Maxine Waters?

These professional politicians don't know anything about business because they've never done it; they've never had other people relying on their business acumen to keep a company afloat. They don't know what it's like to sign the *front* of people's paychecks or painfully have to choose who to lay off and what other areas to cut back. They got elected, and they've lived in the swamp ever since, spending most of their time soliciting large donations and playing the establishment game. And because of longevity, some of the most complicit and least-qualified people, like Joe Biden, have weaseled their way into positions of considerable influence.

Our children and grandchildren will be paying for the decisions that I-don't-have-a-clue people like Maxine Waters are making right now. Somehow this woman has become the chair of the US House Committee on Financial Services without understanding even the essential elements of finance and business. She doesn't live in her district, has made millions, though we're not exactly sure how, and chairs the influential banking committee even though she doesn't understand how a mortgage works. How does this happen? Why does this woman get to make trillion-dollar decisions when she doesn't understand finance? Just because of tenure?

She bumbled her way through testimony with Goldman Sachs, and I couldn't believe what I saw as I watched her asking then Federal Reserve Chairman Ben Bernanke to explain the difference between the federal funds rate and the discount rate, which is a special rate they lend to banks on an overnight basis.[1] "It has nothing to do with the federal funds rate," Bernanke patiently explained. When she pressed the point—because you don't need to know any facts, you just need the sound bite—you could see Bernanke wishing he could be talking to anyone else. "I don't think there's any connection," Bernanke said, shaking his head.[2] After the exchange, CBS financial analyst Jill Schlesinger wrote a piece entitled "Is Maxine Waters Really as Dumb as She Seems?" In the piece, Schlesinger went on to write: "Congresswoman Maxine Waters . . . demonstrates that there is obviously NO intelligence requirement necessary to be named to the House Financial Services Committee."[3]

I couldn't believe she was at it again in April 2019 regarding student loans, when she tried for another "gotcha moment" with seven big bank CEOs, and instead got schooled. The chairwoman of the House Committee on Financial Services didn't know basic facts like how student loans work, how they're financed, or which lenders provide them!

"What are you guys doing to help us with this student loan debt? Who would like to answer first?" she demanded.

She picked Bank of America CEO Brian Moynihan first. "Mr. Moynihan, big bank."

Moynihan paused, then responded, "We stopped making student loans in 2007 or so."[4] She went down the line, each time failing to get her "gotcha moment." Citigroup's Michael Corbat: "We exited student lending in 2009."[5]

It took JPMorgan Chase & Co. CEO Jamie Dimon to finally explain that the Department of Education now provides nearly all student loans—which started around ten years prior, when Obama nationalized student loans.[6]

It's not like she tried to learn anything. You would think that if she embarrassed herself a few times, she might try to educate herself—but no. She's in a safe seat, she's been there a long time, and she's not at risk. Her seniority means she can sit on one of the most powerful committees in Congress, even though she doesn't understand what she's doing. Only in the swamp can this happen.

This woman has been in Congress since 1991.[7] She's in her position simply because she's been in the swamp longer than others. She's making massive decisions about things she doesn't understand and hunting for sound bites when she should be trying to do a less sucky job. The problem is, she doesn't know what she needs to know, but she acts like she does. I've heard of the saying "fake it till you make it." Perhaps let's not apply that to trillion-dollar decisions which our children and grandchildren will be forced to pay for. A college graduate with an economics degree is more qualified and would have a better understanding of finance than Maxine Waters painfully demonstrates!

How do we allow this to continue? The fundamental flaw with DC is that these people get in, they stay forever, there is no accountability, and they don't have to know anything about the trillion-dollar decisions about which they're voting. It's all about the next sound bite, so they can get a good headline in the *New York Times* when they write your fluff piece.

Think she's alone? Bernie Sanders has also been known to ask a similar question, how is it that student loans have a higher interest rate than houses. Someone had to explain to him what collateral is! Home mortgages have the homes as collateral; student loans have nothing. With collateral, the interest rate is lower because there is much less risk to the lender; the bank can't exactly take students' livers if they default.[8] Sadly, it's these kinds of dumbfounded, lifetime, career politicians we're depending on to make decisions and pass laws that spend our hard-earned tax dollars.

The current student loan system encourages career students, those who keep going to class after class and earning degrees in underwater basket weaving while racking up half a million dollars in debt with an education that lands them a job which can't possibly provide enough to pay off the loan. But we encourage these loans because the federal government guarantees them, which disincentivizes colleges from doing anything about their cost structure or their pricing. It's someone else's money—yours, the taxpayer.

Similarly, Democrats either seem too ignorant to understand or simply don't care that if they cut off oil, natural gas, and coal production, they will destroy economies in states like Ohio, Pennsylvania, and Texas, push millions of Americans out of work, and again make us dependent on foreign oil from nations that hate us. Michigan and Wisconsin may not be producing oil and natural gas like Texas or Pennsylvania, but they need trade. Democrat policies would cost millions of jobs and tens of millions in tax revenue when we can least afford it in the aftermath of COVID-19.

When asked during the Democratic debates if he would have any place for fossil fuels like coal and fracking in his administration, Biden stumbled through, saying, "No. We would, we would work it out. We would make sure it's eliminated."[9] Really? Then what?

He reiterated this in a campaign-trail promise he made in February 2020: "We are going to get rid of fossil fuels."[10] Afterward, I'm sure he jumped on his fossil-fueled private plane, flew home, and went straight to his basement.

"No more coal plants," Biden promised.[11] No more fracking.[12]

Between these two moves, Biden would disastrously impact battleground states like Pennsylvania, Ohio, and Michigan, which have a combined 720,000 shale workers.[13] Biden later lied and tried to walk it back, but does he even know what the truth is anymore? Just think of the incredible damage Biden's policies would do to Texas, Oklahoma, and most of the West. Now, we don't have to rape the environment to harvest natural resources; we can do it responsibly. But even if Biden flipped again and only stopped all new leases on federal lands, it would have disastrous consequences for America.

Sounds like pretty standard fare for a Green New Deal mixed-up liberal, but it was merely four years ago in 2016 when Biden was on record with the *Tampa Bay Business Journal* saying that natural gas production in the US was a key to our energy independence. "Energy is the linchpin to economic growth," Biden said. "You don't set up shop if you can't rely on affordable, accessible energy, electricity."[14] In his 2015 speech on the Caribbean Energy Security Initiative, he said,

> Meanwhile, we're in the midst of a seismic shift in the global economy: the ascendancy of the Americas as the epicenter of energy production in the world. We have more oil and gas rigs running in the United States, than all the rest of the world combined. Mexico, Canada and the United States is the new epicenter of energy—not the Arabian Peninsula. It is the new epicenter of energy in the 21st century.[15]

He understood the stakes then. Must have forgotten—you know how the memory starts to go after, well, after you've been through what Biden's been through. When the pressure is on, and Biden faces a decision between America's energy independence or trying to restrict cow farts and appease AOC and the Green New Deal liberals, which do you think he'll choose? Which radical Leftist will have his ear or pull his strings? Because you certainly can't judge his future acts by his voting record or what he mumbles today.

They want to do away with fossil fuels altogether, forcing us to be dependent on people in the Middle East who hate us. Do you want to go back to relying on the Saudis for all our oil? Or maybe we, too, could line up to buy from Russia? Wouldn't that be Putin's dream—the entire West dependent on Russian oil! We spent three years under the farce that DJT was a Russian agent, and now they want to look to these same Russians to provide our energy? The Left would rather submit our country to Putin's mercy than keep America energy independent, all to try to get rid of farting cows in America.

Never mind that our companies will drill better, cleaner, more responsibly, and under more scrutiny than any other place in the world. It's okay for Russia or the Middle East to drill for oil as irresponsibly as they want to—that doesn't harm the earth, right? Sorry, lefty weirdos; we share a common environment. The same air they breathe in China eventually floats its way over here, so you're not going to have the environmental panacea you think you are. Your insane ideas will regulate us into economic collapse, while the rest of the oil-producing nations flourish.

People like Maxine Waters have no business being in the positions they're in, but this is how it works. Congress is not a meritocracy, where people earn more responsibility and power based on their ability. It doesn't reward people for their excellence; it rewards them for being able to play the DC game better than others. It's about tenure, the same problem as our school systems. In DC, you don't need to be smarter, quicker, or more efficient; you just need to lie better and play the sound-bite game.

Not only is this scary because people like Waters are making such huge decisions, but it also seems like someone with her level of ignorance could be easily manipulated by people with real knowledge and understanding. Someone willing to play the swamp game could get someone like Waters to do things she's too ignorant to understand.

If a person like Waters was a Republican, you can bet that the media would try to hold her accountable. They would dig and report and make stuff up as necessary. There would be a level of examination no liberal like Waters seems to experience. This is why a guy like Joe Biden can run for president. Ability doesn't matter. Competence doesn't matter. The record doesn't matter. Conviction doesn't matter. It's all about tenure and liberal privilege.

It's why we almost had Hillary for a president. She had no business getting that close. Had it not been for Bill Clinton, she would never have been a senator. For all the feminists pushing for Hillary, it seems like there are countless other women so much better qualified than Hillary to be the first female president. And she was the best they could do? Hillary was there because of Bill, maybe trying to make up for the many wrongs he had done to her over the years. She did her time in the marriage and the swamp, and the Left thought it was her turn to get her just rewards. They did their best to rig the system, but they weren't counting on two things: Donald J. Trump and the American people.

Contrast Donald Trump with the establishment's waffling ways. He has advocated the same things for decades without wavering. Look at his 1988 interview with Oprah.[16] He starts the conversation by saying, "I'd make our allies pay their fair share," which he's done with the North Atlantic Treaty Organization (NATO). No other president in American history has stood his ground and made them pay what they should have been paying for years. Trump objected to trade imbalances and unfair trade practices to Oprah, and when in office, he did the impossible and got the China trade deal done. He told her that he was tired of seeing the US get ripped off, and when he became president, DJT scrapped the North American Free Trade Agreement (NAFTA) and renegotiated the agreement with Mexico and Canada. Now we have the United States-Mexico-Canada Agreement (USMCA), which is excellent for American companies and workers.

When my father said he would do something in the business world, he delivered on it faster, better, and for less than the other guys. It's how he was so successful. In a world of swamp creatures who tell their constituents what they want to hear, Donald Trump has made a habit out of delivering on the promises he makes and believes in—despite opposition from every corner. My father does what he thinks is right, what he actually believes in, not what is seen as politically expedient.

Biden will say whatever is convenient. He was on the wrong side of the Cold War, fighting Reagan's military buildup that defeated the Russian communist empire-building.[17] From 1984 to 1998, Biden voted against missile defense and for cutting missile programs that kept America safe.[18] His energy policies would again give the Organization of Petroleum Exporting Countries (OPEC) power over our nation and destroy our energy independence. He would raise taxes and bring back the Obama-Biden "recovery"—the worst recovery in American history.[19] All this, while providing federal funding for abortion.

Pick any policy; he's flip-flopped on it during his half-century in office, from immigration to taxes to abortion to big government to incarceration. Pick a position, and I can probably show you three stances Biden has taken on it during his time in the swamp. Believe it or not, Biden once believed in balancing the budget, but we can all see what effect that had on spending for the last fifty years.

The Left says he's the solution for what's wrong in DC. It's just another empty promise that sounds good on paper—until even more extreme liberals start hazing him for jeopardizing federal funding for health services.[20] Biden can't fix DC; he's what's *wrong* with it.

Biden hasn't changed—he's as inconsistent as ever. How can anyone, moderate or liberal, trust what this man says? He changes his position too frequently to know what he thinks is right, if that even matters to him.

The current media pressure against my father, calling him a racist and all the rest, is just a sham. Before he moved to 1600 Pennsylvania Avenue, people knew him to be an advocate of minorities, and he has a history of supporters. As I've said, he was on *Oprah*, and they hung out socially. I've told you about Michael Jackson, Mike Tyson, Herschel Walker, and others. Even Jesse Jackson, to whom my father gave space at 40 Wall Street so he could have a presence there, used to work closely together with my father and had glowing things to say about him.[21] Jackson praised Trump's commitment to minorities and underserved communities in 1998 at his Rainbow/PUSH Coalition Wall Street Project Conference as well as Trump's interest in his 1984 and 1988 campaigns.[22] Reverend Al Sharpton and my father raised money for Sharpton's causes and worked together for decades, and my father gave him discounted rents and was a friend despite Sharpton's legal troubles.[23] These people never accused my father of prejudice—not until the media narrative painted him, along with every other Republican alive, as a racist.

Donald Trump hasn't changed; he's the same man he was before. When the media decided he was a conservative threat to their establishment, he suddenly became an overnight target. It's incredible how, once he showed himself as a conservative, my father was accused of racism after a forty-year track record of working with and helping minorities.

As the president who succeeded in reducing minority un-employment to record lows, DJT is the same sharp-speaking, no-nonsense businessman as he was when he went on *Oprah* over thirty years ago. The issues that drew him to run for president have not changed. His positions have not changed.

That's because his positions are ones of conviction, not expedient talking points—something Joe Biden would never understand.

Neither would these losers . . .

CHAPTER 15
Biggest Losers

You've seen me draw attention to my father's incredible accomplishments, even against ridiculous opposition from the swamp and the deep state who are resisting changes the American people demanded of the presidency. After being spied on, conspired against, unmasked, and impeached on trumped-up charges, not to mention "Russia, Russia, Russia," Trump has successfully pushed through.

All these accomplishments came under incredible pressure, yet he was able to think clearly, strategize, and execute his duties in office, while carrying the burdensome knowledge of targeted attacks against allies like General Flynn, his children, his grandchildren, and himself. They actually subpoenaed my then-four-year-old daughter's financial records and wrote her hate mail!

It's sick and sadistic and shameful, but the DNC and liberal media did everything they could to try to steal victory from my father and subvert the peaceful transition of power, for the first time in over two hundred years of American history. The DNC establishment has not gone quietly into the night. Instead, they've fought viciously. It's mind-boggling—but what's worse is how many people didn't know what the swamp was doing and how many bought into the DNC narrative.

Never before has the peaceful transition of power been as threatened as under my father's first term in office. They branded my father a traitor, an agent of Russia. Most of the major news networks ran with this narrative long after proven false, and they still periodically come back to it when they can't find anything else negative to say. Most people would have curled up in a ball, rolled over, and died under this kind of attack, but my father kept fighting.

For love of country, he succeeded despite it all, and now many people find themselves having fought for the establishment in vain, only to have DJT win anyway. Welcome to his world!

In 2015 when he declared his candidacy in Trump Tower, my father told me on the elevator ride down to his announcement that we would soon find out who our real friends were.[1] He was right.

We've been betrayed, fought, lied to, lied about, stabbed in the back, and so much more, and it has revealed two things: who our real friends are, and who are the biggest losers.

Let's take a look at some of them.

People ask me who my favorite Democrat is. I like to tell them Mitt Romney. You know, Utah's "Republican" representative and backstabbing Never Trumper? Too weak to win his presidential bid and stick to his convictions, he has again proven himself a coward. Instead of standing up for what he says he believes and what the citizens in conservative Utah want, Romney has opposed my father. He wants to be loved by the side that took him down and the same media he didn't have the guts to fight when he took his swing. He begged for my father's support while running for Senate, but as soon as he got his endorsement, he turned and stabbed him in the back as the only Republican who voted in favor of impeachment. Romney is your best friend if he needs you, but the moment he doesn't, he extends no loyalty—to you or to his constituents. Any roadblock he can throw your way, he will. He revealed himself to be a spineless politician, and we may be better off that he was never elected president.

With Republicans like Mitt Romney, who needs Democrats? How desperate must one be to completely sell your convictions, just to carry favor with the media? We knew Romney was a New England moderate, but we didn't know he had become the lapdog of the liberal press, willing to spout out quotes to stay relevant, liked, and on the DC party circuit. What's next? Romney showing up at protests to rip down statues of Lincoln and Grant? I wouldn't be surprised!

Rick Wilson is another example of a wannabe conservative. A professional grifter, he likes to call everyone else out, but we learned he's in a ton of debt. He turned Never Trumper, likely because he felt there was more money in that than in sticking with his supposed convictions. An outspoken Russia hoax advocate, Rick bit off more than he could chew when trying to shame Dominos.[2] As a result, a little research turned up pictures he and his wife posted of "his family on a boat, featuring a confederate flag ice chest . . . which reads 'The South Will Rise Again.'"[3] Taken together with his wife's amazing racist and homophobic comments, the Wilsons quickly became some pretty big losers. If he were a true conservative, these actions would be enough to get him canceled, similar to his failed attempt at canceling Dominos. In another excellent example of the double standard, because he's against Trump, the media doesn't care what he says or does or how hypocritical he is. It just shows that everything Wilson talks about is bullshit. If he gets a pass, everyone should get a pass, but that's not how it works. Plenty of conservatives have been canceled for far less, but because they label him as a conservative who happily bashes Trump, I'm sure he gets plenty of airtime.

George Conway, Kellyanne Conway's husband, is a weak little lemming who used to hang around the campaign office begging for a job. He tried hard, but my father "didn't give him the job he so desperately wanted," though he did have a chance in the Department of Justice (DOJ).[4] George said, "I am profoundly grateful to the president and to the attorney general for selecting me to serve in the Department of Justice. . . . Kellyanne and I continue to support the President and his administration, and I look forward to doing so in whatever way I can from outside the government."[5]

Then George did that thing where you pretend you don't want it after all.[6] When he didn't get the job he wanted on the legal team, desperate George remade himself as a Never Trumper. With his tail between his legs, he cofounded an outspoken, anti-Trump group. Even his own wife criticized the organization, saying they "never achieved what I achieved, which is success as a presidential campaign manager. They all failed."[7]

Imagine his wife going to work day by day to do something she believes in, while he's busy undermining and subverting her and her boss, in a desperate cry for attention. How pathetic—name another "man" who's ever done that.

And in May 2020, here is what President Donald Trump tweeted in response to an ad by Conway's failing Never-Trumper group: "A group of RINO Republicans who failed badly 12 years ago, then again 8 years ago, and then got BADLY beaten by me, a political first timer, 4 years ago, have copied (no imagination) the concept of an ad from Ronald Reagan, 'Morning in America', doing everything possible to get even for all of their many failures."[8]

Again, this loser didn't get the special treatment he wanted, so he turned against my father to try to get noticed.

Since we were new to politics, we didn't have an extensive list of contacts and ended up hiring some real losers. In fact, I would say this was our weakest point—we had to rely on some people we never should have hired.

Jeff Sessions has always been pretty good to me, but my father was loyal to a man who came out for us early but who just wasn't a fighter. He's an awesome grandfather, but he wasn't the attorney general we needed to push back against the swamp. He was a friendly guy, but he didn't know how to play the same game the Democrats played. He didn't realize the deep state would run the show, so when he recused himself, the animals took over the zoo. That's what enabled the $32 million Mueller investigation, which took nearly two years to finish.[9]

So while we're on the topic, let's look at losers Peter Strzok and Lisa Page whose shenanigans happened under Sessions's watch. The *New York Post* said, "Disgraced anti-Trump FBI lovebirds Lisa Page and Peter Strzok conspired to keep the case against Trump's former national security adviser Michael Flynn ongoing when they found out it hadn't been formally closed."[10] This is just a portion of what these two did. Strzok, one of several deputy assistant directors in the FBI Counterintelligence Division, had an influential position in the probes of both Hillary Clinton and my father.[11]

Strzok and Page's affair reached the public eye when their anti-Trump texts revealed details of their relationship and their deep-state bias. Fox News pointed out the DOJ's Office of Professional Responsibility (OPR) slammed Strzok, saying he "had engaged in a 'dereliction of supervisory responsibility' by failing to investigate the potentially classified Clinton emails that had turned up on an unsecured laptop belonging to Anthony Weiner."[12] So, not only did Strzok fail to examine the *real* obstruction—Hillary Clinton's bleaching of hard drives and more—he also was part of railroading General Michael Flynn. Nowadays, he's trying to get his job back, saying his conspiratorial texts on FBI phones should be protected under the First Amendment.

Lisa Page, his lover and fellow anti-Trump elitist, tried to paint herself as a victim, but Fox's Sean Hannity pointed out, "Lisa Page is neither innocent nor a victim. She carried out what was a lengthy affair with the top investigator at the FBI named Peter Strzok."[13] Robert Mueller's investigation didn't get access to their cell phones because of the deep-state bias, but we still know that these two became the poster children for the swamp fighting back. Hannity revealed, "'only eight days after [then-FBI Director] Jim Comey opened his counter-intelligence investigation against the Trump campaign,' the two wrote back-and-forth that they'd stop the president's election."[14] Another article points out that the two wanted to use presidential briefings to find openings into the Trump administration they could exploit to damage DJT.[15] My father told Hannity, "They were trying to infiltrate the administration. . . . Really, it's a coup. It's spying. It's hard to believe in this country we would have had that."[16]

The establishment tried nothing short of an undercover coup to get rid of a duly-elected president, and the media played right along with it. These are the people we're up against—hidden and conspiring until they're brought into the light.

Right in the middle of that was Jim Comey, the most sanctimonious person in American politics—and the human being who is probably the most full of shit. He tries to do these profound tweets like he's this great-thinking man, but he's a bureaucrat through and through, a DC swamp product like few others, a mealy-mouthed bureaucrat in a cheap suit. He did the FBI a disgrace by having a badge, but we all know that he was never one of the hardworking people protecting us by carrying a gun.

The difference between the door kickers on the ground enforcing the law and the bureaucrats who run them couldn't possibly be starker. We love the door kickers; the Comeys of the swamp need to go. Comey is a liar, who never met a camera he didn't love—his entire career was based on publicity, so the media loved him every step of the way. One of the best things my father did was firing him, which put a stop to his attempts at subverting the administration and spying on the president. He corruptly ran one of the most formerly respected institutions in American law enforcement and used the FBI's resources to perpetrate a coup against the president. No one in modern American history has done as much damage to a once-lauded institution in law enforcement. He tried to subvert the will of the American people. Now? He spends his time on Twitter, trying to be a social justice warrior, but he'll always be one of the biggest losers in DC.

John Brennan, the former director of the CIA under Obama, is a real piece of work. As I write this, John Durham, a US attorney brought in by Attorney General William Barr, is investigating the origins of the Russia probe and John Brennan's role in it. The Mises Institute put it well when they described Brennan's part in the drama: "It was Brennan's CIA, after all, that was found guilty of spying on Senate computer servers and threatened to prosecute Intelligence community staffers investigating CIA interrogation practices. He then lied about it repeatedly until investigation into the matter made doing so indefensible."[17] Brennan repeatedly resisted revealing what the CIA had done as it relates to torture. It's incredible how this guy went on to become a liberal media icon as soon as he turned against President Trump.[18] Brennan lied to Congress again in 2017, when he told the House Intel Committee that the fake Russian dossier Hillary covertly funded played no part in starting the Russian hoax investigation. The Inspector General report revealed this to be a lie.[19] Tell me again why he's not facing perjury charges for lying to Congress . . . again? Could it be liberal privilege and the swamp taking care of its own? Make no mistake, I wouldn't have gotten that same privilege and neither would you if you stood with President Trump.

James Clapper, Obama's former director of national intelligence, lied in front of Congress, pure and simple. But again, a perjury trap for a liberal is no big deal, unlike it is for a conservative. In front of Congress, knowingly and flagrantly, Clapper lied about surveying citizens of the United States—and nothing happened. How is that possible? Would an ordinary American have received that kind of treatment? Would I? Would *any* Trump supporter (case in point, Roger Stone)? I doubt it. I think they would get the General Flynn treatment instead: railroaded and hammered and threatened until you confess, so that it doesn't get any worse. Clapper lied when asked, "Does the NSA collect any type of data at all on millions, or hundreds of millions of Americans?" He replied, "No, sir. . . . Not wittingly."[20] Liar! He defended his statement, saying it was the "the least untruthful" he could be.[21] "Least untruthful"? There's one you'll hear in DC that you may not hear anywhere else! When you have liberal privilege, lying under oath is no big deal. Clapper later bragged about surveilling an opposition candidate (Trump) during an election year.[22] How did they get by with this? How does Clapper get to brag about it? Only in DC, and only a liberal could literally laugh about lying to Congress and face absolutely no ramifications.

Oh, and let's not forget the celebrity experts who think their opinion should matter because they're beautiful movie stars. They don't know jack about politics, the economy, immigration, or any other topic they preach about, but God forbid you go against their woke narrative. They'll use all their billions of followers to cancel you! Don't you dare say that all lives matter to Billie Eilish, who will lose her "f*cking mind"[23] or Harvard gal Claira Janover, who will stab you to death if you say all lives matter.[24] So much for progressives being the ones who support free speech and expression! It's all fun and games until someone starts making death threats.

Strzok, Page, Comey, Brennan, and Clapper could all lie because of the positions they hold, and when they get pushed out of government, they get to be contributors on CNN, where their lies fit right in. Think of the numbers of Americans who still watch garbage like CNN—yes, there are still *some who watch it*—where they see former intelligence directors and foolishly assume they are credible and, well, *intelligent*. Easy mistake, but you'll pay for it, if you believe their lies. These losers used their positions to afflict Americans, like trying to overthrow the president of the United States. And then they lie about it, appear on TV so they can keep lying about it, and face zero consequences. Must be a liberal privilege.

Believing them lends credibility to whatever fake narrative the media is trying to push. This dishonesty helps to make it real in the minds of the American people, which is truly disgusting.

What a country we live in! Politics have always been crazy, but we've never seen this kind of blatant corruption on this level before—it's the biggest scandal in American political history, and at least half of America doesn't believe it's happening. Or doesn't care.

The real problem is that these guys lie with no consequences. Rather than facing punishment, they end up like heroes or martyrs. Not exactly a bad consolation prize. Now, CNN trails Fox News in total audience by 1.4 some-odd million viewers, and Fox's Laura Ingraham, Sean Hannity, and Tucker Carlson destroy them for viewers.[25] Still, there are numerous liberal media outlets and so few conservative ones. These losers get jobs telling the American people about the justice system, intelligence agencies, or information about Trump or the attempted coup against him when they are known liars.

Think it doesn't work? How many of you who care where your news comes from actually watch whatever biased propaganda is on TV and swallow their BS whole? The Left has unlimited access to all the liberal networks, giving them the ability to force their story down the throats of the American people. No, we definitely can't depend on the liberal media to do their job. They won't hold anyone accountable on the Left, or tell the truth about anyone on the Right.

If swamp scum like Strzok, Page, Comey, Brennan, and Clapper can lie, cheat, and backstab without repercussions, what hope is there for justice in America? Where's the accountability?

Where are the checks and balances? Where are the watchdogs in the media who expose the truth and oppose corruption at any level, from any party?

In their absence, the responsibility falls to winners like you and my father. It's time to ditch the losers and go with a winner for all Americans—Donald Trump. A man who will always keep America safe.

CHAPTER 16

Not a Beautiful Day in Your Neighborhood

If you don't like something, shouldn't you be able to burn things down, loot whatever store happens to be nearby, and beat up and kill people? If you feel it that strongly, you should surely be able to act on your feelings, right?

That's what happened after George Floyd's tragic death. The country was a tinderbox, and this was the spark that set off months of pent-up fear, learned helplessness, frustration, and rage. What started as peaceful protests regarding George Floyd's death in Minneapolis quickly degenerated into riots as thousands of people flooded the streets. Do you know what fixes a perceived racial inequality? Looting a Target. Or stealing Gucci loafers from Fifth Avenue. There's nothing like stealing a 62-inch flat-screen smart TV to honor the death of George Floyd. Oh, and burning down local businesses, many of them minority owned, like restaurants and auto-parts stores.[1]

COVID-19 fears had kept us cowering in our homes, terrified and unable to go to work or school. Domestic violence exploded as frustrated and scared people aggressively vented their anger.[2] Depression and suicides skyrocketed.[3]

Then, the spark. On May 25, 2020, George Floyd reportedly paid for his cigarettes with a fake twenty-dollar bill, prompting a convenience store employee to call the Minneapolis police. Less than twenty minutes after they arrived, Floyd was dead.[4]

The charges filed against rotten cop Derek Chauvin, who had eighteen prior complaints, weren't enough to calm the situation.[5] People burned buildings down in Minneapolis, but soon others in cities all across the country began protesting and then rioting, vandalizing, looting, burning, hurting others, and even murdering people.[6]

If Dr. Martin Luther King Jr. saw what people are doing in the name of racial equality—the people getting hurt, the buildings looted and burned—he would roll over in his grave. Dr. King's friend, former mayor Andrew Young, cautioned that protests can distract and detract from more significant issues and that all lives matter. "Protests," he wrote, "can't save us now. But partnerships can. The police department can't lead us out of poverty. Instead, it will take the combined efforts of entities like the Federal Reserve, chambers of commerce, Invest Atlanta, the Westside Future Fund, and the creative imagination of the cadre of truly great colleges and universities that grace our city."[7] The civil rights leader advocates peace. When seeing a demonstration in Atlanta that "went bad," he described his thoughts by saying, "I wanna cry."[8]

What's insane to me are the people who support the protests and act surprised when they turn violent. Minnesota Governor Tim Walz put it well: "Let's be very clear. The situation in Minneapolis, is no longer, in any way, about the murder of George Floyd. It is about attacking civil society, instilling fear, and disrupting our great cities."[9]

It is an attack on civil society, and Joe Biden wants to bring it to your neighborhood.

Have you seen the crazy people who cheer for the protests and even the looting—when it's far away? Then as it moves close by, they change their tune. Take Chris Palmer, a reporter who covers the NBA. On a Thursday, Palmer tweeted a photo of a building burning with the caption, "Burn that shit down. Burn it all down."[10] By the wee hours of Sunday morning, with the protesters in *his* neighborhood, he wrote, "They just attacked our sister community down the street. It's a gated community and they tried to climb the gates. They had to beat them back. Then destroyed a Starbucks and are now in front of my building. Get these animals TF out of my neighborhood. Go back to where you live."[11] Can you believe this guy? Later he posted, "Tear up your own shit. Don't come to where we live at and tear our neighborhood up. We care about our community. If you don't care about yours I don't give a shit."[12]

If those words came from a conservative white man, he would be canceled for being a racist—but it's okay because Palmer is part of the liberal press. I hereby nominate Chris Palmer for the Hypocrite of the Year Award, a distinction that could go to anyone on the Left at nearly any time, but I think he embodies the problem we face. Lefties like Chris, Pelosi, Schumer, and most importantly, Biden don't care if protests turn violent, just like Pelosi doesn't care about the needles and literal crap on San Francisco streets. They don't seem to care if rioters burn buildings down, hurt people, or murder innocent victims. As long as they're safe, their possessions aren't looted or on fire, and their Starbucks is open, they're just fine to let people riot and destroy other peoples' stuff.

It's free speech and all that—until the anarchy comes calling on their doorstep. That may be a problem for the Chris Palmers of the world, but Nancy Pelosi, Chuck Schumer, and Joe Biden have security teams. Do you have one? If not, you might want to figure that out now, because you won't be safe in Joe Biden's America. Never has there been a time in recent history where our American citizens could so clearly understand why our fore-fathers created the Second Amendment. The Left's argument for gun control should all but be dead in 2020.

Let's go back just a few years to something you probably don't know exists. Back in 2015, Obama and Biden quietly (as in there was little media coverage) rolled out their Affirmatively Furthering Fair Housing (AFFH) regulation. This radical socialist program should scare anyone who doesn't want the big city's problems in their backyard. Stanley Kurtz, author of *Spreading the Wealth: How Obama Is Robbing the Suburbs to Pay for the Cities*, breaks it down: "In effect, AFFH gives the federal government a lever to re-engineer nearly every American neighborhood—imposing a preferred racial and ethnic composition, densifying housing, transportation, and business development in suburb and city alike, and weakening or casting aside the authority of local governments over core responsibilities, from zoning to transportation to education."[13] Kurtz explains in careful detail how Obama and Biden wanted to rob the suburbs to pay for the cities and their broken, Democrat-made budgets and how Obama and the media kept it quiet until the massive rule was in place. "Ultimately, the regulation amounts to back-door annexation, a way of turning America's suburbs into tributaries of nearby cities," Kurtz wrote in the *National Review*.[14]

Why bring up this Obama-Biden-era piece of liberal trash? Because Biden wants to push AFFH further to destroy America's suburbs by bringing the inner city's violence and crime into

America's backyard. "Biden has embraced Cory Booker's strategy for ending single-family zoning in the suburbs and creating what you might call 'little downtowns' in the suburbs," Kurtz explains while warning about a Biden presidency.[15]

It's a classic example of a liberal wanting to redistribute wealth by bringing the poor up by borrowing the old socialist strategy of destroying the middle class.

Guess what—you need to get accustomed to this if Joe Biden is elected. Obama and Biden's AFFH means suburbs will lose their ability to govern themselves, and high-density government housing will bring the problems of the big cities to your home. If you felt safe because the riots were downtown and you lived a few miles out, kiss that security goodbye. Happy you live in a less urban environment because of the pandemic? Forget it—Biden will bring the population to you. If you like your suburbs, Joe Biden won't let you keep them; in fact, he will destroy them.

He's going to catch hell for this, but as of this writing, my father is considering striking down this Obama-Biden socialist rule. If Biden gets in, he'll take AFFH even further than Obama did. But this isn't an issue of race. It's one of crime and economics. Now that Democrats have finished spending the cities' money, Biden won't hesitate to redistribute the suburbs' resources back into the cities.

Nineteen of the twenty most violent cities in America are run by Democrats.[16] That's no coincidence. Now they want to share that crime with the outlying communities around their cities. How thoughtful of them!

My father established Opportunity Zones to bring investment dollars into the inner cities to build them up; Biden's housing policies will bring the problems of those cities to the suburbs, tearing them down. As Chris Palmer shows us, even people on the Left don't like it when the mobs and riots come into their neighborhood. And make no mistake: in a Biden presidency, they are coming! These idiot rioters burned down affordable housing where they could live, which would make investors hesitant to build there in the future. And now Biden wants to bring those people out to the suburbs so they can burn things there, too. What could go wrong with that plan?

Well, I'll tell you one thing: if rioters repeat what they did to a home in Richmond, Virginia, and burn down your house with *your child inside* and then *block* the emergency crews' access,[17] you may be pretty passionate about stopping Biden's plan. Richmond Police Chief Will Smith said, "This is not the only occupied building that has been set fire to over the last two days. But they prohibited us from getting on scene. We had to force our way to make a clear path for the fire department. Protestors intercepted that fire apparatus several blocks away with vehicles and blocked that fire department's access to the structure fire. Inside that home was a child."[18] *A child!*

I can't even imagine that.

The Richmond mayor put it best: "As soon as you loot a store or set a public bus on fire, you're not demonstrating. You've made it about you. When you block law enforcement from allowing fire services to get to a home that has caught on fire. You are not inspiring change. When you knock out windows of businesses that had nothing to do with this, you are not inspiring change. That's an insult to the cause."[19]

What if your elderly parents were victims of a home invasion and supposedly "peaceful" protesters in the streets *blocked* the police on their way to intervene? How would you feel?

This mayhem doesn't serve a cause other than anarchy, and it must stop. No one deserves to have this anywhere, regardless of whether they're in the city or a suburban area. The virtue-signaling bullshit that we see from people like journalist Chris Palmer is a big part of the problem. It is *never* okay to burn stuff down, loot, injure, or kill people, or endanger innocent children in burning houses—period. To do it in the name of some cause like justice for George Floyd is nothing short of tragic. The great irony of 2020 is that the one thing that everyone in America can agree on is that what happened to George Floyd is a disgrace and should have never happened. In a time where things are very polarized, for once everyone agrees—no one more so than police officers, who recognize that the actions of one bad cop make their own jobs harder, and much more dangerous.

If you're an independent or a moderate who plays along and virtue-signals, so you don't get called a racist, this is no game. It's the socialist Left trying to grab power under the guise of trying to fix inequality. This approach isn't how you build up the poor. You do that by increasing job opportunities like my father did.

Electing Joe Biden means bringing the worst of these liberal-enabled problems into your neighborhood unchecked. Your ability to govern your suburb is stripped away and given to some liberal city bureaucrat swamp creature. Trust me; you do not want that.

You might have been able to identify with protesters seeking justice. But that wasn't what these protests were—these were the preludes to riots that defaced property, burned down homes and businesses, endangered kids, injured people, led to multiple murders, and chased out, injured, and killed the police officers trying to keep us safe. According to the *New York Post*, as of this writing, over seven hundred officers have been injured in the line of duty during the riots.[20] This includes sixty Secret Service agents and forty US Park Police officers injured in protests in DC.[21]

At *The Federalist*, they have a list of the officers killed or wounded in a week of violence, noting that the brave men and women who keep us safe have been "shot, stabbed, run over, and hit with objects."[22] Thirteen officers in Las Vegas were injured in the riots, with one shot in the back of the head and others fired on while at a courthouse. Four officers were shot in St. Louis. A vehicle intentionally hit three officers in Buffalo, and another stuck an officer in New York. In Davenport, rioters ambushed officers and shot one. In Chicago, 132 officers were injured during the riots.[23] I could go on and on. These are the men and women trying to protect us, and they're now the targets of sick "defund the police" efforts, which we'll return to in a moment.

Law enforcement officers aren't the only ones hurt by rioters. David Dorn, an African American retired police captain from St. Louis, responded to an alarm and was shot by looters stealing TVs. This seventy-seven-year-old man, trying to protect his community while others go crazy around him, was in a sickening video that was live-streamed on Facebook as he bled out in the street where rioters left him to die.[24] Where are the BLM protests on his behalf?

If you Google it, you can see another video of him down in the street. You can see the phone in his hand, maybe from trying to talk to his loved ones a final time. He paid the ultimate price, giving his life for others. Many more were killed in the heat of the rioting, including Italia Kelly, who was shot while trying to leave a protest turning violent in Davenport, Iowa.[25]

Marquis Tousant died that night in Davenport, too. They found him near the site where rioters had shot multiple times into an unmarked police truck.[26] At least twenty-eight people have died in incidents related to the protests and riots that followed George Floyd's death, as I write this.[27]

My father called state governors to account, telling them to "dominate" their streets and protect their citizens. It worked. "The streets of America didn't spontaneously become peaceful last week," said White House director of strategic communications, Alyssa Farah.[28] "It was a direct result of President Trump calling on governors and mayors to surge the National Guard in their states and restore law and order on America's streets so that peaceful protesters could demonstrate safely," she continued.[29]Not to mention to keep our cops *and* our citizens safe from riots.

Amid all this insanity, an even crazier level of radical leftism has cropped up: defund the police. In case you've naively listened for months to the media trying to play down what this means and convince you it was actually something else, AOC helpfully explains it clearly: "Defunding police means defunding police," she said in a statement. "It does not mean budget tricks or funny math. It does not mean moving school police officers from the NYPD budget to the Department of Education's budget so that the exact same police remain in schools."[30] The fake news media has tried to paint this as just another slogan, but it's not. It's radical leftist idiot-ology. It's not reasonable, and it's not proportional to the supposed offense. It is the relentless progressive agenda that Leftists will use to remake America into a failed state like the Democrat-run inner cities already are.

Defunding the police is one of the dumbest ideas in history—an idea worthy of AOC. She and others want to take money away from the people who keep us safe and protect our schools, and instead spend it on social programs. Nearly three hundred of the injuries to the nation's law enforcement happened in New York City, and de Blasio wants to cut *one billion dollars* from the NYPD.[31] That alone is idiotic, but then AOC raised the bar to a whole new level of stupidity by even criticizing de Blasio's move. There is no end to the absurdity of her socialist agenda. She has good company with Ilhan Omar, another liberal nutcase who wants to abolish the Minneapolis police[32] because it didn't go far enough.

Dems are being cautious with this one—Sanders came out against it, and Joe Biden's campaign at first issued a weak statement before he later called for urgent reform but fell short of calling it "defunding."[33] As usual with Joe Biden and his lack of conviction, in early July he said police have "become the enemy."[34] This is for certain, one way to cause more senseless deaths like George Floyd's in the future is to call police the enemy. It will drive experienced, well-trained officers to leave their jobs and careers in law enforcement, only to be replaced by less-experienced candidates who have vied for jobs against fewer applicants. Cities are no longer getting the cream of the crop, as evidenced by the massive amount of retirements across countless police departments. And who would blame them?

Polling data shows that as of this writing, 64 percent of Americans opposed the defund movement or even shuffling money around.[35] However, as we've seen throughout this book, there is not a position Biden takes on which he won't flip-flop. When you think about how weak he is, how uncertain and muddled, it's not a stretch to believe that he'll support it if his handlers decide that defunding is the future of the Democrat Party.

The fact that defunding the police has become a mainstream idea shows just how weak people have become and how willing they are to give in to the mob. You can see the irony when de-fund-the-police protesters ask for *police protection* for their pro-test. How stupid is this? They recognize the need for security and then ask for it from the very people they want to marginalize.[36]

As idiotic as it is, other liberal mayors are sure to follow de Blasio's example as he cuts a billion from the NYPD budget. Rather than do anything proactive for the city like stopping looting and rioting, fixing the disasters he has caused, and finding the billion dollars that his wife made disappear from her pet project, the mayor is busy painting BLM murals on streets for cheap photo ops. We already saw how anarchists in Seattle pushed the police out of their own precinct to occupy several blocks in Seattle's radical Capitol Hill.[37] Do you want the CHAZ brigade (Capitol Hill Autonomous Zone) coming to your backyard? What do you think would happen if conservatives took up arms and cut off six blocks of a major US city? They would be ransacked in hours! Are you okay with that? Chris Palmer may be fine with it, as long as he doesn't live in any of those places.

But I'm not—I'm not okay with that happening anywhere, because if liberal pressure has this effect on officers, who is to say if, when the next protest comes, they'll protect my neighborhood or yours? This is anarchy, and for weeks Seattle didn't stop it—they brought in portable toilets and dumpsters. Wouldn't want the anarchists to have bad hygiene, now would we? They're not very "autonomous" if they still must receive city services.

Radio host Jason Rantz told Tucker Carlson, "The city has ceded this land to these individuals. And the implications of that cannot be overstated. If folks think right now, maybe they live in Los Angeles or New York, 'Oh, it's not gonna happen here,' yeah, it's gonna happen there. We're allowing it to happen here."[38]

The craziness won't end. Literally, as I write this, what would have been unthinkable only a few months ago has happened. Representatives Rashida Tlaib and Ayanna Pressley announced the BREATHE Act this July 2020:

> Under the bill, federal funds to local police and federal agencies would be slashed and diverted to pay for health care, education, environmental housing programs. It would eliminate federal programs and agencies used to finance Immigration and Customs Enforcement (ICE) and the controversial Department of Defense 1033 program, which transfers excess military equipment to civilian law enforcement agencies.

> Other provisions include abolishing surveillance tactics disproportionately used to target minority communities, electronic monitoring—including ankle monitors, smartphone apps and other tools—ending civil asset forfeiture, ending the "three strikes" law and repealing laws that criminalize illegal immigration.

> In addition, it would offer a 50 percent match of savings for states to close down detention facilities and prisons, the elimination of gang databases and the forgiving of all fees and surcharges within the justice system.

> The reparations provisions include passing the Commission to Study Reparation Proposal for African-Americans Act and establishing commissions to "design reparations" for mass incarceration to include those caught up in the War on Drugs, border and police violence and the "sys-

temic violation of the U.S. Government's treaty obligations to Tribal nations."[39]

Antifa, the leftist terrorist anarchy group, loves this stuff.
John Miller, New York's Deputy Commissioner for Intelligence
and Counterterrorism, described the prep work Antifa put into
the protests and showed this is indeed a well-executed treachery.
They raised bail money, lined up medics in expectation of violence, aimed at wealthier neighborhoods, and employed bicycle
scouts to move ahead of demonstrators and scope out police presence.[40] Miller explained that of the 686 arrests at that time, one
out of seven were from outside New York City.[41] In other words,
Antifa brought in people from different areas and even states to
stage a well-organized, destructive, and dangerous riot.[42] For all
their talk of being anti-Fascists, Antifa sounds, acts, and mimics
the actual Fascists that swept across Europe in the last century.
The label itself is an oxymoron. Let's just call them what they
are—actual fascists.

This is a frightening level of sophistication and coordination
for an anarchist group, since anarchy is supposed to be "a
state of lawlessness or political disorder due to the absence of
governmental authority."[43] It's not just the inner cities; these
extreme Leftists could show up anywhere. A Biden win and weak
presidency controlled by liberal activists in DC will encourage
them, and they will bring this to cities and small towns all across
the country. If this continues, it's coming to a town next to you.

And with that, as I have mentioned earlier, the argument for
gun control is over. The Left has proven they don't care about
people's safety when it serves their political agenda. They'll defund the cops and tell them not to engage and protect homes

and businesses. And then where does that leave you? Maybe, like Mark and Patricia McCloskey, you might pick up your guns and stand outside your home when supposedly "peaceful" protesters break down the wrought-iron gate to your community and start trespassing.[44] Right or wrong with how this couple handled themselves (and the media is trying to pin the blame on them and not the protesters who were breaking the law and damaging private property), the McCloskeys feared the police would not protect them, since there was a chance the police would get shamed or defunded for it. "The gate came down, and a large crowd of angry, aggressive people poured through," Mark McCloskey said. "I was terrified that we'd be murdered within seconds. Our house would be burned down, our pets would be killed."[45]

If you're a gun manufacturer, you couldn't ask for better publicity. People everywhere are watching this, and even if McCloskey held his AR like he was on the 1980s *A-Team*, he became a momentary focal point for people who are unwilling to let this crap destroy their homes and take their lives. Liberal mayors and other leaders have told police to stand down, and next time it could be your community in the crosshairs, and your underfunded police told to pack it up and allow them to torch your house or business.

At various places in the country like Clay County, Florida, Sheriff Darryl Daniels and others recognize the threat. Daniels seems to think he and his deputies are there to uphold the Constitution. What a crazy notion! While he supports people's option to protest peacefully, "the second you step out from up under the protection of the Constitution," Daniels said, "we'll be waiting on you and give you everything you want: all the publicity, all the pain, all the glamour and glory for all that five minutes will give you."[46] An African American, Daniels said that he would deputize legal gun owners to protect the country from rioters if the need arose. "Lawlessness?" Daniels commented. "That's unacceptable in this country."[47] Damn right, Sheriff Daniels. He's not the first to think about making extra deputies, and he will not be the last. But he and others form the strong base of law-abiding people who won't stand back and let crazy anarchists and rioters destroy our country.

Joe Biden is weak. He's caved to the liberal mob, and he will try to destroy suburbs and eventually defund the police or whatever else they tell him to do because he has no convictions and is nothing more than a puppet. If his next handler wants to defund the police, he'll kowtow to that; it's just a matter of who is pulling his strings.

Not only is he weak, his support is uncertain because no one really knows what they're getting with him or when he'll flip and betray them. Outside of a Lancaster, Pennsylvania, recreation center where protesters for both sides showed up, BLM protesters were there to protest that Biden had not met with other BLM protesters earlier in Pennsylvania. So, let's make sure we get this straight—the protesters were there to protest that Biden hadn't met with other protesters. Okay, got it. The BLMers were there to complain *against* Biden for *not* going far enough. They were carrying "Defund the Police" banners. These people are supposed to be his base, and his headquarters is in nearby Wilmington, Delaware. This should be his home court! When they saw people there to support Trump, however, it put the BLMers in a bind. So many things to protest, so little time! One BLM protester, Kareem Anthony, was no Biden supporter and criticized him for his 1994 crime law. "I would rather eat dirt than to support him," said Anthony, a transgender African American person.[48]

So, in his backyard, with an African American who is *supposed* to vote for Biden simply because Biden is a Democrat, Uncle Joe is treated like dirt. And these are his supporters!

In June 2020, President Trump signed the Safe Policing for Safe Communities executive order with Republican support.[49] This is strong action to address citizens' concerns while showing my father's unswerving commitment to law and order and to the enforcement officers who make that possible. "We need to bring law enforcement and communities closer together, not to drive them apart," he said.[50]

Not that he's getting any credit, but the order will *ban chokeholds*. It will also offer incentives to departments for meeting higher standards and learning better de-escalation skills, among other things.[51] It will also create a database of cops with black marks on their records like George Floyd's killer Derek Chauvin and provide grants so police departments can get help from social services.[52]

As he issued the order, my father spoke out:

Without the police, there is chaos. Without law, there is anarchy. Without safety, there is catastrophe. We need leaders at every level of government with the moral clarity to state these obvious facts. Americans believe we must support the brave men and women in blue who police our streets and keep us safe. Americans also believe we must improve accountability, increase transparency, and invest more in police training, recruiting, and community engagement. Reducing crime and raising standards are not opposite goals. They are not mutually exclusive. They work together.[53]

While Biden is hiding out in his basement, my father provides the strong leadership this country needs. Rotten apples like Derek Chauvin need more accountability. Our country's police can be modernized, but 99 percent of our law enforcement officers are amazing people doing an incredibly difficult job, with little thanks, with relatively low pay. We need to support them in every way we can, not defund them.

Defunding the police isn't a movement; it's a mistake.

PART III

WINNING

CHAPTER 17

Promises Kept

Despite incredible opposition from the Left and the deep state, President Trump has delivered on the promises he made, and more. Against all odds, he has taken on the establishment on both sides to achieve record-breaking results for the American people who put him in office. He has accomplished more in one term than Joe Biden has in his entire career.

With the Democrat field cleared out and the bewildered Joe Biden somehow still standing with half a century of failures dogging his career, the Left now says that Biden is the one to bring the change DC needs. He made DC what it is; he isn't changing shit. The lifelong politician and DC swamp creature cannot do what needs to be done. Donald Trump has and will continue to do so.

We're accustomed to politicians talking a big game without taking action. Now we have a leader who delivers on his promises, and this alone is the reason to make sure DJT gets four more years. If he achieved so much under all the incredible pressure, lies, and harassment the Democrats threw at him, what can he do in four more years?

Because our economy was fundamentally sound before the pandemic, we weathered COVID-19 better than many feared, and, already, we are seeing signs of recovery. In May and June 2020, 7.5 million jobs were created, the largest two-month gain in history.

Do you want Donald Trump, the man who created a robust economy, to lead the recovery? Or do you want Biden, who, together with Obama, managed the worst recovery from a recession in American history? DJT broke every economic and employment record, and he set us on solid footing, so that only a global pandemic could slow us down—but it couldn't stop us. He did it before, so let's make sure he gets to do it again.

Talk is cheap. Results are what matter. Let's remember the great accomplishments of Donald Trump.

My father has done what was right and needed to be done, regardless of what side of the aisle he needed to work with, and his prison reform is a great example of this. The First Step Act provides sentencing reform by reducing the number of people we incarcerate. For years, politicians in DC knew minority communities were being disproportionately hurt by our criminal laws. Not a historically Republican issue, we needed someone to write new laws. As a country, we spend an ever-increasing amount per inmate (over $36,000 a year in 2017)[1] and rising, and according to research, we incarcerate four-and-a-half times more individuals than the world's median prison population rate.[2] Under Joe Biden's failed crime bill, he didn't solve any problems, just separated families, and crippled communities. The first African American president wanted comprehensive criminal justice reform yet accomplished almost nothing. It took Trump to bring reforms. He has aggressively promoted second-chance hiring of former inmates.

My father created Opportunity Zones because he saw the chance to benefit some of our poorest communities by bringing them fresh investments and possibilities. Why did he do it? Because these citizens needed help, and my father swore to be the president for *all* Americans, not for just those who voted for him.

We've already talked extensively about his record-low unemployment for minority groups, and combined with his creation of a robust economy, prison reform, and Opportunity Zones, all these achievements demonstrate beyond any doubt that DJT is helping all Americans, regardless of race, color, creed, income, or voting record. All of them were the right thing to do and they're working. What my father does is for the right reasons; what Joe Biden did for half a century was only to advance his career and get him to the next office. And let's not forget enriching his family in the process. No Biden Left Behind is his motto!

Measure only those four accomplishments against what Biden says (usually on a teleprompter) and what he's done. Sure, he can (sometimes) still manage to sound like a good little progressive with his comments about race, economic inequality, redistribution of wealth, "free" health care, and so on. But his record shows these things are mere talking points. Biden opposed integration and busing. His failed crime bill disproportionately hurt African American and minority communities, as we saw earlier. To this day, he continually shoots himself in the foot with racial gaffes and dumb statements. And his policies have proven ineffective in actually *helping* people, and instead have crippled them and made them dependents with no hope for a better future. This is the guy who's going to bring us all together?

My father likes to joke that he's appointed more judges than all but one president—George Washington. From the Supreme

Court to more than two hundred federal judges, one of Trump's most lasting accomplishments for America are the constitutionalist, conservative judges who will serve long after DJT's final term is over.

What about immigration? We spent awhile diving into the hypocrisy of the Democrats and saw that, before Trump, they liked the idea of a physical barrier along the southern border and voted for it. Trump made campaign promises, and he acted, announcing tariffs on Mexico unless they agreed to be part of the solution instead of sending us their troubles. Arrests along the border dramatically diminished as the flow of migrants from Central America declined, revealing that Trump's pressure on Mexico worked.[3]

My father replaced one of the worst trade agreements in history—NAFTA. His shrewd bargaining skills persuaded Canada and Mexico to take us seriously, and he negotiated a much better deal, which Nancy Pelosi delayed bringing to the House floor for a vote for about a year, because she would rather hurt the American people than give Trump a win.[4] She finally relented and the United States-Mexico-Canada Agreement (USMCA) was signed. This agreement helps farmers sell more of their dairy products, poultry, and eggs; improves the protection and enforcement of our trade secrets and intellectual property rights; expands market opportunities for US businesses to export electronic payment services, and provides many more benefits. Another win for America!

Earlier in this book, I said many people doubted he could ever make a trade deal with China. They wondered, if our president puts tariffs on products from China, will that make our next iPhones (created by a US company but assembled in China) more expensive? Will it hurt farmers? Will it drive up the cost of electronics? But our country has endured a massively one-sided trade inequality with China, so my father accomplished that trade deal! Afterward, the glaring need to bring our manufacturing home and restore America's preeminence in trade became incredibly obvious to everyone when China threatened to cut off our supply of medicine during the COVID-19 pandemic. Suddenly, the problem with China became clear to everyone and revealed that my father was correct. China is a competitor, Mr. Biden, and to be taken very seriously—but America can lead the world in trade again under Donald J. Trump's leadership.

Few even talk about Right to Try, but this may go down as one of the biggest no-brainer accomplishments of my father's first years in office. This landmark initiative removed liabilities from major drug companies to allow terminal patients to try experimental medications that could be unavailable for years on the market. These medications might have shown promise in trials but haven't received final FDA approval, which often takes many years. This initiative not only gave patients hope but, in many instances, actually worked.

Take the case of Jackson Silva, who as a newborn in 2014, started showing signs of pain and was diagnosed with a form of spinal muscular atrophy. When his parents were informed that nothing could be done, they found a clinical trial in Ohio. "Jackson was the third child in the world to receive treatment. And while 90% of children with SMA pass away before the age of two, and 50% pass away before 6 months old, Jackson is still here because of the investigational drug he is receiving. Jackson's parents want all children with SMA to have access to this drug, not just the lucky few who have been accepted into a clinical trial."[5] For those interested, please visit RightToTry.Org.

Why didn't someone do it sooner? Because it took an outsider, not a swamp creature, to see how stupid the existing system was. If they tell you you're going to die, why not try a Hail Mary? None of the DC establishment thought enough outside the box to come up with this, and it just serves to contrast career politicians who their whole lives *can't think outside of a box* and a career businessman who made his money through innovation and simplifying systems.

I love to talk about energy independence because this is such a polarizing topic between liberals and conservatives. While the Left wants us counting cow farts and shutting down air travel so we can all eat vegan and ride our bikes, Trump has led the way to making America energy independent, exporting more oil than we import for the first time since 1949 when record-keeping of this kind began![6]

"Trump's Energy Independence Policy Executive Order reverses the regulations on American jobs and energy production," says a White House briefing.[7] He ended Obama-era regulations that would have cost businesses nearly $40 billion a year and raised electricity prices for most of the country,[8] and consequently, your electric bills. Thanks to good clean coal, abundant natural gas, responsible oil drilling, and lifting "job-killing restrictions on the production of oil, natural gas, and shale energy,"[9] Trump positioned America to be an exporter of energy, no longer held hostage to OPEC or other Middle Eastern countries who hate us. Oil, gas, and coal are certainly going to be mined in this world because we need them to heat our homes, fuel our cars and airplanes, cook our food, and much more. Would you rather the US did it, under careful oversight and sensible precautions, or that China or Russia do it without consideration for our shared environment? I'll get my energy American made, thank you very much.

The state of the Veterans Administration (VA) when Trump took office was shameful and inexcusable. We should take better care of men and women who have fought for our country than anyone else. They should come first, especially before we medically treat illegal immigrants, and we need to ensure that every single one of these brave soldiers receives the best possible care. Anything less is unacceptable.

My father began removing bureaucrats who had done nothing but show up because they had tenure. He enacted reforms such as the MISSION Act, which, in part, improves the VA's ability to retain the best medical providers; therefore, veterans have the opportunity to receive the best health care possible, and dramatically more of them have the freedom to get it from the VA or local community providers. This law proves that both sides of the aisle can work together to take care of our vets. DJT signed the Veterans Benefits and Transition Act and the Forever GI Bill Housing Payment Fulfillment Act. Together, they ensure that vets receive the money they are owed and that they won't be punished for VA delays, resulting in an inability to pay their mortgage or student loans on time, which hits them with penalties or lost class time.[10]

Veteran friends of mine have been thrilled that someone finally took the initiative to do something, and they report real changes in their ability to get health care and VA benefits without having to travel and wait in stupidly long lines. How could our care for the veterans who laid their lives on the line for our country have gotten this bad? Trump has exchanged this bloated, inefficient system that lets vets fall through the cracks with a simpler, efficient program that allows far more of our brave men and women to decide where they want to get their health care, including the private sector.[11] Instead of just 8 percent, now 40 percent of our veterans can choose.[12]

So, what causes a person to be able to choose what they need from a variety of options? Competition. And competition, as we know from the success of the free market and the failure of communism, is a good thing. It drives us all to be better. It's like accountability; you have to deliver and perform in order to get the business. Now vets can go to professionals who will provide excellent medical care. Another campaign promise delivered!

Lazy bureaucrats in the VA have been driving care into the ground for decades, but bureaucracy everywhere throughout the swamp makes real improvement impossible—unless you start cutting the red tape. Deregulation has been a massive issue for my father. He came out with guns blazing (or should I say scissors slashing) as he demanded we cut unnecessary regulations. To determine which rules weren't working for the American people, he sent letters asking this question to US government departments, and he listened to their feedback. Then, when he began cutting regulations, he had an excellent idea of what needed to go. For every new rule, he wanted to repeal two. Along the way, repeals have climbed as high as twenty-two repealed for every new regulation implemented. Twenty-two idiotic regulations cut for every sensible one we enact. Now that's progress!

If Joe Biden gets voted into office, you can say hello to all the productivity-destroying red tape again because he owes his career and his family's livelihood to the swamp. All the regulations are a huge issue for businesspeople. Business creates jobs, contributes to our Gross Domestic Product (GDP), and pays corporate taxes. When it's easier for businesspeople to innovate, employ, and earn money, guess what? It's going to result in more people making things, providing services, getting paid, and, in turn, paying personal taxes. More people will be off welfare and working in good jobs that contribute to our economic system, rather than taking from the system. To Democrats, who want more and more people reliant on the federal government, this is an anathema. They can't handle people taking the initiative and working hard without their regulatory helicopter oversight. DC does not know what's best for your business; they don't understand business at all! Their only interest is protecting their bureaucracy.

Donald J. Trump's policy of deregulation has opened the throttle on our economy. Cutting the red tape is a huge reason the Trump economy was growing stronger daily before COVID-19, and why the virus amounted to a speed bump for us rather than an economic death sentence like it would have been under Biden and Obama. Our underlying healthy economy will recover. With continued deregulation, DJT knows that business, trade, and the entire free market system will flourish, putting even more Americans to work and making our country great again. Does that sound good? Or do you want more of DC's red tape? Something you may not know is that Trump waived 817 regulations to accelerate the fight against COVID-19.[13] In doing so, he freed brilliant scientists and doctors to work toward developing critical vaccines and therapies.

Cutting regulations has been a considerable part of the economic boom under my father. Obama told America that our jobs were gone, never to return, but Trump has proven this wasn't true. From tax reform to deregulation, my father has created an economy that allows the free market to work. Obama could have done these things, but he didn't fight for any of them. Why? Because liberals love regulations (just look at the EU), and regulations kill growth.

The newest crop of far-Left crazies want communism, the antithesis of the free market. Trump's war on regulations and high taxes have resulted in record-low unemployment numbers in half a century and the highest increases in wage growth for the lowest earners, with wage growth the fastest it's been in a decade.[14] Read that again—income inequality hasn't grown under Trump; it has shrunk. A White House document puts it so perfectly: "The unemployment rates for African Americans, Hispanic Americans, Asian Americans, veterans, individuals with disabilities, and those without a high school diploma have all reached record lows under President Trump."[15] All across the country, 2.4 million Americans were lifted out of poverty thanks to good jobs, with poverty rates among African Americans reaching record lows.[16] Those manufacturing jobs Obama said were gone? Magically, they're back.[17]

Before COVID-19, the US economy enjoyed its longest period of expansion ever, beating out the 1991–2001 boom and setting record unemployment numbers.[18] One investment strategist at UBS, Justin Waring, put it like this in 2019: "If voters went to the ballot box today, it would be the strongest economy in U.S. election history."[19] The economic misery index, a sum of inflation and unemployment numbers, was so low, my father tweeted, "In many ways this is the greatest economy in the HISTORY of America and the best time EVER to look for a job!"[20] According to CNBC, under Trump, "The S&P 500 has returned more than 50% since President Trump was elected, more than double the average market return of presidents three years into their term, according to Bespoke Investment Group."[21]

My father lowered the corporate tax rate from 35 percent to 21 percent—from one of the highest in the world to one that invites businesses that moved offshore to return (and bring their money back, too, to the tune of $1 *trillion* dollars).[22] The most significant tax reform package in history resulted in six million

Americans receiving wage increases, bonuses, and more benefits.[23] Instead of us telling businesses like Target how much they should pay their workers, this tax reform allowed American businesses through the free market system to invest in themselves and their workers, organically raising pay. I wish I had space to share examples of all the companies who raised wages or benefits, but they range from Visa to McDonald's to main street mom-and-pops. According to Fox Business, "A family of four with an annual income of $73,000 is seeing a 60 percent reduction in federal taxes—totaling to more than $2,058. According to the Heritage Foundation, the typical American family will be almost $45,000 better off over the next decade because of higher take-home pay and a stronger economy."[24] I would say that sounds like pretty good results, despite media misinformation campaigns that say 83 percent of the tax breaks go to the wealthiest 1 percent, which has been disproven by numerous fact-check sites.[25] Biden, on the other hand, has already promised he'll repeal Trump's tax breaks,[26] so if he gets in, kiss all these benefits goodbye. They won't survive a Biden presidency.

As of June 2020, the US stock market (and therefore your 401K) had regained the losses from the pandemic and is on a trajectory to fully recover all it lost and more.[27] Business leaders are showing a lot of confidence in the market; if they were uncertain about it, the Dow Jones Industrial Average would have remained at 18,000 points or worse. But instead, the markets bounced back and reclaimed their losses in about one month.

As I write this, we just received new job numbers that show a record gain of 4.8 million jobs in June 2020, beating the May record and knocking unemployment down to 11.1 percent.[28] These gains absolutely destroyed estimates, showing the fundamentals of the American economy are still strong. While Democrats are doing their best to keep their states shut down and their residents from returning back to work so they become dependent on government, Trump is putting America back to work.

What about foreign policy? My father reversed decades of policy toward North Korea. He was the first US president to step across the border into North Korea, showing he will sit down and talk with anyone.[29] It's always better to have open lines of communication than not, and the fruit of his efforts will become obvious over time.

Obama literally sent a plane in the night with pallets of cash totaling $400 million to Iran, which was only part of a larger deal totaling $1.7 billion![30] Iran is a hostile nation, known as the world's leading sponsor of terror, who is working hard to develop nuclear technology it could use to destroy Israel, us, or anyone else their hate points them toward. Trump reversed that failed Iran nuclear deal with tough measures and maximum pressure because he believes the cash Obama gave Iran should have gone to hardworking Americans. Unlike previous politicians like Joe Biden, Trump wants us out of Middle Eastern wars and wants to sever relationships with people whose ideology paints us as the Great Satan, and their sworn enemy. Why do we continue to send billions of dollars to those who hate us, burn our flag, and chant "Death to America" in their streets? We are not the world's police, and it's not our job to oust dictators and try to force democracy on people who only listen to the strength of the next warlord.

According to The Bureau of Investigative Journalism, Obama carried out "a total of 563 strikes, largely by drones, targeted Pakistan, Somalia and Yemen during Obama's two terms, compared to 57 strikes under Bush. Between 384 and 807 civilians were killed in those countries, according to reports logged by the Bureau."[31] Media backlash against Obama? Negligible. Trump continues to use the same technology as Obama to kill terrorists, and he's crucified or ignored, depending on whether the result fits the narrative of the dishonest media and Dems. My father has been the only one trying to end wars which have gone on for far too long. You would think the liberal elite would support that. I wonder where Michael Moore is when we call to end wars? My father believes in a strong America, but he doesn't believe we need to be rebuilding the world at our expense. America first!

Since my father took office, we have taken out some major terrorists who have masterminded countless attacks and killed US service members and anyone else who doesn't agree with them. In February 2017, we eliminated bombmaker Ibrahim al-Asiri, who designed explosives that bypassed airport security and Abu al-Khayr al-Masri, the most senior al-Qa'ida member in Syria and the likely successor to amir Ayman al-Zawahiri, limiting al-Qa'ida's ability to execute external attacks. In 2019 we took out Asim Umar and Hamza bin Laden, al-Qa'ida senior leader and son of deceased al-Qa'ida founder Osama bin Laden. That same year, we permanently removed Abu Hassan al-Muhajir, an ISIS spokesman. In 2020, Qassim al-Rimi and Hajji Taysir. The list goes on, but you won't hear about it—because that would show Trump's agenda is working.

We conducted a military operation that caused the death of Abu Bakr al-Baghdadi on October 26, 2019. The founder of ISIS, the "most ruthless and violent terror organization anywhere in the world," was dead.[32] Taking out al-Baghdadi was on my father's list and was a top priority for his administration. Remarkably, instead of celebrating a better world without this cowardly terrorist who blew himself up with a suicide vest, nutty Nancy Pelosi and others criticized my father! Can you see how sick the swamp really is?

Even worse than Nancy Pelosi is the mainstream media, who you would think would rejoice in the death of someone who has doused journalists in gasoline and lit them on fire; enslaved, trafficked, and raped young women; and thrown homosexuals from rooftops—but no! The *Washington Post*, where supposedly "Democracy Dies in Darkness," wrote an obituary where they described this scum as an "Austere Religious Scholar."[33] Imagine how warped you must be to highlight this and whitewash his deranged criminal and terrorist past, simply because Donald Trump took out the world's leading terrorist. When Obama gave the order to kill Osama bin Laden (which Biden was vehemently against, probably the only American), America rejoiced and rightfully so, but Trump Derangement Syndrome wouldn't allow the Left to celebrate this victory for freedom. They should be ashamed, but, as we have seen, they have no shame!

But that was nothing next to the criticism Trump received when the US took out Iranian Islamic Revolutionary Guard Corps-Quds Force leader Qasem Soleimani. The Department of Defense statement read like this:

> General Soleimani was actively developing plans to attack American diplomats and service members in Iraq and throughout the region. General Soleimani and his Quds Force were responsible for the deaths of hundreds of American and coalition service members and the wounding of thousands more. He had orchestrated attacks on coalition bases in Iraq over the last several months—including the attack on December 27—culminating in the death

and wounding of additional American and Iraqi personnel. General Soleimani also approved the attacks on the U.S. Embassy in Baghdad that took place this week.[34]

This is a piece-of-shit terrorist we took out, and you would have thought Trump had killed Gandhi. Pelosi called it "provocative and disproportionate."[35] Soleimani was responsible for hundreds of American deaths and had organized an attack just days before. I would say that's a proportional response, but that didn't stop Pelosi and all of her leftist buddies from trying to restrict Donald J. Trump's executive authority to continue the kinds of strikes that we have used since Bush. In 2001, Congress authorized the use of military force in the war on terror. "The President is authorized to use all necessary and appropriate force against those nations, organizations, or persons he determines planned, authorized, committed, or aided the terrorist attacks that occurred on September 11, 2001, or harbored such organizations or persons, in order to prevent any future acts of international terrorism against the United States by such nations, organizations or persons."[36] Sounds like DJT was acting within his authority.

Let's not forget Soleimani was also the primary architect of the IED campaign that our enemies used against our heroic soldiers, which maimed and killed thousands of our bravest Americans. He is believed to be one of the prime people responsible for designing and implementing this IED warfare on our young men and women in the Middle East. That said, it's no surprise that the Left still went to great lengths to defend him.

But again, we see that the liberal swamp creatures of this country are more interested in anything that can hurt Donald Trump than what's best for you.

We believe in a strong defense. The safety of our fellow Americans is the president's top priority.

Over the years I've discussed with my friend, former ambassador Rick Grenell, his experiences representing the US in Germany. Germany is a prime example of a NATO member who hadn't thought it necessary to contribute their part to our joint defense. Rick and I agreed the concept that NATO countries must pay their dues isn't new, but it took Trump to take a hard approach and demand they actually do it. They're supposed to spend 2 percent of their GDP on national defense, but no one held them accountable, even though they depended on us to protect them from Russia and China. Not only had they refused to pay their fair share for many years, they expected the US taxpayer to assist in their defense. It gets even worse; not only weren't they meeting their obligations, they were actually enriching the Russians through gas deals. So, the very people making lucrative deals were outraged when called out for not keeping their end of the deal.

Some NATO countries have trusted China with their 5G cellular network infrastructure, never mind that China could cut off their connections or use the technology for espionage, despite America's warnings of the potential significant consequences.[37] These countries don't think these others are a threat—and even if they were, they think we'll come to save their asses (on our dime) if things go south quickly. They are almost as bad as the Democrats here at home!

By late 2019, the NATO allies had moved toward an agreement to pay their share—minus France, who refused, because they probably like being conquered.[38] Instead of us paying nearly 100 percent, my father got the NATO allies to contribute $150 billion to their own self-interest, with hopes for $400 billion.[39] No one else has ever come close to this.

Jack Wilson, chairman of the Republican Party of Virginia, put my father's accomplishments like this, and I love it: "On criminal justice reform, education, Opportunity Zones, tax cuts, bringing back American jobs from China and removing the United States from endless wars, President Trump continues to smash the failed institutions Joe Biden got us into for nearly a half-century."[40]

From elevating the lives of our most disadvantaged citizens, to creating our booming economy and making our country safer, Donald Trump has done what he said he would do. His policies have put America on the right track and ensured that our economy is strong enough to quickly rebound from the pandemic closedown, even with Democrat governors dragging their feet.

There is something profoundly revealing about a man who makes promises, then flip-flops on them for nearly half a century like Joe Biden. There is something special about a man who makes bold promises, then keeps them. Not only are his promises kept, but they benefit an entire nation. That's the kind of accomplishment we need in a president. Donald Trump is that man.

A man America needs for four more years.

CHAPTER 18

He Did It Before and He Can Do It Again

The choice before us couldn't be more striking.

In July 2020, Joe Biden said his administration "won't just rebuild this nation—we'll transform it," frightening words for every American who loves their freedom and this great country.

The radical Left and their co-conspirators in the media are intent on controlling what you believe, what you own, what you say, what you worship, what our history says, what you post, what you earn, and everything that's made America great.

Emboldened by a virus sent to us by China and a murderous police officer, they believe the time is right to blindside us and take America out. Their great Wizard of Odd, Joe Biden, is the perfect candidate to control from behind their curtain. Squads, media propogandists, Marxists, Socialists, deer-in-the-headlights leaders in the Democrat Party are licking their chops to tell Creepy Joe how *they* fundamentally want to change this country.

A Biden presidency will lead us full circle back to Barack Obama's "pastor" Jeremiah Wright. He shouted, "It's not God bless America, it's God damn America," which summarizes the Democrat Party today.[1]

That's their legacy, and it's overtaking their party. *Their goal is not a more exceptional America; their goal is the defeat of America. They are after you, what you have, how you earned it, and anything you hold dear. In their demented minds—it's THEIRS.*

The question at the forefront of everyone's mind is, who can return America to greatness again after COVID-19—Joe Biden or Donald Trump? My father campaigned on making America great again after a succession of neocons and liberals tried their best to run it into the ground. As a successful businessman, he understood what would be required to accomplish this. Trump still knows what it takes to succeed, Joe Biden never will! Joe Biden's liberal policies failed to bring substantial growth when he and Obama were in office, and they will hurt American families. He will raise taxes, open our borders, destroy our most vulnerable workers' jobs, and be a puppet for whatever leftist extremist holds the most-woke clout.

Donald Trump has never been and never will be a "politician"—not like the establishment swamp creatures such as Biden. Trump is a capitalist who built his fortune and became a success through lots of tough work, an indomitable spirit, and sharp wit. DJT is a pragmatist who understands the real world and tells it like it is without all the politically correct BS. He has signed the front of the paychecks for countless workers who depended on him to deliver the goods, while career politicians like Biden have only signed the back of donors' checks.

Trump has done the things in the real world that swamp creatures like Biden can never understand because they've never done them. Trump's experience is what gives him such a decisive advantage and, in turn, an advantage for the American people. A special skill set no one in DC possesses, and he's willing to use it to help you and your family.

Because so many Dems have never actually done anything other than play in the swamp, when they try to govern, they think it's about restrictions and regulations. They don't care how difficult their asinine restrictions make it on ordinary Americans—the very people whose taxes fund their idiotic little projects and pay their salaries. These bureaucrats, rising on tenure and not competence, are the heart of what is wrong in DC. None of them are a better example of this problem than Joe Biden, a myopic opportunist who has made his entire career about enriching his family with his many taxpayer-funded positions. For all his decades in politics, he remains ignorant of the way the real world prospers.

My father understands an incredible breadth of topics. Many real estate developers specialize in one kind of construction, like my grandfather, who built apartment housing. Trump is one of the very few who have done it all. He has built high-rises, office buildings, resorts, golf courses, condos, casinos, apartments, and so many more—all in different areas of the world for diverse communities. Instead of a viewpoint limited to one perspective like Democrats who decide their point of view is the only valid one, Trump has embraced many ways of thinking to accomplish his goals with excellence in a large variety of settings. Hell, he's even done reality TV and has an incredible understanding of pop culture! Because of his hands-on involvement, my father understands the working class like few other leaders.

From an entrepreneur starting a company to a college graduate getting a first car loan to a couple refinancing their house, my father understands everyday Americans—and he knows how to help them in the ways that matter most. Not handouts, jobs. Not illegals first, Americans first. Not a weak America dependent on foreign energy, an America that's strong and energy independent, responsibly using her resources for the good of her people and *then* the world.

Trump's insight into people has enabled him to negotiate effectively with everyone: massive corporate conglomerates, Chinese communists, even me as a young kid for my allowance. Democrats don't understand the first thing about negotiation, and they never would have played hardball with the Chinese as my father did. DJT comprehended what Chinese trade imbalances and currency manipulation do to our country and what it means when China doesn't play by the rules and steals our intellectual property and jobs. But because the establishment swamp monsters have never really *done* anything in the real world, they don't understand how China's actions affect our country, or care about the subsequent job losses. Can you imagine AOC trying to comprehend foreign trade? No, never mind—don't put that idea in her head.

There was no single economic metric, including optimism, where Trump has not destroyed the Obama-Biden administration's record. Whether it's the stock market, your 401k, unemployment, or jobless claims, there is not one aspect where they outperformed Trump.

Now, you'll never hear that from the media, who try to make Obama out to be this economic genius. In truth, he oversaw the slowest recovery in American history. Biden and Obama waved goodbye to our manufacturing jobs and happily placed workers on unemployment rolls, telling my father there was no magic wand to bring these jobs back. Well, as we've seen in this book, they were wholly and utterly wrong.

There is a "magic wand," but Obama didn't have it. Biden certainly doesn't have it and definitely can't find it. It's called commonsense conservative values—something completely lacking on the Left. When combined with the actual business experience to apply them, commonsense values cause job growth to explode! Obama was a community organizer. We shouldn't be surprised that he didn't know what the hell he was doing (except pursuing his leftist ideology at the cost of the American worker). Yet we, the American people, threw him the keys to a few trillion-dollar economy. Biden has spent his whole life getting slimy and scaly in DC, saying whatever would get him a win and whoring himself out for donations. He's never had a real job, but he's made a pretty cushy life for himself and his family members, who have profited from his public post for fifty freaking years.

Joe Biden wants to use your family to enrich his at the expense of the men and women of this country, by stepping on the backs of hardworking Americans.

How can you expect these guys to run the most exceptional economy in the free world? You can't! The only reason these political creatures ever get in office or stay there is that they have the full backing of the greatest marketing team on the planet, the fake news media.

They survive by liberal privilege.

The establishment has grown wealthy from their ill-gotten gains, and few have gotten as many gains as the Bidens. Jim has peddled access to Joe to the tune of millions, and Hunter has reaped the rewards of his last name from MBNA to Amtrak to Ukraine to China. And all the while, Lost Uncle Joe has skinny-dipped, lied, and bumbled his way to the top on the taxpayer's dime.

Now he expects a reward for all his years of "hard work" by being elected president. He is the example of all that's wrong with DC; he's a weak, failing puppet with no mind left of his own and will undoubtedly be directed by the loudest people on the Left.

I acknowledge, as the son of a billionaire, I've benefited from my father's name. However, we did it with our own money—we achieved success through lots and lots of hard work, innovating in the free market against incredible competition, and while keeping thousands gainfully employed. We took chances, made mistakes, and learned from them—because that's what capitalists do! And from those lessons, my father learned what works, and then he taught me. He has put all that to work for America.

Trump didn't need to be president. He didn't do it expecting people to like him or be kind to him. He did it because it needed to be done to make America great again.

From the moment Donald Trump entered the race, the establishment recognized the threat—an outsider with the experience and skills to reveal how inept and corrupt they are. A man unafraid to take bold risks and offer new approaches to the way it's always been done. Everything was on the table if it would make America great again. It frightened them, so they attacked.

Every attack you've seen since then has been the swamp fighting back. The liberal-privileged know that if Donald Trump exposes them, all the wealth and ill-gotten gains they've made for themselves, their family, and their friends through DC cronyism is at risk. Once people see the swamp's corruption contrasted by DJT's success under extreme pressure, they'll see how ugly, corrupt, inefficient, and duplicitous it is.

When Donald Trump is reelected, it will be the swamp's last stand.

If Trump wins despite all they've done to attack him—all the BS, all the media bias, all the times he's done the right thing but received no credit—that tells me America can keep going. It says this great system our Founding Fathers created has life in it yet, the corrupt establishment hasn't trampled all the good from it, and there's hope. It tells me the greedy, selfish, corrupt politicians who are only looking out for their interests while forgetting their constituency have not had the last laugh. They haven't killed what originally made America great.

We can save it.

In 2016, Donald Trump went around the country making promises—some of the same guarantees that many politicians have made before him. He took it a little further, was a little more aggressive, and didn't kowtow to the raging mob on the things he knew were important to Americans. He is the first president in modern times who has delivered on what he promised. He has led and run a promises-made, promises-kept agenda, and he's done it under unprecedented resistance from the Democrats, Hollywood pop culture, the establishment, and media. He's been attacked with scandalous, baseless accusations that dragged on for years and cost taxpayers millions of dollars, not to mention lost productivity that his enemies wasted attacking him instead of getting things done for our country. And despite it all, DJT was still able to deliver on his promises.

He said he could bring back manufacturing, and he did— and we need it now more than ever in the post–COVID-19 world. Instead of telling them to "learn to code," like Biden so hypocritically did, he's brought their jobs back. My father said he would renegotiate the worst deal for the American worker ever, NAFTA—a disastrous trade debacle Joe Biden voted into law in 1993—and on July 1, 2020, Trump's USMCA trade deal began.[2] My father has already shown he's capable of creating unprecedented job and low-unemployment numbers. As I write this, we see the incredible job gains as America recovers from the coronavirus pandemic. The stock market has already rebounded, and I just noticed that retail sales are skyrocketing. It will take time to regrow the economy, but the fundamentals are still sound, and the guy who did it once is the guy who can *and will* do it again.

If my father could accomplish so many things under unprecedented opposition, what would happen if something really unrealistic occurred? Something crazy like the Democrats actually working *with* us for the benefit of the American people? Maybe we should let Donald Trump be a builder, which is what he does. What if we worked together to put Americans back to work fixing our dilapidated infrastructure, which so desperately needs it? We might be able to get the rest of the things done that DJT wants to do for America. There is still more to be done together.

I believe my father's words in a recent speech at Mount Rushmore bear repeating to offer hope to keep America great.

Angry mobs are trying to tear down statues of our Founders, deface our most sacred memorials, and unleash a wave of violent crime in our cities. Many of these people have no idea why they are doing this, but some know exactly what they are doing. They think the American people are weak and soft and submissive. But no, the American people are strong and proud, and they will not allow our country, and all of its values, history, and culture, to be taken from them. . . .

The violent mayhem we have seen in the streets of cities that are run by liberal Democrats, in every case, is the predictable result of years of extreme indoctrination and bias in education, journalism, and other cultural institutions.

Against every law of society and nature, our children are taught in school to hate their own country, and to believe that the men and women who built it were not heroes, but that they were villains. The radical view of American history is a web of lies—all perspective is removed, every virtue is obscured, every motive is twisted, every fact is distorted, and every flaw is magnified until the history is purged and the record is disfigured beyond all recognition. . . .

Those who seek to erase our heritage want Americans to forget our pride and our great dignity, so that we can no longer understand ourselves or America's destiny. In toppling the heroes of 1776, they seek to dissolve the bonds of love and loyalty that we feel for our country, and that we feel for each other. Their goal is not a better America, their goal is the end of America.

In its place, they want power for themselves. But just as patriots did in centuries past, the American people will stand in their way—and we will win, and win quickly and with great dignity. . . .

They would tear down the principles that propelled the abolition of slavery in America and, ultimately, around the world, ending an evil institution that had plagued humanity for thousands and thousands of years. Our opponents would tear apart the very documents that Martin Luther King used to express his dream, and the ideas that were the foundation of the righteous movement for

Civil Rights. They would tear down the beliefs, culture, and iden-
tity that have made America the most vibrant and tolerant society
in the history of the Earth.

My fellow Americans, it is time to speak up loudly and strongly
and powerfully and defend the integrity of our country.

The choice before us is not the most important vote in your life-
time, it's the most important decision in our nation's lifetime.[3]

People may tell you they want to vote for Biden because they're "woke" and want to appease the mob, but I have a hard time believing that people will knowingly go into a voting booth and vote to earn 30 percent less and destroy their 401k. I don't believe they will choose to let anarchy run wild and show up at their front door, demanding to take all they have worked so hard for. I don't think the average American will go in a voting booth and vote to put an impossible burden on our health-care system, further worsen their children's education, or give their jobs away to illegal workers or China. Know that's what you will get if you choose Joe Biden and his America-hating teammates.

Those voting *against* Trump are voting *for* all these things. They are voting for higher taxes, a stagnant or ruined economy, and rampaging rioters in the streets. At the same time, police stand by, impotent, and our great national history is rewritten to fit Marxist ideals. Yeah, you can vote for Biden, but this is what you'll get. The choice is yours, America, and it couldn't be more clear. Vote for Biden, and you'll get a sock puppet for the radical Left who will do whatever trendy, destructive, and shortsighted thing the loudest voices on the Left tell him to do because he has no convictions of his own. You'll get flip-flops and crooked deals, massive mistakes like NAFTA, an unwillingness to kill terrorists like Osama bin Laden, and turning a blind eye to China's desire to dominate us militarily and in global trade. People tend to vote their self-interest. And if you're going to vote against your job, wages, savings, the stock market, your 401k, health care, and common sense, Biden is your man.

You may not agree with everything my father says or how he says it, but if you want to live in a safe, secure America with the lowest unemployment on record, there is no more obvious choice than voting for Donald J. Trump. Joe Biden has had fifty freaking years to get it right, and he can't. He's been on the wrong side of every policy decision he's ever made, yet now they say Biden will fix what's wrong in DC. That's impossible; Joe Biden *is* what's wrong with DC—if he fixed it, he would have to fire himself.

The swamp has failed you. They have taken your money and given it to everyone else, wasted it in stupid deals, or just completely lost it. Or they will give it to their filthy buddies in the corrupt backroom deals that made Hunter and Jim Biden rich. But they won't go quietly; they're not toothless. They're embedded in the deep state, in the leadership of formerly great institutions like the FBI that have been corrupted by partisan leaders and outright crooks. They're desperately fighting back because they see that the outsider, Donald Trump, isn't part of their little club, and he's coming for them. This is the way they think. This is why they needed an insurance policy. They want you to do what they say, when they say. They want you to repeat their talking points mindlessly, without having your own opinion. The only option is their opinion; otherwise, they cancel you. They want to dictate your values, which change by the hour. They will not protect you or your property or your rights, because they will give preferential treatment to the dependents they court as their voters. They'll support riots and anarchy because it's woke, and they will drive this country into the ground.

Honestly, America, can you see yourself voting to destroy all you hold dear? Do you remember when Obama said that if you like your doctors, you can keep them? If you want all the Democrats' promises, you can have them—and it will be just like every Democrat promise for the last fifty years. It will come at an unimaginable cost, be corrupted by greed and waste, and benefit America last, if at all.

That is the Left's mantra: America *last*. It's what the globalists want—to drive us into the ground, so we're no longer the envy of every nation on earth. They don't want America to be the leader and set the standard for trade, fairness, human rights, innovation, and wealth production. They want to destroy our suburbs and remake them as dysfunctional as our inner cities, tear down our monuments, and remake us all into victims of identity politics.

I wrote this book because the fake news media won't do their jobs. I have tried to fill the void they left and provide you with what you need to know to make a decision. We're at a pivotal point in our country's history. Actually, we're at *the* crucial point in our country's history. We've just taken a big hit, but we're strong. America isn't a country of survival; it's a nation of people who overcome despite incredible odds and find a way to succeed and make our lives better, no matter what.

How will we best recover? Will it be another Biden recovery, which was the worst in history? Will our inner-city poverty reshape our suburbs? Will rioting and looting become the new normal and the way people object to anything they don't like? Will taxes cripple our working class—the few that still have jobs when the Left takes them away? Will we once again be dependent on energy from countries that hate us? Will our country be only a place of liberal privilege?

Or will we help Donald J. Trump do it again—improve employment to record levels again, help the stock market hit unprecedented gains again, protect all lives, born and unborn, and restore America's dominance in trade again? President Trump will rebuild our infrastructure, create jobs for the most impoverished workers, and raise their pay quicker than ever before in history. He will confront the anarchists and restore law and order, lead with new law enforcement training that respects and brings no excessive force for all suspects, and cut off the head of the swamp once and for all.

If you want to even recognize your country in four years, you have to stand up now. With your help and a belief in the founding principle of our nation, Donald J. Trump will Make America Great Again!

APPENDIX

THE BEST OF THE WORST JOE BIDEN QUOTES

You might think that conservatives have taken crazy Joe Biden out of context—but that would be false. Nothing exemplifies how crazy he truly is than by reading his own words. He might not remember these words, but we'll try to refresh his memory and maybe that of the media who should be talking about them!

REAL BIDEN

June 1, 1974

"When it comes to issues like abortion, amnesty, and acid, I'm about as liberal as your grandmother. I don't like the Supreme Court decision on abortion. I think it went too far. I don't think that a woman has the sole right to say what should happen to her body. I support a limited amnesty, and I don't think marijuana should be legalized.'

It's hard to predict which Joe Biden will show—take a look at his career and you will find every shade of position—but the reality is, the Democrat Party is for unapologetic abortion, including Governor Ralph Northam's position of seemingly post-term abortion. The Left has lost its mind on this issue, and Joe Biden will be swayed by the far Left.

October 1975

"I think the concept of busing . . . that we are going to integrate people so that they all have the same access and they learn
to grow up with one another and all the rest, is a rejection of the
whole movement of black pride, is a rejection of the entire black
awareness concept where black is beautiful, black culture should
be studied, and the cultural awareness of the importance of their
own identity, their own individuality."[2]

October 2, 1975

Biden commented in the Congressional Record, "I do not
buy the concept, popular in the 60's which said: 'we have suppressed the black man for 300 years, and the white man is now far
ahead in the "race" for everything our society offers. In order to
even the score, we must now give the black man a "head start" or
even hold the white man back to even the race.' I don't buy that."[3]

Considering his entire party made reparations an issue, I am
not the least bit surprised that Joe Biden has flipped his position.
This is the guy that was against reparations, before he was for
them, before somehow, he confused the entire room with his position. Joe will do anything to get your support, but we all know
it's not authentic.

October 2, 1975

"I am philosophically opposed to quota-systems; they insure
mediocrity. The new integration plans being offered are really just
quota-systems to assure a certain number of blacks, Chicanos, or
whatever in each school. That, to me, is the most racist concept
you can come up with; what it says is, 'in order for your child, with
curly black hair, brown eyes, and dark skin to be able to learn anything, he needs to sit next to my blond-haired, blue-eyed son.'"[4]

October 12, 1975

"I think the Democratic Party could stand a liberal George Wallace—someone who's not afraid to stand up and offend people, someone who wouldn't pander but would say what the American people know in their gut is right."[5]

Forty-five years later, the Democrats still haven't produced someone who refuses to pander. In fact, pandering has become the foundation of their party platform.

September 27, 1977

"Unless we do something about this, my children are going to grow up in a jungle, the jungle being a racial jungle with tensions having built so high that it is going to explode at some point. We have got to make some move on this."[6]

Yikes! No comment necessary. I would add some snark, but it speaks for itself. And they call conservatives racist?

April 3, 1987

"The first year in law school I decided I didn't want to be in law school and ended up in the bottom two-thirds of my class and then decided I wanted to stay and went back to law school and in fact ended up in the top half of my class." Biden lied about his academic record at Syracuse Law School. He graduated 76th out of 85 students.[7]

Not a stable genius! Wouldn't be the first or last time that Joe Biden lied or cheated trying to get ahead.

September 18, 1987

During his first presidential run, Joe Biden plagiarized content from a speech by Neil Kinnock without giving credit to the

British Labour Party leader. According to the *Washington Post*, he "plagiarized portions of speeches made by former President John F. Kennedy and Sen. Robert F. Kennedy (D-N.Y.). It effectively led to him dropping out of the race."[8]

Biden later called the accusations of plagiarism "much ado about nothing," after being caught red-handed.

It seems taking the easy way is the Biden way always! It also seems Biden has a long history of not being able to come up with a thought of his own!

January 1995

"When I argued that we should freeze federal spending, I meant Social Security as well. I meant Medicare and Medicaid. I meant veterans' benefits. I meant *every* single, solitary thing in the government. And I not only tried it once, I tried it twice, I tried it a third time, and I tried it a fourth time."[9]

While my father has called for restrained spending, it's ironic that under Obama and Biden's leadership, there wasn't one spending bill they didn't seem to support. In fact, they often made them larger. Perhaps instead of cutting Social Security, Biden could have cut the bloated bureaucracy and endless wars his buddy Barack spent endlessly on.

July 2004

"Hell, I might be president now if it weren't for the fact I said I had an uncle who was a coal miner. Turns out I didn't have anybody in the coal mines, you know what I mean? I tried that crap—it didn't work."[10]

March 2006

"It's going to be very difficult. I do not view abortion as a choice and a right. I think it's always a tragedy, and I think that it should be rare and safe, and I think we should be focusing on how to limit the number of abortions. There ought to be able to have a common ground and consensus as to do that."[11]

Now, bullied by the left-wing mob, Biden supports no restrictions on terminating pregnancies up until the time of birth. What else will they push him around on?

June 17, 2006

"In Delaware, the largest growth of population is Indian Americans, moving from India. You cannot go to a 7-11 or a Dunkin' Donuts unless you have a slight Indian accent. I'm not joking."[12]

November 2006

"I voted for a fence, I voted, unlike most Democrats—and some of you won't like it—I voted for 700 miles of fence. . . . And the reason why I add that parenthetically, why I believe the fence is needed does not have anything to do with immigration as much as drugs. And let me tell you something, folks, people are driving across that border with tons, tons, hear me, tons of everything from byproducts for methamphetamine to cocaine to heroin and it's all coming up through corrupt Mexico."[13]

Trump says the same thing and was slammed for it, WTF?

January 31, 2007

Joe said this of Barack Obama, "I mean, you got the first mainstream African-American who is articulate and bright and clean and a nice-looking guy. I mean, that's a storybook, man."[14]

Joe Biden sounds like a character out of *Blazing Saddles*, not a nominee for the Democrat Party in 2020. Can we even spell "woke"?

September 10, 2008

"Hillary Clinton is as qualified or more qualified than I am to be Vice President of the United States of America. Let's get that straight. She's a truly close, personal friend. She is qualified to be President of the United States of America. She's easily qualified to be Vice President of the United States of America. Quite frankly, it might have been a better pick than me. But she's first rate."[15]

From one crook to another. Biden knows corruption when he sees it; he's perfected it for half a century. Of course, he thinks she was qualified.

July 2010

Biden delivered a eulogy for a former KKK leader, Sen. Robert Byrd: "He was a friend, he was a mentor, and he was a guide."[16]

August 2012

While campaigning for Obama, Biden told an audience that included many African Americans, "Look at what they [Republicans] value, and look at their budget. And look what they're proposing. [Romney] said in the first 100 days, he's going to let the big banks write their own rules—unchain Wall Street. They're going to put y'all back in chains."[17]

Can this guy be any more of an imbecile?

January 2018

Bragging about getting the prosecutor fired who was investigating the Ukranian natural gas company Burisma, Biden said, "I was supposed to announce that there was another billion-dollar loan guarantee. And I had gotten a commitment from Poroshenko and from Yatsenyuk that they would take action against the state prosecutor. And they didn't . . . So they said they had—they were walking out to a press conference. I said, 'Nah, I'm not going to—or, we're not going to give you the billion dollars.' They said, 'You have no authority. You're not the president. The president said—.' I said, 'Call him.' I said, 'I'm telling you, you're not getting the billion dollars.' I said, 'You're not getting the billion.' I'm going to be leaving here in, I think it was about six hours. I looked at them and said, 'I'm leaving in six hours. If the prosecutor is not fired, you're not getting the money.' Well, son of a bitch. He got fired. And they put in place someone who was solid at the time."[18]

The Democrats forced a sham impeachment on President Trump for far less. Would they or the weak Republicans, like Senator Lindsey Graham, even look at this malfeasance?

August 2019

The *Washington Post* exposed Biden for fabricating a war story repeatedly told throughout his tenure as vice president and on the 2020 campaign trail. On the stump, Biden often recounts a trip he made to Afghanistan while serving as vice president, frequently shifting the details of the trip, which the *Post* reported was demonstrably false. According to the *Post*, Biden visited the Middle Eastern country in 2008 when he was a senator, not vice president, and got nearly every other significant detail of the trip wrong, several times.

Are you even surprised at this point that he lies about anything to create a narrative?

August 2019

Biden tells a moving story (later proven by the *Washington Post* as completely false) about pinning a medal on a reluctant navy captain in honor of his daring attempt to rescue a downed comrade in Afghanistan. He said the soldier shouted this before the pinning, "Sir, I don't want the damn thing!" Biden shouted, recounting the apocryphal event. "Do not pin it on me, sir! Please, sir. Do not do that! He died. He died!"

"This is the God's truth," he added. "My word as a Biden."[19]

Clearly doesn't mean much. Nothing is sacred to this guy. How can you make up a story of a dead or wounded soldier to move the political needle? It's despicable.

August 2019

Biden was asked, "How many genders are there?"

"There are at least three."

A follow-up question was, "What are they?"

"Don't play games with me, kid," grabbing the arm of the questioner. "By the way, the first one to come out for marriage was me."[20]

Call me crazy, but I don't like a man claiming to be a woman playing against my daughters in competitive sports. My daughters are great athletes, but to pretend that a natural-born male doesn't have any biological advantages is asinine. The Democrats want to redefine biology and, in the process, will destroy your daughter's athletic career, Title IX, and women's sports in general. Men who became women are dominating competitive sports and breaking records regularly. Let's stop pretending they have no advantage. Women who became men, not so much.

I couldn't care less how you identify, or what you wear, or what pronouns you use—but the second you start impacting some young lady's life and her dream and goals, by discarding every aspect of biology known to men, it becomes too much. The goalposts are constantly moving; you can never be woke enough.

Woke Joe Biden says there is "no room for compromise" on "transgender equality."[21] Sounds like he wants boys competing against your daughter.

Donald Trump was the first to not be against gay marriage when he was running for president.

August 8, 2019

"We should challenge students in these schools to have advanced placement programs in these schools," Biden said. "We have this notion that if you're poor, you cannot do it. Poor kids are just as bright and just as talented as white kids. Wealthy kids, black kids, Asian kids—no, I really mean it."[22]

October 2019

Biden claimed to have gone to Delaware State University, a historically black college, not the University of Delaware where he actually went to college.

"I got started out at an HBCU, Delaware State. Now, I don't want to hear anything negative about Delaware State here. They're my folks."[23]

Pander. Pander. Pander.

February 2020

When a college student asked Biden about turning his campaign around, he asked if she's been to a caucus in the past. When she says "yes," Biden angrily responded, "No, you haven't. You're a lying, dog-faced, pony soldier."[24]

May 2020

Biden said in an interview on *The Breakfast Club* with African

American radio host Charlamagne tha God, "If you have a problem figuring out whether you're for me or Trump, then you ain't black."[25]

June 2020

At a town hall event with Biden, Don Cheadle said, "Do we really think that this is as good as we can be as a nation?" Biden responded, "I don't think the vast majority of people think that. There are probably anywhere from 10 to 15 percent of the people out there that are just not very good people." That's thirty to fifty million Americans.[26]

June 25, 2020

"Now we have over 120 million dead from COVID."[27]

Big news to me and everyone else in the country. It might be true if Biden was in charge.

LOST BIDEN

September 2008

"When the stock market crashed, FDR got on the TV and didn't just talk about, you know, the princes of greed. He said, 'Look, here's what happened.'"[28]

(Franklin Delano Roosevelt wasn't president in 1929, Herbert Hoover was. TVs weren't available in homes, and President Hoover would address the nation through the radio.)

September 9, 2008

"I'm told Chuck Graham, state senator, is here. Stand up Chuck, let 'em see you. Oh, God love you. What am I talking about. I'll tell you what, you're making everybody else stand up, though, pal." Biden, telling Missouri state senator Chuck Graham to stand up. Graham is confined to a wheelchair.[29]

October 2008

"Look, John's [McCain] last-minute economic plan does nothing to tackle the number-one job facing the middle class, and it happens to be, as Barack says, a three-letter word: jobs. J-O-B-S, jobs."[30]

February 6, 2009

Joe Biden speaking to House Democrats, "If we do everything right, if we do it with absolute certainty, there's still a 30 percent chance we're going to get it wrong."[31]

March 2010

Speaking of Irish Prime Minister Brian Cowen's mother, who is alive, "His mom lived in Long Island for 10 years or so, God rest her soul. Although, she's, wait—your mom's still alive. It was your dad passed. God bless her soul. I gotta get this straight."[32]

March 2012

Biden, forgetting D-Day, the Revolutionary War, and World War I and II, said this about the raid that killed bin Laden: "You can go back 500 years. You cannot find a more audacious plan. Never knowing for certain. We never had more than a 48 percent probability that he was there."[33]

He also voted against the raid.

April 2012

"What I'm trying to say without boring you too long at

breakfast, and you all look dull as hell, I might add. The dullest audience I have ever spoken to. Just sitting there, staring at me. Pretend you like me!"[34]

Clearly not an easy task.

May 2012

"My mother believed and my father believed that if I wanted to be president of the United States, I could be. I could be Vice President!"[35]

June 2012

"Make sure of two things. Be careful—microphones are always hot, and understand that in Washington, D.C., a gaffe is when you tell the truth. So, be careful."[36]

August 2012

"Folks, I can tell you I've known eight presidents, three of them intimately."[37]

August 2019

"I want to be clear; I'm not going nuts."[38]

August 2019

When asked about his impression of a New Hampshire town, Biden said, "I've been here a number of times. I love this place. Look, what's not to like about Vermont in terms of the beauty of it?"[39]

August 2019

"Those kids in Parkland came up to see me when I was vice

president." Biden had been out of office more than a year when that shooting occurred.[40]

August 2019

"We choose unity over division. We choose science over fiction. We choose truth over facts."[41]

September 2019

"They [parents] don't—they don't know quite what to do," Biden said. "Play the radio, make sure the television—excuse me, make sure you have the record player on at night . . . make sure that kids hear words."[42]

September 2019

Biden confused Afghanistan with Iraq. "The whole purpose of going to Afghanistan was to not have a counterinsurgency, meaning that we're going to put that country together," Biden said. "It will not be put together. It's three different countries. Pakistan owns the three counties—the three provinces in the east. They're not any part of—the Haqqani's run it."[43]

November 2019

At the Democratic debate, Biden proudly proclaimed he was endorsed by "the only African-American woman that's ever been elected to the Senate."

Standing next to him, Kamala Harris, an African-American, responded, "Nope. That's not true. The other one is here!"[44]

November 2019

Biden confused Iowa for Ohio. "How many unsafe bridges do

you still have here in the state of Ohio?" Biden asked a group of Cedar Rapids, Iowa, voters. "I mean Iowa, and I was just in Ohio because they have more."[45]

December 2019

Meeting with an Iowa newspaper, Biden said, "Look what's going on in Venezuela right now . . . Millions of people are crossing the border destabilizing Bolivia."[46]

Bolivia does not share a border with Venezuela. The two are separated by seven hundred miles—a lot of it, Amazon rain forest.

December 2019

"Anybody who can go down 300 to 3,000 feet in a mine, sure in hell can learn to program as well," he said. "Anybody who can throw coal into a furnace can learn how to program, for god's sake," he said later.[47]

January 2020

Biden mixed up his sister and wife. "By the way, this is my little sister Valerie!" Biden said as he grabbed his wife's hand. "And I'm Jill's husband," he added when reaching for his sister's.[48]

February 2020

Biden forgot which office he is running for. "My name is Joe Biden. I'm a Democratic candidate for the United States Senate . . . if you don't like me, you can vote for the other Biden."[49]

February 2020

"I had the great honor of meeting him [Nelson Mandela]. I

had the great honor of being arrested with our U.N. ambassador on the streets of Soweto trying to get to see him on Robben Island."[50] This never happened.

March 2020

Biden lied, or just forgot, when he said, "One of the things that I did early on in my career as a U.S. Senator was I was one of the sponsors of the Endangered Species Act. And one of the other things we've done is we, in the state of Delaware, set up the coastal zone legislation which means that they can't build any factories or anything within one mile of the estuary of the Delaware River and the Atlantic Ocean and the Chesapeake."[51] I know this makes no sense, that's why this Lost Joe quote is here.

March 2020

Trying to recite the Declaration of Independence, Biden said, "We hold these truths to be self-evident. All men and women are created, by the, you know, you know the thing."[52]

March 2020

"You are actively trying to end our Second Amendment right and take away our guns," the construction worker told Biden.

The former vice president responded, "You're full of shit. . . . I support the Second Amendment. The Second Amendment—just like right now, if you yelled 'fire,' that's not free speech. . . . I'm not taking your gun away at all. You need 100 rounds?"

The worker again accused Biden of "trying to take our guns."

"I did not say that!" the former vice president shouted. "I did not say that."

The man claimed he saw Biden say as much in "a viral video."

"It's a viral video like the other ones they're putting out that are simply a lie," said the 2020 Democratic primary candidate, putting his finger in the man's face and claiming that it was "AR-14s" that he was targeting.

The construction worker said, "This is not OK, all right?"

"Don't tell me that, pal," said Biden, his finger still in the man's face, "or I'm going to go out and slap you in the face."

"You're working for me, man!" the worker responded.

"I'm not working for you," said Biden. "Don't be such a horse's ass."[53]

May 2020

"I'm prepared to say that I have a record of over 40 years and that I'm going to beat Joe Biden!" Biden said.[54]

ACKNOWLEDGMENTS

As I finish writing this book, I can't help but to reflect on all the people who have made this project possible—those who have helped me succeed in life and continue to support me every single day. I could write an entire book about the individuals who have made an impact on me. To each of you, I am very grateful. There are too many friends and mentors to mention here, but please know that I value each one of you. THANK YOU for all you have done in the past, in the present, and, without a doubt, will do in the future.

To my father, President Donald J. Trump. Our entire family is proud of you and everything you have accomplished. When you set a goal, you always achieve it! You continue to amaze not only your family, but the entire world. Thank you for always fighting for me, our family, our nation, and the values that Make America Great! You and Melania are the Gold Standard.

To my beloved children, as you get older you will appreciate the sacrifices our family continues to make. I fight every day so you can have the opportunities that I had growing up. You mean everything to me, and you will always be my little monsters. I love you all very much!

To my princess, Kimberly, over the past two years I have been impressed by you so much—especially your love of country, your work ethic, and your drive to always win. I am lucky to have you in my life and I love you.

To my four siblings for always sticking together, fighting for our father, and always standing up for each other. From dawn to dusk, we strive to win. Thank you for everything you have all done for me. Love you.

To Jared for always being calm, cool, and reasonable. You make all of our days easier because you look out not only for the family, but for the best interests of this nation.

To Sergio Gor for being a great and loyal friend. This book wouldn't have happened without you. To many more adventures ahead.

To Charlie Kirk for fighting to make America Great Again and directing the next generation of youth in the right direction.

To all those who assisted with this book project, especially Alan, Adam, John, Linda, Michelle, Josh, Clint, Whitney, Kristopher, Marianne, Arthur, and Amanda. Thank you for the professionalism and support!

To the entire Trump Organization team who continue to excel in everything they do. No one works harder and more efficiently than you. We are blessed to have such amazing talent!

To the Deplorables, it is an honor to be in this fight with you to save our beloved nation. Never forget, I consider it a privilege to be one of you!

NOTES

PART I
Chapter 1: Fake News, You're Fired!

[1] Brian Flood. "Broadcast news slams Trump with 96 percent negative coverage since impeachment inquiry began, study says," Fox News, November 12, 2019. https://www.foxnews.com/media/broadcast-news-trump-impeachment-inquiry-negative-coverage.

[2] Christine M. Flowers. "Let's be honest about the persecution of Christians in Sri Lanka and beyond | Christine Flowers," *Philadelphia Inquirer*, April 26, 2019. https://www.inquirer.com/opinion/sri-lanka-bombing-christians-hillary-clinton-20190426.html.

[3] Brian Flood. "Media outlets mum on Bloomberg News' policy to investigate Trump, not Democrats, study shows," Fox News, December 4, 2019. https://www.foxnews.com/media/media-bloomberg-news-trump-democrats.

[4] Brian Flood. "Media outlets mum on Bloomberg News' policy to investigate Trump, not Democrats, study shows," Fox News, December 4, 2019. https://www.foxnews.com/media/media-bloomberg-news-trump-democrats.

[5] Brian Flood. "Media outlets mum on Bloomberg News' policy to investigate Trump, not Democrats, study shows," Fox News, December 4, 2019. https://www.foxnews.com/media/media-bloomberg-news-trump-democrats.

[6] Zach Montellaro. "Bloomberg's final bill: $1 billion for a 104-day campaign," *Politico*, April 20, 2020. https://www.politico.com/news/2020/04/20/bloomberg-1-billion-104-day-campaign-197216.

[7] Katherine J Igoe. "Where Did 'Amtrak Joe,' Joe Biden's Nickname, Come From?," *Marie Claire*, May 4, 2020. https://www.marieclaire.com/politics/a32363173/joe-biden-amtrak-joe-meaning.

[8] Hayes Thomas. "Whoopie Goldberg Explaining Roman Polanski Child Rape wasn't Legitimate Rape," YouTube, August 21, 2012. https://www.youtube.com/watch?v=nZskUvAGyjQ.

[9] RNC Research. "Former Obama Adviser Axelrod: Biden seemed 'confused,' 'defensive,' 'mired in the past'," Twitter, June 27, 2019. https://twitter.com/RNCResearch/status/1144443114754646016.

[10] RNC Research. "CNN panel slams Joe Biden's 'weak performance:' 'undermined the electability argument'," Twitter, June 27, 2019. https://twitter.com/RNCResearch/status/1144451493652836352.

[11] Matt Wolking. "Joe Biden's 'campaign has kept him a little bit in bubble wrap .... He hasn't been subjected to that many questions, that many unpredictable moments where he can easily go off script,'" Twitter, June 27, 2019. https://twitter.com/MattWolking/status/1144328221384728577.

[12] The *LNP* | LancasterOnline Editorial Board. "By shutting out this newspaper's reporters, Biden campaign sends wrong message to Lancaster [editorial]," *LNP* | LancasterOnline, June 26, 2020. https://lancasteronline.com/opinion/editorials/by-shutting-out-this-newspapers-reporters-biden-campaign-sends-wrong-message-to-lancaster-editorial/article_0140e830-b761-11ea-9e4d-0f0eb17abf99.html.

[13] Eliza Relman and Sonam Sheth. "Here are all the times Joe Biden has been accused of acting inappropriately toward women and girls," *Business Insider*, May 4, 2020. https://www.businessinsider.com/joe-biden-allegations-women-2020-campaign-2019-6.

[14] Alan Reynolds. "How One Model Simulated 2.2 Million U.S. Deaths from COVID-19," Cato Institute, April 21, 2020. https://www.cato.org/blog/how-one-model-simulated-22-million-us-deaths-covid-19.

[15] Robert Romano. "Biden flips on China travel ban," *Ceres Courier*, April 8, 2020. https://www.cerescourier.com/opinion/editorial/biden-flips-china-travel-ban.

[16] NBC Bay Area staff. "Nancy Pelosi Visits San Francisco's Chinatown Amid Coronavirus Concerns," NBC Bay

Area, February 24, 2020. https://www.nbcbayarea.com/news/local/nancy-pelosi-visits-san-franciscos-chinatown/2240247.

[17] Gregg Re. "After attacking Trump's coronavirus-related China travel ban as xenophobic, Dems and media have changed tune," Fox News, April 1, 2020. https://www.foxnews.com/politics/dems-media-change-tune-trump-attacks-coronavirus-china-travel-ban.

[18] Rebecca Savransky. "Obama to Trump: 'What magic wand do you have?'," *The Hill*, June 1, 2016. https://thehill.com/blogs/blog-briefing-room/news/281936-obama-to-trump-what-magic-wand-do-you-have.

[19] Chuck DeVore. "The Trump Manufacturing Jobs Boom: 10 Times Obama's Over 21 Months," *Forbes*, October 6, 2018. https://www.forbes.com/sites/chuckdevore/2018/10/16/the-trump-manufacturing-jobs-boom-10-times-obamas-over-21-months/#55e8a3595850.

[20] Chuck DeVore. "The Trump Manufacturing Jobs Boom: 10 Times Obama's Over 21 Months," *Forbes*, October 6, 2018. https://www.forbes.com/sites/chuckdevore/2018/10/16/the-trump-manufacturing-jobs-boom-10-times-obamas-over-21-months/#55e8a3595850.

[21] Chuck DeVore. "Trump's Policy 'Magic Wand' Boosts Manufacturing Jobs 399% in First 26 Months Over Obama's Last 26," *Forbes*, March 11, 2019. https://www.forbes.com/sites/chuckdevore/2019/03/11/trumps-policy-magic-wand-boosts-manufacturing-jobs-399-in-first-26-months-over-obamas-last-26/#1d6d2d7120a6.

[22] Alexandra Kelley. "Biden tells coal miners to 'learn to code,'" *The Hill*, December 31, 2019. https://thehill.com/changing-america/enrichment/education/476391-biden-tells-coal-miners-to-learn-to-code.

[23] Talia Lavin. "The Fetid, Right-Wing Origins of 'Learn to Code,'" *New Republic*, February 1, 2019. https://newrepublic.com/article/153019/fetid-right-wing-origins-learn-code.

[24] Oliver Darcy. "CNN settles lawsuit with Nick Sandmann stemming from viral video controversy," CNN Business, January 7, 2020. https://www.cnn.com/2020/01/07/media/cnn-settles-lawsuit-viral-video/index.html.

Chapter 2: Unfit to Serve

[1] Ian Schwartz. "Biden Confuses Wife and Sister in Super Tuesday Speech," RealClear Politics, March 4, 2020. https://www.realclearpolitics.com/video/2020/03/04/biden_confuses_wife_and_sister_in_super_tuesday_speech.html.

[2] Benjamin Fearnow. "Joe Biden Says He's Running For 'United States Senate' While in South Carolina; Supporters Say It's Rhetorical," *Newsweek*, February 25, 2020. https://www.newsweek.com/joe-biden-says-hes-running-united-states-senate-while-south-carolina-supporters-say-its-1489034.

[3] Lawrence K. Altman, M.D. "THE DOCTORS WORLD; Subtle Clues Are Often the Only Warnings Of Perilous Aneurysms," *New York Times*, February 23, 1988. https://www.nytimes.com/1988/02/23/science/the-doctors-world-subtle-clues-are-often-the-only-warnings-of-perilous-aneurysms.html.

[4] Lawrence K. Altman, M.D. "Many Holes in Disclosure of Nominees' Health," *New York Times*, October 19, 2008. https://www.nytimes.com/2008/10/20/us/politics/20health.html.

[5] Michael Brant-Zawadzki, M.D., F.A.C.R., "Joe Biden's Aneurysm Rupture: A Stroke of Fortune," Hoag. https://www.hoag.org/specialties-services/neurosciences/latest/joe-biden-s-aneurysm-rupture-a-stroke-of-fortune.

[6] Brain Aneurysm Foundation. "Statistics and Facts," Bafound.org. https://bafound.org/about-brain-aneurysms/brain-aneurysm-basics/brain-aneurysm-statistics-and-facts.

[7] Terence P. Jeffrey. "FLASHBACK: Brain Surgeon Told Biden He Had Less Than 50% Chance of 'Being Completely Normal,'" CNSNews, June 5, 2013. https://cnsnews.com/article/washington/terence-p-jeffrey/flashback-brain-surgeon-told-biden-he-had-less-50-chance-being.

[8] Terence P. Jeffrey. "FLASHBACK: Brain Surgeon Told Biden He Had Less Than 50% Chance of 'Being Completely Normal,'" CNSNews, June 5, 2013. https://cnsnews.com/article/washington/terence-p-jeffrey/flashback-brain-surgeon-told-biden-he-had-less-50-chance-being.

[9] David Whelan. "Obama's Doctor Knocks ObamaCare," *Forbes*, June 18, 2009. https://www.forbes.

com/2009/06/18/obama-doctor-knocks-obamacare-business-healthcare-obamas-doctor.html#70fdfb202294.

[10] Sam Dorman. "Obama's former doc says Biden 'not a healthy guy' after reviewing medical info: Report," Fox News, December 19, 2019. https://www.foxnews.com/politics/obamas-doc-biden-not-healthy.

[11] Sam Dorman. "Obama's former doc says Biden 'not a healthy guy' after reviewing medical info: Report," Fox News, December 19, 2019. https://www.foxnews.com/politics/obamas-doc-biden-not-healthy.

[12] Charles Creitz. "Biden camp denies ex-VP confused D-Day with Pearl Harbor Day during fundraiser," Fox News, May 27, 2020. https://www.foxnews.com/politics/joe-biden-confuses-d-day-pearl-harbor-day-discussion-pennsylvania-wolf.

[13] Terence P. Jeffrey. "FLASHBACK: Brain Surgeon Told Biden He Had Less Than 50% Chance of 'Being Completely Normal,'" CNSNews, June 5, 2013. https://cnsnews.com/article/washington/terence-p-jeffrey/flashback-brain-surgeon-told-biden-he-had-less-50-chance-being.

[14] Chris Riotta. "Joe Biden confuses Nevada with New Hampshire in speech after second primary vote," *Independent*, February 12, 2020. https://www.independent.co.uk/news/joe-biden-nevada-new-hampshire-primary-state-confusing-gaffe-a9330701.html.

[15] Trump War Room. "Joe Biden Forgets What Office He's Running For," YouTube, February 25, 2020. https://www.youtube.com/watch?v=umbTUOzgz8M.

[16] S. E. Cupp. "The president is not well: The umpteenth reminders of Trump's mental state and the consequences," *New York Daily News*, May 5, 2020. https://www.nydailynews.com/opinion/ny-oped-the-president-is-not-well-20200505-37i32k3q55c55bnnk6hdkgxvga-story.html.

[17] American Psychiatric Association. "APA Calls for End to 'Armchair' Psychiatry," Psychiatry.org, January 9, 2018. https://www.psychiatry.org/newsroom/news-releases/apa-calls-for-end-to-armchair-psychiatry.

[18] Dan Merica. "Dr. Ronny Jackson's glowing bill of health for Trump," CNN Politics, January 16, 2018. https://www.cnn.com/2018/01/16/politics/dr-ronny-jackson-donald-trump-clean-bill-of-health/index.html.

[19] Dan Merica. "Dr. Ronny Jackson's glowing bill of health for Trump," CNN Politics, January 16, 2018. https://www.cnn.com/2018/01/16/politics/dr-ronny-jackson-donald-trump-clean-bill-of-health/index.html.

Chapter 3: Puppet on a String

[1] Serena Lin. "PROFILE: Dr. Bandy Lee and the psychiatric case against Donald Trump," *Yale Daily News*, May 13, 2020. https://yaledailynews.com/blog/2020/05/13/profile-dr-bandy-lee-and-the-psychiatric-case-against-donald-trump.

[2] "President Obama Endorses Joe Biden's Presidential Bid," C-SPAN, April 14, 2020. https://www.c-span.org/video/?471214-1/president-obama-endorses-joe-bidens-presidential-bid.

[3] Gregg Re. "Usama bin Laden wanted to kill Obama so 'totally unprepared' Biden would be president, declassified docs show," Fox News, April 23, 2020. https://www.foxnews.com/politics/osama-bin-laden-wanted-to-kill-obama-so-biden-would-be-president-declassified-docs-show.

[4] Josh Feldman. "Fmr DefSec Gates Offers Trump Praise on Foreign Policy, but Bothered by 'His Treatment and Words about Military People,'" Mediaite, June 14, 2020. https://www.mediaite.com/tv/fmr-defsec-gates-offers-trump-praise-on-foreign-policy-but-bothered-by-his-treatment-and-words-about-military-people.

[5] Bloomberg Politics. "Beto O'Rourke: 'Hell Yes, We're Going to Take Your AR-15's,'" YouTube, September 13, 2019. https://www.youtube.com/watch?v=7vEnTjs2RVo.

[6] John Verhovek, Kesley Walsh, and Molly Nagle. "Biden gets testy with auto worker over 2nd Amendment claim," ABC News, March 10, 2020. https://abcnews.go.com/Politics/biden-testy-auto-worker-2nd-amendment-claim/story?id=69505754.

Chapter 4: The Wrong Side of History

[1] Joint Center for Housing Studies of Harvard University. 2014. https://www.jchs.harvard.edu/sites/default/files/jchs-housing_americas_older_adults_2014-ch2_0.pdf.

[2] Eric Levitz. "Will Black Voters Still Love Biden When They Remember Who He Was?," *New York Intelligencer*, March 12, 2019. https://nymag.com/intelligencer/2019/03/joe-biden-record-on-busing-incarceration-racial-justice-democratic-primary-2020-explained.html.

[3] Grace Panetta. "Joe Biden worried in 1977 that certain de-segregation policies would cause his children to grow up 'in a racial jungle,'" *Business Insider*, July 15, 2019. https://www.businessinsider.com/biden-said-desegregation-would-create-a-racial-jungle-2019-7.

[4] Eric Levitz. "Will Black Voters Still Love Biden When They Remember Who He Was?," *New York Intelligencer*, March 12, 2019. https://nymag.com/intelligencer/2019/03/joe-biden-record-on-busing-incarceration-racial-justice-democratic-primary-2020-explained.html.

[5] Xuan Thai and Ted Barrett. "Biden's description of Obama draws scrutiny," CNN, February 9, 2007. https://www.cnn.com/2007/POLITICS/01/31/biden.obama.

[6] Maggie Fitzgerald. "Black and Hispanic unemployment is at a record low," CNBC, October 4, 2019. https://www.cnbc.com/2019/10/04/black-and-hispanic-unemployment-is-at-a-record-low.html.

[7] Jimmy Atkinson. "Democratic Presidential Candidates Positions on Opportunity Zones," OpportunityDb, March 2, 2020. https://opportunitydb.com/2020/03/democratic-presidential-candidates-positions-on-opportunity-zones.

[8] Martin Crutsinger and Darlene Superville. "Trump administration seeks to boost Opportunity Zones," Fox Business, April 17, 2019. https://www.foxbusiness.com/markets/trump-administration-seeks-to-boost-opportunity-zones.

[9] Sheryl Gay Stolberg and Astead W. Herndon. "'Lock the S.O.B.s Up': Joe Biden and the Era of Mass Incarceration," *New York Times*, June 25, 2019. https://www.nytimes.com/2019/06/25/us/joe-biden-crime-laws.html.

[10] Paris Dennard. "Joe Biden questions my blackness one moment, defends racist 1994 crime bill the next," *USA Today*, May 25, 2020. https://www.usatoday.com/story/opinion/2020/05/25/joe-biden-you-aint-black-racism-trump-column/5254434002.

[11] Ranya Shannon. "3 Ways the 1994 Crime Bill Continues to Hurt Communities of Color," Center for American Progress, May 10, 2019. https://www.americanprogress.org/issues/race/news/2019/05/10/469642/3-ways-1994-crime-bill-continues-hurt-communities-color.

[12] Council of Economic Advisers. "Historic U.S. Job Market Continues as African-American Unemployment Rate Hits New Low," The White House, November 1, 2019. https://www.whitehouse.gov/articles/historic-u-s-job-market-continues-african-american-unemployment-rate-hits-new-low.

[13] "80 Named as Recipients of Ellis Island Awards," *New York Times*, October 16, 1986. https://www.nytimes.com/1986/10/16/nyregion/80-named-as-recipients-of-ellis-island-awards.html.

[14] "Jesse Jackson Praises Trump's Commitment to Minorities, 'Under-served Communities' Video," C-SPAN, January 14, 1998. https://www.c-span.org/video/?c4773388/user-clip-1999-jesse-jackson-praises-trumps-commitment-minorities-under-served.

[15] Janell Ross. "Joe Biden didn't just compromise with segregationists. He fought for their cause in schools, experts say," NBC News, June 25, 2019. https://www.nbcnews.com/news/nbcblk/joe-biden-didn-t-just-compromise-segregationists-he-fought-their-n1021626.

[16] Paris Dennard. "Joe Biden questions my blackness one moment, defends racist 1994 crime bill the next," *USA Today*, May 25, 2020. https://www.usatoday.com/story/opinion/2020/05/25/joe-biden-you-aint-black-racism-trump-column/5254434002.

[17] Jeva Lange. "Clinton stirs anger by claiming she carries hot sauce in her bag, like Beyoncé," *The Week*, April 18, 2016. https://theweek.com/speedreads/619127/clinton-stirs-anger-by-claiming-carries-hot-sauce-bag-like-beyonc.

[18] "Biden refuses to apologise for working with racist senators," BBC, June 20, 2019. https://www.bbc.com/news/world-us-canada-48696126.

Chapter 5: A Tale of Two Bidens

[1] Mix Clip Max. "Creepy Joe Biden Hair Sniffing Compilation," YouTube, April 2, 2019. https://www.youtube.com/watch?v=_H5NJZMDumY.

[2] Sean Hannity. "Biden Awkwardly Kisses Granddaughter at Campaign Stop," Twitter, February 3, 2020. https://twitter.com/seanhannity/status/1224352898647195650.

[3] David Choi. "More women have come forward accusing Joe Biden of uncomfortable physical contact, bringing the total to 7," *Business Insider*, April 4, 2019. https://www.businessinsider.com/joe-biden-new-accusers-inappropriate-touching-report-2019-4.

[4] David Choi. "More women have come forward accusing Joe Biden of uncomfortable physical contact, bringing the total to 7," *Business Insider*, April 4, 2019. https://www.businessinsider.com/joe-biden-new-accusers-inappropriate-touching-report-2019-4.

[5] David Choi. "More women have come forward accusing Joe Biden of uncomfortable physical contact, bringing the total to 7," *Business Insider*, April 4, 2019. https://www.businessinsider.com/joe-biden-new-accusers-inappropriate-touching-report-2019-4.

[6] Eliza Relman and Sonam Sheth. "Here are all the times Joe Biden has been accused of acting inappropriately toward women and girls," *Business Insider*, May 4, 2020. https://www.businessinsider.com/joe-biden-allegations-women-2020-campaign-2019-6.

[7] Eliza Relman and Sonam Sheth. "Here are all the times Joe Biden has been accused of acting inappropriately toward women and girls," *Business Insider*, May 4, 2020. https://www.businessinsider.com/joe-biden-allegations-women-2020-campaign-2019-6.

[8] Eliza Relman and Sonam Sheth. "Here are all the times Joe Biden has been accused of acting inappropriately toward women and girls," *Business Insider*, May 4, 2020. https://www.businessinsider.com/joe-biden-allegations-women-2020-campaign-2019-6.

[9] Jeannie Suk Gersen. "A Fair Examination of the Allegations Against Joe Biden Can Strengthen the #MeToo Movement," *New Yorker*, May 6, 2020. https://www.newyorker.com/news/our-columnists/a-fair-examination-of-tara-reades-allegation-can-strengthen-the-metoo-movement.

[10] Jeannie Suk Gersen. "A Fair Examination of the Allegations Against Joe Biden Can Strengthen the #MeToo Movement," *New Yorker*, May 6, 2020. https://www.newyorker.com/news/our-columnists/a-fair-examination-of-tara-reades-allegation-can-strengthen-the-metoo-movement.

[11] Grateful American. "Larry King Live August 11, 1993: Tara Reade's Mother Calling in to Allege Joe Biden's Sexual Assault," YouTube, April 26, 2020. https://www.youtube.com/watch?v=bBTwwOHV6vQ.

[12] Matt Fountain. "Exclusive: 1996 court document confirms Tara Reade told of harassment in Biden's office," *The Tribune*, May 9, 2020. https://www.sanluisobispo.com/news/politics-government/article242527331.html.

[13] Lisa Lerer and Sydney Ember. "Examining Tara Reade's Sexual Assault Allegation Against Joe Biden," *New York Times*, May 22, 2020. https://www.nytimes.com/2020/04/12/us/politics/joe-biden-tara-reade-sexual-assault-complaint.html.

[14] Eliza Relman and Sonam Sheth. "Here are all the times Joe Biden has been accused of acting inappropriately toward women and girls," *Business Insider*, May 4, 2020. https://www.businessinsider.com/joe-biden-allegations-women-2020-campaign-2019-6.

[15] Emma Green. "Is It Fair to Compare Joe Biden to Brett Kavanaugh?," *The Atlantic*, May 5, 2020. https://www.theatlantic.com/politics/archive/2020/05/tara-reade-biden-feminism/611152.

[16] Fox News. "New video raises questions about Kavanaugh accuser's testimony," YouTube, September 5, 2019. https://www.youtube.com/watch?v=zW7qGXkyZcc.

[17] "COBRA COBRA COBRA," Urban Dictionary, May 2, 2020. https://www.urbandictionary.com/define.php?term=COBRA%20COBRA%20COBRA.

[18] Steven Nelson. "Biden Swims Naked, Upsetting Female Secret Service Agents, Book Claims," *U.S. News &*

World Report, August 1, 2014. https://www.usnews.com/news/blogs/washington-whispers/2014/08/01/biden-swims-naked-upsetting-female-secret-service-agents-book-claims.

[19] Ronald Kessler. "Joe Biden's disrespect for the Secret Service," *Washington Times*, May 13, 2020. https://www.washingtontimes.com/news/2020/may/13/joe-bidens-disrespect-for-the-secret-service.

[20] Steven Nelson. "Biden Swims Naked, Upsetting Female Secret Service Agents, Book Claims," *U.S. News & World Report*, August 1, 2014. https://www.usnews.com/news/blogs/washington-whispers/2014/08/01/biden-swims-naked-upsetting-female-secret-service-agents-book-claims.

[21] Ronald Kessler. "Joe Biden's disrespect for the Secret Service," *Washington Times*, May 13, 2020. https://www.washingtontimes.com/news/2020/may/13/joe-bidens-disrespect-for-the-secret-service.

[22] Bari Weiss. "Resignation Letter," Bariweiss.com, July 14, 2020. https://www.bariweiss.com/resignation-letter.

[23] Greg Garrison. "Cancel Pastor Chris Hodges? Church of the Highlands faces social media firestorm," AL.com, June 14, 2020. https://www.al.com/news/2020/06/cancel-pastor-chris-hodges-church-of-the-highlands-faces-social-media-firestorm.html.

[24] Greg Garrison. "Cancel Pastor Chris Hodges? Church of the Highlands faces social media firestorm," AL.com, June 14, 2020. https://www.al.com/news/2020/06/cancel-pastor-chris-hodges-church-of-the-highlands-faces-social-media-firestorm.html.

[25] Greg Garrison. "Cancel Pastor Chris Hodges? Church of the Highlands faces social media firestorm," AL.com, June 14, 2020. https://www.al.com/news/2020/06/cancel-pastor-chris-hodges-church-of-the-highlands-faces-social-media-firestorm.html.

Chapter 6: It Didn't Work

[1] Jonathan Turley. "The unmasking of Joe Biden," *The Hill*, May 14, 2020. https://thehill.com/opinion/white-house/497711-the-unmasking-of-joe-biden.

[2] John Santucci and Allison Pecorin. "DC Alcoholic Beverage Control Board rejects challenge to Trump hotel," ABC News, September 25, 2019. https://abcnews.go.com/Politics/dc-alcoholic-beverage-control-board-rejects-challenge-trump/story?id=65864511.

[3] Kevin D. Williamson. "Social justice warriors are waging a dangerous 'Cancel Cultural Revolution,'" *New York Post*, June 13, 2020. https://nypost.com/2020/06/13/social-justice-warriors-are-waging-a-cancel-cultural-revolution.

[4] Kevin D. Williamson. "Social justice warriors are waging a dangerous 'Cancel Cultural Revolution,'" *New York Post*, June 13, 2020. https://nypost.com/2020/06/13/social-justice-warriors-are-waging-a-cancel-cultural-revolution.

[5] Emily Larson. "Cocaine pipe and 'white, powdery substance' found in Hunter Biden's rental car in 2016," *Washington Examiner*, May 17, 2019. https://www.washingtonexaminer.com/news/police-report-cocaine-pipe-found-in-hunter-bidens-rental-car-in-2016/.

[6] Maureen MacDonald. "Peaceful Transition of Power," *Prologue Magazine*, Winter 2000, Vol. 32, No. 2. https://www.archives.gov/publications/prologue/2000/winter/inaugurations.

[7] Oliver Staley. "The type of diversity boardrooms prize most is age—and they can't even manage that," Quartz, April 25, 2018. https://qz.com/work/1260792/the-type-of-diversity-boardrooms-prize-most-is-age-and-they-cant-even-manage-that.

[8] Margie Fishman. "Joe Biden leaves D.C. on—what else?—Amtrak," *USA Today*, January 20, 2017. https://www.usatoday.com/story/news/politics/2017/01/20/biden-returns-delaware-amtrak-inauguration/96840088.

[9] Aime Williams, Sun Yu, and Roman Olearchyk. "Hunter Biden's web of interests," *Financial Times*, October 8, 2019. https://www.ft.com/content/3904f888-e8ef-11e9-a240-3b065ef5fc55.

[10] Peter Schweizer, *Profiles in Corruption* (New York: HarperCollins, 2020), 60.

[11] Bradford Betz. "Massive bribe to stop Ukraine probe of Burisma founder intercepted," Fox News, June 14, 2020. https://www.foxnews.com/world/burisma-bribe-stop-ukraine-probe-intercepted.

[12] Council of Europe. "Ukraine most corrupt country in Europe after Russia," Coe.int, February 2018. https://

www.coe.int/en/web/corruption/completed-projects/enpi/newsroom-enpi/-/asset_publisher/F0LygN4lv4rX/content/ukraine-most-corrupt-country-in-europe-after-russia?inheritRedirect=false.

[13] Paul Ausick. "25 Boards of Directors with Shocking Pay Packages," 24/7 Wall St., January 11, 2020. https://247wallst.com/special-report/2018/11/29/25-boards-of-directors-with-shocking-pay-packages.

[14] Tim McLaughlin. "U.S. company directors compensated more than ever, but now risk backlash," Reuters, November 8, 2019. https://www.reuters.com/article/us-compensation-directors-insight/u-s-company-directors-compensated-more-than-ever-but-now-risk-backlash-idUSKBN1XI1PF.

[15] Schweizer, Profiles, 61.

[16] https://www.realclearpolitics.com/video/2019/09/27/flashback_2018_joe_biden_brags_at_cfr_meeting_about_withholding_aid_to_ukraine_to_force_firing_of_prosecutor.html.

[17] Schweizer, Profiles, 62.

[18] Aime Williams, Sun Yu, and Roman Olearchyk. "Hunter Biden's web of interests," Financial Times, October 8, 2019. https://www.ft.com/content/3904f888-e8ef-11e9-a240-3b065ef5fc55.

[19] U.S.A. v. Galanis et al., Case No. 1:16-cr-00371, United States District Court for the Southern District of New York, Rosemont Seneca Bohai account statements from Morgan Stanley Private Wealth Management, Gx301; Novatus Holding PTE. Ltd.—'3' for 6/7/13 re: Net Element, Inc., June 10, 2013, File # 1-34887, http://www.secinfo.com/d141Nx.x1165.htm; Nicholas Trickett, "Watch the Throne: Trans-Caspian Pipeline Meets Succession Politics in Kazakhstan," Diplomat, February 16, 2017, https://thediplomat.com/2017/02/watch-the-throne-trans-caspian-pipeline-meets-succession-politics-in-kazakhstan.

[20] U.S.A. v. Galanis et al., Case No. 1:16-cr-00371, United States District Court for the Southern District of New York, Rosemont Seneca Bohai account statements from Morgan Stanley Private Wealth Management, Gx301; Shamim Adam and Laurence Arnold, "A Guide to the Worldwide Probes of Malaysia's 1MDB Fund," Bloomberg, March 7, 2018, https://www.bloomberg.com/news/articles/2018-03-07/malaysia-s-1mdb-fund-spawns-worldwide-probes-quicktake.

[21] U.S.A. v. Galanis et al., Case No. 1:16-cr-00371, United States District Court for the Southern District of New York, Rosemont Seneca Bohai account statements from Morgan Stanley Private Wealth Management, Gx301.

[22] Schweizer, Profiles, 62–63.

[23] Schweizer, 64.

Chapter 7: Family First

[1] Tim O'Donnell. "Hunter Biden reportedly received a 2.8 carat diamond from a Chinese energy tycoon," The Week, July 1, 2019. https://theweek.com/speedreads/850429/hunter-biden-reportedly-received-28-carat-diamond-from-chinese-energy-tycoon.

[2] Peter Schweizer, Profiles in Corruption (New York: HarperCollins, 2020), 55.

[3] Josh Lederman. "Biden's trip to China with son Hunter in 2013 comes under new scrutiny," NBC News, October 2, 2019. https://www.nbcnews.com/politics/2020-election/biden-s-trip-china-son-hunter-2013-comes-under-new-n1061051.

[4] Schweizer, Profiles, 55.

[5] Schweizer, 55.

[6] Aime Williams, Sun Yu, and Roman Olearchyk. "Hunter Biden's web of interests," Financial Times, October 8, 2019. https://www.ft.com/content/3904f888-e8ef-11e9-a240-3b065ef5fc55.

[7] Emily Jacobs. "Hunter Biden still listed on board of Chinese company he was to resign from: report," New York Post, October 8, 2019. https://nypost.com/2020/04/15/hunter-biden-still-listed-as-board-member-of-chinese-company-report.

[8] Simon Denyer. "From diet pills to underwear: Chinese firms scramble to grab Ivanka Trump trademark," Washington Post, March 8, 2017. https://www.washingtonpost.com/world/asia_pacific/from-diet-pills-to-

underwear-chinese-firms-scramble-to-grab-ivanka-trump-trademark/2017/02/24/9a6ecea4-fa96-11e6-9b3e-ed886f4f4825_story.html.

[9] Blue Nile. "2.80-Carat Round Cut Diamond," Bluenile.com, 2020. https://www.bluenile.com/diamond-details/LD12514972.

[10] Tim O'Donnell. "Hunter Biden reportedly received a 2.8 carat diamond from a Chinese energy tycoon," *The Week*, July 1, 2019. https://theweek.com/speedreads/850429/hunter-biden-reportedly-received-28-carat-diamond-from-chinese-energy-tycoon.

[11] Adam Entous. "Will Hunter Biden Jeopardize His Father's Campaign?," *New Yorker*, July 1, 2019. https://www.newyorker.com/magazine/2019/07/08/will-hunter-biden-jeopardize-his-fathers-campaign.

[12] Schweizer, *Profiles*, 59.

[13] Schweizer, 59.

[14] Schweizer, 60.

[15] Veronica Stracqualursi. "Biden downplays Chinese economic competition, drawing criticism from Republicans and Sanders," CNN Politics, May 2, 2019. https://www.cnn.com/2019/05/02/politics/joe-biden-china-threat-united-states/index.html.

[16] Geoff Herbert. "Hunter Biden fathered child with woman while dating brother's widow, DNA test reveals," *Syracuse.com*, November 21, 2019. https://www.syracuse.com/us-news/2019/11/hunter-biden-fathered-child-with-woman-while-dating-brothers-widow-dna-test-reveals.html.

[17] Schweizer, *Profiles*, 48.

[18] Schweizer, 48.

[19] Brent Scher. "Biden: I Tried to 'Prostitute Myself' to Big Donors During First Senate Run," *Washington Free Beacon*, March 27, 2019. https://freebeacon.com/politics/biden-i-tried-to-prostitute-myself-to-big-donors-during-first-senate-run.

[20] Schweizer, *Profiles*, 71.

[21] Ben Schreckinger. "Biden Inc.," *Politico Magazine*, August 2, 2019. https://www.politico.com/magazine/story/2019/08/02/joe-biden-investigation-hunter-brother-hedge-fund-money-2020-campaign-227407.

[22] Ben Schreckinger. "Biden Inc.," *Politico Magazine*, August 2, 2019. https://www.politico.com/magazine/story/2019/08/02/joe-biden-investigation-hunter-brother-hedge-fund-money-2020-campaign-227407.

[23] Schweizer, *Profiles*, 72.

[24] Charlie Gasparino. "The Ties that Biden," Fox Business, October 22, 2012. https://www.foxbusiness.com/politics/the-ties-that-biden.

[25] Charlie Gasparino. "The Ties that Biden," Fox Business, October 22, 2012. https://www.foxbusiness.com/politics/the-ties-that-biden.

[26] Charlie Gasparino. "The Ties that Biden," Fox Business, October 22, 2012. https://www.foxbusiness.com/politics/the-ties-that-biden.

[27] Charlie Gasparino. "The Ties that Biden," Fox Business, October 22, 2012. https://www.foxbusiness.com/politics/the-ties-that-biden.

[28] Schweizer, *Profiles*, 74.

[29] Charlie Gasparino. "The Ties that Biden," Fox Business, October 22, 2012. https://www.foxbusiness.com/politics/the-ties-that-biden.

[30] Peter Schweizer. "How five members of Joe Biden's family got rich through his connections," *New York Post*, January 18, 2020. https://nypost.com/2020/01/18/how-five-members-of-joe-bidens-family-got-rich-through-his-connections.

[31] Schweizer, *Profiles*, 84–89.

[32] Schweizer, 79–80.

[33] Schweizer, 79–80.

[34] Schweizer, 77.

[35] Schweizer, 77.

[36] Schweizer, 77.

[37] Schweizer, 77.

[38] Schweizer, 47.

[39] Ryan Parry, Alan Butterfield, and Josh Boswell. "EXCLUSIVE: Joe Biden's brother Frank owes dead man's family $1 MILLION for 8omph car crash - but has never paid a cent in 20 years and the Democratic candidate did NOTHING to help," *Daily Mail*, February 6, 2020. https://www.dailymail.co.uk/news/article-7908559/Joe-Bidens-brother-Frank-owes-1-million-dead-mans-family-2020-Democrat-did-help.html.

[40] Schweizer, *Profiles*, 80.

[41] Schweizer, 82.

Chapter 8: Beijing Biden

[1] Emily Larsen. "Biden downplays China again after bowing to pressure last time," *Washington Examiner*, May 13, 2019. https://www.washingtonexaminer.com/news/biden-downplays-china-again-after-bowing-to-pressure-last-time.

[2] Andrew Buncombe. "US and China in war of words as Beijing threatens to halt supply of medicine amid coronavirus crisis," *Independent*, March 13, 2020. https://www.independent.co.uk/news/world/americas/us-politics/coronavirus-china-us-drugs-trump-rubio-china-virus-xinhua-hell-epidemic-a9400811.html.

[3] Nicholas Laughlin. "Nearly 3 in 4 Americans Blame the Chinese Government for America's High Death Rate," Morning Consult, May 8, 2020. https://morningconsult.com/form/nearly-3-in-4-americans-blame-the-chinese-government-for-americas-high-death-count.

[4] Kat Devlin, Laura Silver, and Christine Huang. "U.S. Views of China Increasingly Negative Amid Coronavirus Outbreak," Pew Research Center, April 21, 2020. https://www.pewresearch.org/global/2020/04/21/u-s-views-of-china-increasingly-negative-amid-coronavirus-outbreak.

[5] Yanzhong Huang. "U.S. Dependence on Pharmaceutical Products from China," Council on Foreign Relations, August 14, 2019. https://www.cfr.org/blog/us-dependence-pharmaceutical-products-china.

[6] Ana Swanson. "Coronavirus Spurs U.S. Efforts to End China's Chokehold on Drugs," *New York Times*, March 11, 2020. https://www.nytimes.com/2020/03/11/business/economy/coronavirus-china-trump-drugs.html.

[7] Doug Palmer and Finbarr Bermingham. "U.S. policymakers worry about China 'weaponizing' drug exports," *Politico*, April 10, 2020. https://www.politico.com/news/2019/12/20/policymakers-worry-china-drug-exports-088126.

[8] Doug Palmer and Finbarr Bermingham. "U.S. policymakers worry about China 'weaponizing' drug exports," *Politico*, April 10, 2020. https://www.politico.com/news/2019/12/20/policymakers-worry-china-drug-exports-088126.

[9] Marc A. Thiessen. "Explain the Chinese spy, Sen. Feinstein," *Washington Post*, August 9, 2018. https://www.washingtonpost.com/opinions/explain-the-chinese-spy-sen-feinstein/2018/08/09/0560ca60-9bfd-11e8-b60b-1c897f17e185_story.html.

[10] Donald G. McNeil and Zolan Kanno-Youngs. "C.D.C. and W.H.O. Offers to Help China Have Been Ignored for Weeks," *New York Times*, February 7, 2020. https://www.nytimes.com/2020/02/07/health/cdc-coronavirus-china.html.

[11] Barnini Chakraborty. "Chinese doctor who first raised the alarm over COVID-19 vanishes," Fox News, April 1, 2020. https://www.foxnews.com/world/chinese-doctor-critics-who-first-raised-the-alarm-over-covid-19-vanishes.

[12] Ana Swanson. "Coronavirus Spurs U.S. Efforts to End China's Chokehold on Drugs," *New York Times*, March 11, 2020. https://www.nytimes.com/2020/03/11/business/economy/coronavirus-china-trump-drugs.html.

[13] Charles E. Grassley and Ron Johnson. "Grassley, Johnson Seek Hunter Biden Travel Records in Conflict-of-Interest Probe," Grassley.senate.gov, February 5, 2020. https://www.grassley.senate.gov/news/news-releases/grassley-johnson-seek-hunter-biden-travel-records-conflict-interest-probe.

[14] Charles E. Grassley. "Grassley Raises Concerns Over Obama Admin Approval of U.S. Tech Company Joint

Sale to Chinese Government and Investment Firm Linked to Biden, Kerry Families," United States Senate Committee on Finance, August 15, 2019. https://www.finance.senate.gov/chairmans-news/grassley-raises-concerns-over-obama-admin-approval-of-us-tech-company-joint-sale-to-chinese-government-and-investment-firm-linked-to-biden-kerry-families.

[15] Owen Churchill. "Senator wants inquiry into whether 'conflict of interest' led to US approval of deal involving Chinese state company and Joe Biden's son," *South China Morning Post*, August 16, 2019. https://www.scmp.com/news/china/diplomacy/article/3023025/senator-wants-inquiry-whether-conflict-interest-led-us.

[16] Charles E. Grassley. "Grassley Raises Concerns Over Obama Admin Approval of U.S. Tech Company Joint Sale to Chinese Government and Investment Firm Linked to Biden, Kerry Families," United States Senate Committee on Finance, August 15, 2019. https://www.finance.senate.gov/chairmans-news/grassley-raises-concerns-over-obama-admin-approval-of-us-tech-company-joint-sale-to-chinese-government-and-investment-firm-linked-to-biden-kerry-families.

[17] Gregg Re. "Usama bin Laden wanted to kill Obama so 'totally unprepared' Biden would be president, declassified docs show," Fox News, April 23, 2020. https://www.foxnews.com/politics/osama-bin-laden-wanted-to-kill-obama-so-biden-would-be-president-declassified-docs-show.

[18] David N. Bossie. "David Bossie: Biden wrong on China his entire career—let's look at the record," Fox News, May 15, 2020. https://www.foxnews.com/opinion/biden-wrong-china-career-check-record-david-bossie.

[19] David N. Bossie. "David Bossie: Biden wrong on China his entire career—let's look at the record," Fox News, May 15, 2020. https://www.foxnews.com/opinion/biden-wrong-china-career-check-record-david-bossie.

[20] David N. Bossie. "David Bossie: Biden wrong on China his entire career—let's look at the record," Fox News, May 15, 2020. https://www.foxnews.com/opinion/biden-wrong-china-career-check-record-david-bossie.

[21] Ronn Blitzer. "FBI Director Wray says half of bureau's 5,000 counterintelligence cases are related to China," Fox News, July 7, 2020. https://www.foxnews.com/politics/fbi-director-wray-says-half-of-bureaus-5000-counterintelligence-cases-are-related-to-china.

[22] Christian Whiton. "Biden Is Weak on China," *National Interest*, May 13, 2020. https://nationalinterest.org/feature/biden-weak-china-153971.

[23] David N. Bossie. "David Bossie: Biden wrong on China his entire career—let's look at the record," Fox News, May 15, 2020. https://www.foxnews.com/opinion/biden-wrong-china-career-check-record-david-bossie.

[24] Veronica Stracqualursi and Sheena Jones. "Harvard professor among three charged with lying about Chinese government ties," CNN Politics, January 28, 2020. https://www.cnn.com/2020/01/28/politics/harvard-professor-chinese-nationals-arrest-espionage/index.html.

[25] Ken Dilanian. "American universities are a soft target for China's spies, say U.S. intelligence officials," NBC News, February 2, 2020. https://www.nbcnews.com/news/china/american-universities-are-soft-target-china-s-spies-say-u-n1104291.

[26] Katie Pavlich. "Pavlich: Joe Biden's China problem," *The Hill*, April 29, 2020. https://thehill.com/opinion/katie-pavlich/495156-pavlich-joe-bidens-china-problem.

[27] Ken Dilanian. "American universities are a soft target for China's spies, say U.S. intelligence officials," NBC News, February 2, 2020. https://www.nbcnews.com/news/china/american-universities-are-soft-target-china-s-spies-say-u-n1104291.

[28] Ken Dilanian. "American universities are a soft target for China's spies, say U.S. intelligence officials," NBC News, February 2, 2020. https://www.nbcnews.com/news/china/american-universities-are-soft-target-china-s-spies-say-u-n1104291.

[29] Christian Whiton. "Biden Is Weak on China," *National Interest*, May 13, 2020. https://nationalinterest.org/feature/biden-weak-china-153971.

[30] Kelly Sadler. "Beijing Biden is not the leader we need amidst the COVID-19 crisis," *Washington Times*, April 15, 2020. https://www.washingtontimes.com/news/2020/apr/15/beijing-biden-not-leader-need-amidst-covid-19.

[31] The White House, Office of the Vice President. "Remarks by the Vice President at Sichuan University," The White House, August 21, 2011. https://obamawhitehouse.archives.gov/the-press-office/2011/08/21/remarks-vice-president-sichuan-university.

[32] Christian Whiton. "Biden Is Weak on China," *National Interest*, May 13, 2020. https://nationalinterest.org/feature/biden-weak-china-153971.

[33] Josh Feldman. "Fmr DefSec Gates Offers Trump Praise on Foreign Policy, but Bothered by 'His Treatment and Words about Military People,'" Mediaite, June 14, 2020. https://www.mediaite.com/tv/fmr-defsec-gates-offers-trump-praise-on-foreign-policy-but-bothered-by-his-treatment-and-words-about-military-people.

[34] Veronica Stracqualursi. "Biden downplays Chinese economic competition, drawing criticism from Republicans and Sanders," CNN Politics, May 2, 2019. https://www.cnn.com/2019/05/02/politics/joe-biden-china-threat-united-states/index.html.

[35] Sherisse Pham. "How much has the US lost from China's IP theft?," CNN Business, March 23, 2018. https://money.cnn.com/2018/03/23/technology/china-us-trump-tariffs-ip-theft/index.html.

[36] Natalie Winters. "Biden: China Provides Jobs, 'Fuels World's Prosperity,'" *National Pulse*, April 21, 2020. https://thenationalpulse.com/coronavirus/biden-china-trade.

[37] The National Bureau of Asian Research. "The IP Commission Report," The Commission on the Theft of American Intellectual Property, May 2013. http://ipcommission.org/report/IP_Commission_Report_052213.pdf.

[38] Jeff Cox. "China trade deficit has cost the US 3.7 million jobs this century, report says," CNBC, January 30, 2020. https://www.cnbc.com/2020/01/30/china-trade-deficit-has-cost-us-3point7-million-jobs-this-century-epi-says.html.

[39] Jacqueline Varas. "The Details of Trump's Phase One Trade Deal with China," American Action Forum, January 21, 2020. https://www.americanactionforum.org/insight/the-details-of-trumps-phase-one-trade-deal-with-china/#ixzz6PkZolxgf.

PART II:
Chapter 9: A Suicide Note for America

[1] Charlotte Lydia Riley. "For Labour, the 2019 election echoes 'the longest suicide note in history,'" *Washington Post*, December 14, 2019. https://www.washingtonpost.com/outlook/2019/12/14/labour-election-echoes-longest-suicide-note-history.

[2] Tracey Tully and Sean Piccoli. "He Was Charged With 4 Bank Heists, and Freed. Then He Struck Again, Police Say," *New York Times*, January 19, 20200. https://www.nytimes.com/2020/01/19/nyregion/bank-robber-bail-reform-nyc.html.

[3] Mary Murphy. "Prosecutor says NY judges are 'anguished' as they release suspects under bail reform law," PIX 11, December 26, 2019. https://www.pix11.com/news/local-news/prosecutor-says-judges-are-anguished-as-they-release-suspects-under-bail-reform-law.

[4] Mary Murphy. "Prosecutor says NY judges are 'anguished' as they release suspects under bail reform law," PIX 11, December 26, 2019. https://www.pix11.com/news/local-news/prosecutor-says-judges-are-anguished-as-they-release-suspects-under-bail-reform-law.

[5] Tammy Bruce. "Tammy Bruce: Legislating failure and chaos with bail reform in New York," Fox News, January 18, 2020. https://www.foxnews.com/opinion/bail-reform-new-york-tammy-bruce.

[6] Tammy Bruce. "Tammy Bruce: Legislating failure and chaos with bail reform in New York," Fox News, January 18, 2020. https://www.foxnews.com/opinion/bail-reform-new-york-tammy-bruce.

[7] Branko Marcetic. "Joe Biden, Anti-Immigrant Enabler," *Jacobin*, April, 2019. https://www.jacobinmag.com/2019/04/joe-biden-anti-immigrant-deportation-policies.

[8] Tucker Carlson. "American Dystopia: San Francisco in decline," Fox News, January 6, 2020. https://www.foxnews.com/transcript/american-dystopia-san-francisco-in-decline.

[9] Tucker Carlson. "American Dystopia: San Francisco in decline," Fox News, January 6, 2020. https://www.foxnews.com/transcript/american-dystopia-san-francisco-in-decline.

[10] Tucker Carlson. "American Dystopia: San Francisco in decline," Fox News, January 6, 2020. https://www.foxnews.com/transcript/american-dystopia-san-francisco-in-decline.

[11] Stanley Kurtz. "Biden and Dems Are Set to Abolish the Suburbs," *National Review*, June 30, 2020. https://www.nationalreview.com/corner/biden-and-dems-are-set-to-abolish-the-suburbs.

[12] Stanley Kurtz. "Biden and Dems Are Set to Abolish the Suburbs," *National Review*, June 30, 2020. https://www.nationalreview.com/corner/biden-and-dems-are-set-to-abolish-the-suburbs.

[13] Stanley Kurtz. "Biden and Dems Are Set to Abolish the Suburbs," *National Review*, June 30, 2020. https://www.nationalreview.com/corner/biden-and-dems-are-set-to-abolish-the-suburbs.

Chapter 10: Cheering on the Crisis

[1] Centers for Disease Control and Prevention. "2009 H1N1 Pandemic," CDC.gov, June 11, 2019. https://www.cdc.gov/flu/pandemic-resources/2009-h1n1-pandemic.html.

[2] Natasha Korecki. "Biden has fought a pandemic before. It did not go smoothly.," *Politico*, May 4, 2020. https://www.politico.com/news/2020/05/04/joe-biden-contain-h1n1-virus-232992.

[3] Peggy Peck. "Obama Declares H1N1 a National Emergency," MedPage Today, October 24, 2009. https://www.medpagetoday.com/infectiousdisease/swineflu/16606.

[4] Robert Romano. "Biden flips on China travel ban," *Ceres Courier*, April 8, 2020. https://www.cerescourier.com/opinion/editorial/biden-flips-china-travel-ban.

[5] Miriam Valverde. "Joe Biden's claim about Donald Trump's 'slow' travel restriction needs context," Politifact, April 13, 2020. https://www.politifact.com/factchecks/2020/apr/13/joe-biden/joe-bidens-claim-about-donald-trumps-slow-travel-r.

[6] Stephanie Soucheray. "Coroner: First US COVID-19 death occurred in early February," Center for Infectious Disease Research and Policy, April 22, 2020. https://www.cidrap.umn.edu/news-perspective/2020/04/coroner-first-us-covid-19-death-occurred-early-february.

[7] "Report: Biden's Swine Flu Pandemic Response 'Not the Panacea Portrayed by Biden Campaign,'" Donaldjtrump.com, May 4, 2020. https://www.donaldjtrump.com/media/report-bidens-swine-flu-pandemic-response-not-the-panacea-portrayed-by-biden-campaign.

[8] Gregg Re. "After attacking Trump's coronavirus-related China travel ban as xenophobic, Dems and media have changed tune," Fox News, April 1, 2020. https://www.foxnews.com/politics/dems-media-change-tune-trump-attacks-coronavirus-china-travel-ban.

[9] "Coronavirus: Biden Slams Trump's 'Xenophobic' Europe Travel Ban, Says He'll 'Lead with Science,'" Bloomberg QuickTake News, March 12, 2020. https://www.youtube.com/watch?v=aAdzW-mRKTk.

[10] Jonathan Easley. "Biden: Trump's coronavirus response has been 'nakedly xenophobic,'" *The Hill*, May 18, 2020. https://thehill.com/homenews/campaign/498350-biden-trumps-coronavirus-response-has-been-nakedly-xenophobic.

[11] Natasha Korecki. "Biden has fought a pandemic before. It did not go smoothly.," *Politico*, May 4, 2020. https://www.politico.com/news/2020/05/04/joe-biden-contain-h1n1-virus-232992.

[12] Ben Elgin and John Tozzi. "Hospital Workers Make Masks from Office Supplies Amid U.S. Shortage," *Bloomberg*, March 17, 2020. https://www.bloomberg.com/news/articles/2020-03-18/hospital-makes-face-masks-covid-19-shields-from-office-supplies.

[13] Christine Dolan. "How Obama's failure to resupply respirators in federal stockpile created a 2020 crisis," JusttheNews.com, March 31, 2020. https://justthenews.com/politics-policy/coronavirus/how-obamas-failure-resupply-respirators-federal-stockpile-created-2020.

[14] Christine Dolan. "How Obama's failure to resupply respirators in federal stockpile created a 2020 crisis," JusttheNews.com, March 31, 2020. https://justthenews.com/politics-policy/coronavirus/how-obamas-failure-resupply-respirators-federal-stockpile-created-2020.

[15] Jordan Fabian and Josh Wingrove. "Trump Says U.S. Ordered 500 Million N95 Masks to Combat Virus," *Bloomberg*, March 18, 2020. https://www.bloomberg.com/news/articles/2020-03-18/trump-says-u-s-ordered-500-million-n95-masks-to-combat-virus.

[16] Marguerite Ward. "Apple, Ford, and GM are stepping up to address global shortages of ventilators, hand sanitizer, face masks, and gowns. Here's a running list of companies helping out.," *Business Insider*, May 5, 2020. https://www.businessinsider.com/coronavirus-companies-helping-meet-shortages-of-ventilators-gowns-masks-hand-sanitizer-healthcare.

[17] Charles Clifford. "Nancy Pelosi visits San Francisco's Chinatown to encourage people amid fears of coronavirus," KRON4, February 24, 2020. https://www.kron4.com/news/bay-area/nancy-pelosi-visits-san-franciscos-chinatown-to-encourage-people-amid-fears-of-coronavirus.

[18] Donald J. Trump. Twitter, April 16, 2020. https://twitter.com/realDonaldTrump/status/1250852583318736896?ref_src=twsrc%5Etfw%7Ctwcamp%5Etweetembed%7Ctwterm%5E1250852583318736896&ref_url=https%3A%2F%2Fwww.snopes.com%2Ffact-check%2Fpelosi-tweet-chinatown-tourism%2F.

[19] Katie Pavlich. "Pavlich: Joe Biden's China problem," *The Hill*, April 29, 2020. https://thehill.com/opinion/katie-pavlich/495156-pavlich-joe-bidens-china-problem.

[20] Allyson Chiu and Timothy Bella. "'I don't believe you need 40,000 or 30,000 ventilators': Trump questions New York's plea for critical equipment," *Washington Post*, March 30, 2020. https://www.washingtonpost.com/nation/2020/03/27/coronavirus-trump-fox-ventilator.

[21] Rich Lowry. "Rich Lowry: The ventilator crisis that wasn't," *Salt Lake Tribune*, April 22, 2020. https://www.sltrib.com/opinion/commentary/2020/04/21/rich-lowry-ventilator.

[22] Rich Lowry. "Rich Lowry: The ventilator crisis that wasn't," *Salt Lake Tribune*, April 22, 2020. https://www.sltrib.com/opinion/commentary/2020/04/21/rich-lowry-ventilator.

[23] Rich Lowry. "Rich Lowry: The ventilator crisis that wasn't," *Salt Lake Tribune*, April 22, 2020. https://www.sltrib.com/opinion/commentary/2020/04/21/rich-lowry-ventilator.

[24] Brad Templeton. "Car Companies Are Making Ventilators, but Ventilator Companies, Hackers and CPAP Companies Are Working Harder," *Forbes*, April 20, 2020. https://www.forbes.com/sites/bradtempleton/2020/04/20/car-companies-are-making-ventilators-but-ventilator-companies-hackers-and-cpap-companies-are-working-harder/#25a694707ec7.

[25] Ian Schwartz. "DFC CEO: 'There's Been No American That Has Needed A Ventilator That Has Not Received One,'" RealClear Politics, April 14, 2020. https://www.realclearpolitics.com/video/2020/04/14/dfc_ceo_theres_been_no_american_that_has_needed_a_ventilator_that_has_not_received_one.html.

[26] Brian Mann. "Cuomo to End Daily COVID-19 Briefings That Drew National Attention," NPR, June 17, 2020. https://www.npr.org/sections/coronavirus-live-updates/2020/06/17/879582054/cuomo-to-end-daily-covid-19-briefings-that-drew-national-attention.

[27] Natalie Rahhal. "Can hydroxychloroquine work after all? Coronavirus patients treated early with the drug touted by Trump were 50% less likely to die, study finds," *Daily Mail*, July 3, 2020. https://www.dailymail.co.uk/health/article-8487315/50-fewer-COVID-19-patients-died-treated-hydroxychloroquine.html.

[28] Andy Sullivan. "Divided by COVID-19: Democratic U.S. areas hit three times as hard as Republican ones," Reuters, May 21, 2020. https://www.reuters.com/article/us-health-coronavirus-usa-divided/divided-by-covid-19-democratic-u-s-areas-hit-three-times-as-hard-as-republican-ones-idUSKBN22X14I.

[29] Bernard Condon, Jennifer Peltz, and Jim Mustian. "AP count: Over 4,500 virus patients sent to NY nursing homes," The Associated Press, May 22, 2020. https://apnews.com/5ebc0ad45b73a899efa81f098330204c.

[30] Bernard Condon, Jennifer Peltz, and Jim Mustian. "AP count: Over 4,500 virus patients sent to NY nursing homes," The Associated Press, May 22, 2020. https://apnews.com/5ebc0ad45b73a899efa81f098330204c.

[31] Stephanie Ruhle. "Gov. Cuomo: Placing blame on his office for nursing home deaths is 'a political charade,'" MSNBC, June 22, 2020. https://www.msnbc.com/stephanie-ruhle/watch/gov-cuomo-placing-blame-on-his-office-for-nursing-home-deaths-is-a-political-charade-85675589943.

[32] Brie Stimson. "Pennsylvania health official draws fire after her mother leaves care facility as coronavirus patients return," Fox News, May 14, 2020. https://www.foxnews.com/politics/pennsylvania-health-official-draws-fire-after-her-mother-leaves-care-facility-as-coronavirus-patients-return.

[33] Brie Stimson. "Pennsylvania health official draws fire after her mother leaves care facility as coronavirus patients return," Fox News, May 14, 2020. https://www.foxnews.com/politics/pennsylvania-health-official-draws-fire-after-her-mother-leaves-care-facility-as-coronavirus-patients-return.

[34] Emily Zanotti. "Transgender Pennsylvania Health Director Melts Down in Press Conference after Reporter Uses Wrong Pronoun," *Daily Wire*, May 14, 2020. https://www.dailywire.com/news/transgender-pennsylvania-health-director-melts-down-in-press-conference-after-reporter-uses-wrong-pronoun.

[35] "Covid-19 is hitting Democratic states harder than Republican ones," *The Economist*, May 22, 2020. https://www.economist.com/graphic-detail/2020/05/22/covid-19-is-hitting-democratic-states-harder-than-republican-ones.

[36] "Covid-19 is hitting Democratic states harder than Republican ones," *The Economist*, May 22, 2020. https://www.economist.com/graphic-detail/2020/05/22/covid-19-is-hitting-democratic-states-harder-than-republican-ones.

[37] Sam Kumar. "Tyrannical overreach of liberal politicians," *Reno Gazette-Journal*, May 14, 2020. https://www.rgj.com/story/opinion/columnists/2020/05/14/tyrranical-overreach-liberal-politicians-sam-kumar/5190245002.

[38] Paul Egan. "FEMA: Michigan has not requested major disaster declaration for coronavirus," *Detroit Free Press*, March 26, 2020. https://www.freep.com/story/news/local/michigan/2020/03/25/fema-michigan-disaster-declaration-coronavirus/5077623002.

[39] Craig Mauger. "Protesters, some armed, enter Michigan Capitol in rally against COVID-19 limits," *Detroit News*, April 30, 2020. https://www.detroitnews.com/story/news/local/michigan/2020/04/30/protesters-gathering-outside-capitol-amid-covid-19-restrictions/3054911001.

[40] The Editorial Board. "Should Florida Bail Out New York?," *Wall Street Journal*, May 17, 2020. https://www.wsj.com/articles/should-florida-bail-out-new-york-11589746538.

[41] Christine L. Himes. "One Quarter of Older Americans Live in California, Florida, and Texas," Population Reference Bureau, March 16, 2019. https://www.prb.org/which-us-states-are-the-oldest.

[42] Google News. "Coronavirus (COVID-19)," July 13, 2020. https://news.google.com/covid19/map?hl=en-US&mid=%2Fm%2F059rby&gl=US&ceid=US%3Aen.

[43] Google News. "Coronavirus (COVID-19)," July 13, 2020. https://news.google.com/covid19/map?hl=en-US&mid=%2Fm%2Fo2xry&gl=US&ceid=US%3Aen.

[44] Kara Seymour. "PA Woman Gets $200 Ticket for Driving During Stay-at-Home Order," MSN, April 6, 2020. https://www.msn.com/en-us/news/us/pa-woman-gets-200-ticket-for-driving-during-stay-at-home-order/ar-BB12ey47.

[45] Adam Schrader. "Kentucky cops to record churchgoers' license plates to enforce coronavirus quarantines," *New York Post*, April 10, 2020. https://nypost.com/2020/04/10/kentucky-to-record-churchgoers-license-plates-amid-coronavirus.

[46] Matthew Glowicki. "Judge allows drive-in service at Louisville church, says Fischer 'criminalized' Easter," *Reno Gazette-Journal*, April 11, 2020. https://www.rgj.com/story/news/2020/04/11/covid-19-kentucky-judge-grants-churchs-request-hold-services/2976560001.

[47] "Covid-19 is hitting Democratic states harder than Republican ones," *The Economist*, May 22, 2020. https://www.economist.com/graphic-detail/2020/05/22/covid-19-is-hitting-democratic-states-harder-than-republican-ones.

[48] "Covid-19 is hitting Democratic states harder than Republican ones," *The Economist*, May 22, 2020. https://www.economist.com/graphic-detail/2020/05/22/covid-19-is-hitting-democratic-states-harder-than-republican-ones.

[49] "54,555 sq mi," Wikipedia, July 8, 2020. https://en.wikipedia.org/wiki/New_York_(state). "65,757.70 sq mi," Wikipedia, July 1, 2020. https://en.wikipedia.org/wiki/Florida.

[50] The Editorial Board. "Should Florida Bail Out New York?," *Wall Street Journal*, May 17, 2020. https://www.wsj.com/articles/should-florida-bail-out-new-york-11589746538.

[51] Bob McManus. "De Blasio and 'co-mayor' wife have wasted $1.8B of taxpayer money," *New York Post*, February 28, 2019. https://nypost.com/2019/02/28/de-blasio-and-co-mayor-wife-have-wasted-1-8b-of-taxpayer-money.

[52] Aaron Colen. "NYC Mayor De Blasio's wife spent $900 million in taxpayer money—with no record of how it was used," *The Blaze*, March 1, 2019. https://www.theblaze.com/news/nyc-mayor-de-blasios-wife-spent-900-billion-in-taxpayer-money-with-no-record-of-how-it-was-used.

[53] Julia Marsh. "McCray's 'Thrive' initiative on track to spend $1B in 5 years," *New York Post*, February 27, 2019. https://nypost.com/2019/02/27/mccrays-thrive-initiative-on-track-to-spend-1b-in-5-years.

[54] Julia Marsh. "McCray's 'Thrive' initiative on track to spend $1B in 5 years," *New York Post*, February 27, 2019. https://nypost.com/2019/02/27/mccrays-thrive-initiative-on-track-to-spend-1b-in-5-years.

[55] "What Do the Worst-Run States Have in Common? They're Run by Tax-and-Spend Democrats," *Investor's Business Daily*, October 9, 2018. https://www.investors.com/politics/editorials/worst-run-states-big-spending-democrats.

[56] "What Do the Worst-Run States Have in Common? They're Run by Tax-and-Spend Democrats," *Investor's Business Daily*, October 9, 2018. https://www.investors.com/politics/editorials/worst-run-states-big-spending-democrats.

[57] Arthur Schwartz. "They're not frauds like your colleague," Twitter, June 1, 2020. https://twitter.com/ArthurSchwartz/status/1267612913122136070.

[58] Julia Musto. "Bystander blasts hypocrisy by MSNBC crew: They deserved to be called out for 'mask-shaming,'" Fox News, May 28, 2020. https://www.foxnews.com/media/man-calls-out-msnbc-reporters-hypocrisy-on-masks.

[59] Aaron Blake and JM Rieger. "New York Mayor Bill de Blasio's repeated comments downplaying the coronavirus," *Washington Post*, April 1, 2020. https://www.washingtonpost.com/politics/2020/04/01/new-york-mayor-bill-de-blasios-repeated-comments-downplaying-coronavirus.

[60] Aaron Blake and JM Rieger. "New York Mayor Bill de Blasio's repeated comments downplaying the coronavirus," *Washington Post*, April 1, 2020. https://www.washingtonpost.com/politics/2020/04/01/new-york-mayor-bill-de-blasios-repeated-comments-downplaying-coronavirus.

Chapter 11: *Te Damos La Bienvenida Legalmente* (We Welcome You Legally)

[1] Neli Esipova, Anita Pugliese, and Julie Ray. "More Than 750 Million Worldwide Would Migrate If They Could," Gallup, December 10, 2018. https://news.gallup.com/poll/245255/750-million-worldwide-migrate.aspx.

[2] Donald Trump Jr., *Triggered* (New York: Center Street, 2019), 29, 31, 33.

[3] Trump, *Triggered*, 25.

[4] Trump, 90.

[5] Donald J. Trump. "President Trump Sends a Letter on Border Security to Congress," The White House, January 4, 2019. https://www.whitehouse.gov/articles/president-trump-sends-letter-border-security.

[6] Andrew Kaczynski. "Joe Biden once said a fence was needed to stop 'tons' of drugs from Mexico," CNN Politics, May 10, 2019. https://www.cnn.com/2019/05/10/politics/kfile-biden-drugs-fence-2006/index.html.

[7] Jens Manuel Krogstad, Jeffrey S. Passel, and D'Vera Cohn. "5 facts about illegal immigration in the U.S.," Pew Research Center, June 12, 2019. https://www.pewresearch.org/fact-tank/2019/06/12/5-facts-about-illegal-immigration-in-the-u-s.

[8] Jens Manuel Krogstad, Jeffrey S. Passel, and D'Vera Cohn. "5 facts about illegal immigration in the U.S.," Pew Research Center, June 12, 2019. https://www.pewresearch.org/fact-tank/2019/06/12/5-facts-about-illegal-immigration-in-the-u-s.

[9] Niall McCarthy. "Immigrants in the U.S. Sent Over $148 Billion to Their Home Countries in 2017," *Forbes*, April 8, 2019. https://www.forbes.com/sites/niallmccarthy/2019/04/08/immigrants-in-the-u-s-sent-over-148-billion-to-their-home-countries-in-2017-infographic/#6a6a43dc11f6.

[10] United States Commission on Civil Rights. "The Impact of Illegal Immigration on the Wages and Employment Opportunities of Black Workers," Usccr.gov, October 14, 2010. https://www.usccr.gov/pubs/docs/IllegImmig_10-14-10_430pm.pdf.

[11] "U.S. Const. art I, § 8, cl. 4," Constitution Annotated. https://constitution.congress.gov/browse/article-1/section-8.

[12] U.S. Citizenship and Immigration Services. "Citizenship Through Naturalization," Uscis.gov, April 17, 2019. https://www.uscis.gov/us-citizenship/citizenship-through-naturalization.

[13] Donald J. Trump. "President Trump Sends a Letter on Border Security to Congress," The White House, January 4, 2019. https://www.whitehouse.gov/articles/president-trump-sends-letter-border-security.

[14] Samantha Raphelson, Jeremy Hobson, and Chris Bentley. "California Sanctuary Law Divides State in Fierce Immigration Debate," NPR, October 17, 2018. https://www.npr.org/2018/10/17/657951176/california-sanctuary-law-divides-state-in-fierce-immigration-debate.

[15] Sam Dorman. "ICE: Hundreds of illegal aliens charged with rape, other crimes after release from Southern California jail," Fox News, February 6, 2020. https://www.foxnews.com/us/inmates-rearrested-rape-california-jail-ice.

[16] Donald J. Trump. "President Trump Sends a Letter on Border Security to Congress," The White House, January 4, 2019. https://www.whitehouse.gov/articles/president-trump-sends-letter-border-security.

[17] Charlie Lapastora. "Mexican drug cartels fueling meth comeback in US, with seizures at 'historically high levels,'" Fox News, September 20, 2017. https://www.foxnews.com/us/meth-border-mexican-drug-cartels.

[18] "Twice-deported man charged in killing of Iowa mom and her 2 children," CBS News, July 19, 2019. https://www.cbsnews.com/news/des-moines-murder-mother-children-iowa-guatemalan-charged-previously-deported-2019-07-19.

[19] Jonathan Bandler and Matt Spillane. "Lois Colley's killer sentenced after family speaks out, killer asks forgiveness," Rockland/Westchester Journal News, June 13, 2019. https://www.lohud.com/story/news/local/westchester/north-salem/2019/06/13/lois-colley-killer-sentencing/1440028001.

[20] Barnini Chakraborty. "Undocumented immigrant pleads not guilty to raping, killing 92-year-old NY woman," Fox News, February 6, 2020. https://www.foxnews.com/us/undocumented-immigrant-pleads-not-guilty-to-raping-killing-92-year-old-ny-woman.

[21] Daniel Horowitz. "Oklahoma mother murdered: Suspect is illegal alien deported 5 times," Conservative Review, April 1, 2019. https://www.conservativereview.com/news/oklahoma-mother-murdered-suspect-illegal-alien-deported-5-times.

[22] Steve King. "Illegal Immigration Stories," Steveking.house.gov. https://steveking.house.gov/illegal-immigration-stories#_ftnref142.

[23] Steve King. "Illegal Immigration Stories," Steveking.house.gov. https://steveking.house.gov/illegal-immigration-stories#_ftnref141.

[24] Ken Blackwell. "Sanctuary city policies are a threat to decent people," The Hill, October 22, 2019. https://thehill.com/opinion/immigration/466977-sanctuary-city-policies-are-a-threat-to-decent-people.

[25] Brian Flood. "Viral video: CNN guest says calling 911 on home intruder 'comes from a place of privilege,' sparks reaction," Fox News, June 8, 2020. https://www.foxnews.com/media/viral-video-cnn-guest-calling-911-home-intruder-placeof-privelege.

[26] Jens Manuel Krogstad, Jeffrey S. Passel, and D'Vera Cohn. "5 facts about illegal immigration in the U.S.," Pew Research Center, June 12, 2019. https://www.pewresearch.org/fact-tank/2019/06/12/5-facts-about-illegal-immigration-in-the-u-s.

[27] Jens Manuel Krogstad, Jeffrey S. Passel, and D'Vera Cohn. "5 facts about illegal immigration in the U.S.," Pew Research Center, June 12, 2019. https://www.pewresearch.org/fact-tank/2019/06/12/5-facts-about-illegal-immigration-in-the-u-s.

[28] Tami Luhby. "Democrats want to offer health care to undocumented immigrants. Here's what that means," CNN Politics, September 11, 2019. https://www.cnn.com/2019/09/11/politics/undocumented-immigrants-health-care-democrats/index.html.

[29] Ryan Nunn, Jana Parsons, and Jay Shambaugh. "A dozen facts about the economics of the US health-care system," Brookings, March 10, 2020. https://www.brookings.edu/research/a-dozen-facts-about-the-economics-of-the-u-s-health-care-system.

[30] Investopedia. "What Country Spends the Most on Education?," Investopedia.com, July 7, 2019. https://www.investopedia.com/ask/answers/020915/what-country-spends-most-education.asp.

[31] Ryan Nunn, Jana Parsons, and Jay Shambaugh. "A dozen facts about the economics of the US health-care system," Brookings, March 10, 2020. https://www.brookings.edu/research/a-dozen-facts-about-the-economics-of-the-u-s-health-care-system.

[32] Investopedia. "What Country Spends the Most on Education?," Investopedia.com, July 7, 2019. https://www.investopedia.com/ask/answers/020915/what-country-spends-most-education.asp.

[33] Drew Desilver. "U.S. students' academic achievement still lags that of their peers in many other countries," Pew Research Center, February 15, 2017. https://www.pewresearch.org/fact-tank/2017/02/15/u-s-students-internationally-math-science.

[34] Drew Desilver. "U.S. students' academic achievement still lags that of their peers in many other countries," Pew Research Center, February 15, 2017. https://www.pewresearch.org/fact-tank/2017/02/15/u-s-students-internationally-math-science.

[35] Anthony Principi. "Veterans Affairs reform is now reality under President Trump," *The Hill*, November 11, 2019. https://thehill.com/opinion/civil-rights/469825-veterans-affairs-reform-is-now-reality-under-president-trump.

[36] Sarah Almukhtar and Rod Nordland. "What did the U.S. get for $2 trillion in Afghanistan?," *New York Times*, December 9, 2019. https://www.nytimes.com/interactive/2019/12/09/world/middleeast/afghanistan-war-cost.html.

[37] Joseph W. Kane and Adie Tomer. "Shifting into an era of repair: US infrastructure spending trends," Brookings, May 10, 2019. https://www.brookings.edu/research/shifting-into-an-era-of-repair-us-infrastructure-spending-trends.

[38] Robert Bellafiore. "Summary of the Latest Federal Income Tax Data, 2018 Update," Tax Foundation, November 13, 2018. https://taxfoundation.org/summary-latest-federal-income-tax-data-2018-update.

[39] Amy Bingham. "Mitt Romney's 47 Percent: Who Does Not Pay Income Taxes?," ABC News, September 18, 2012. https://abcnews.go.com/Politics/OTUS/mitt-romneys-47-percent-pay-income-taxes/story?id=17263629.

[40] Louis Jacobson. "Rand Paul's claim about taxes went over poorly on *The View*, but it was pretty accurate," Politifact, October 17, 2019. https://www.politifact.com/factchecks/2019/oct/17/rand-paul/fact-checking-rand-pauls-appearance-view.

Chapter 12: Buying Votes with Your Money

[1] Melissa Etehad. "Young people don't see a future in Afghanistan, so they're leaving," *Washington Post*, August 13, 2016. https://www.washingtonpost.com/world/asia_pacific/young-people-dont-see-a-future-in-afghanistan-so-theyre-leaving/2016/08/12/8737d2a8-5e3e-11e6-84c1-6d27287896b5_story.html.

[2] Miriam Valverde. "Donald Trump's international comparison of 'merit-based' immigration, fact-checked," Politifact, May 24, 2019. https://www.politifact.com/factchecks/2019/may/24/donald-trump/donald-trumps-international-comparison-merit-based.

[3] Miriam Valverde. "Donald Trump's international comparison of 'merit-based' immigration, fact-checked," Politifact, May 24, 2019. https://www.politifact.com/factchecks/2019/may/24/donald-trump/donald-trumps-international-comparison-merit-based.

[4] Mireille Paquet. "Canada's merit-based immigration system is no 'magic bullet,'" The Conversation, February 21, 2018. https://theconversation.com/canadas-merit-based-immigration-system-is-no-magic-bullet-90923.

[5] Vindu Goel. "As Coronavirus Disrupts Factories, India Curbs Exports of Key Drugs," *New York Times*, March 6, 2020. https://www.nytimes.com/2020/03/03/business/coronavirus-india-drugs.html.

[6] Gary D. Cohn and Kevin Hassett. "Tax Reform Has Delivered for Workers," *Wall Street Journal*, December 22, 2019. https://www.wsj.com/articles/tax-reform-has-delivered-for-workers-11577045463.

[7] Maggie Fitzgerald. "Black and Hispanic unemployment is at a record low," CNBC, October 4, 2019. https://www.cnbc.com/2019/10/04/black-and-hispanic-unemployment-is-at-a-record-low.html.

[8] The Council of Economic Advisers. "President Trump's Policies Continue to Benefit All Americans, Especially the Disadvantaged," The White House, September 10, 2019. https://www.whitehouse.gov/articles/president-trumps-policies-continue-benefit-americans-especially-disadvantaged.

[9] The Council of Economic Advisers. "President Trump's Policies Continue to Benefit All Americans, Especially the Disadvantaged," The White House, September 10, 2019. https://www.whitehouse.gov/articles/president-trumps-policies-continue-benefit-americans-especially-disadvantaged.

[10] Neli Esipova, Anita Pugliese, and Julie Ray. "More Than 750 Million Worldwide Would Migrate If They Could," Gallup, December 10, 2018. https://news.gallup.com/poll/245255/750-million-worldwide-migrate.aspx.

[11] Aamna Mohdin. "The EU countries that desperately need migrants to avoid shrinkage—and those that don't," Quartz, July 11, 2018. https://qz.com/1325640/the-european-countries-that-desperately-need-migrants-to-avoid-demographic-decline-and-those-that-dont.

[12] Michael Gibson. "San Francisco's Slow-Motion Suicide," National Review, April 8, 2019. https://www.nationalreview.com/2019/04/san-francisco-decline-failed-government-policies.

[13] Garrett Parker. "How Nancy Pelosi Achieved a Net Worth of $120 Million," Money Inc, January 2019. https://moneyinc.com/nancy-pelosi-net-worth.

[14] Sarah Sanders. "Statement from the Press Secretary," The White House, February 15, 2018. https://www.whitehouse.gov/briefings-statements/statement-press-secretary-27.

[15] The White House. "Remarks by President Trump at South Dakota's 2020 Mount Rushmore Fireworks Celebration Keystone, South Dakota," Whitehouse.gov, July 4, 2020. https://www.whitehouse.gov/briefings-statements/remarks-president-trump-south-dakotas-2020-mount-rushmore-fireworks-celebration-keystone-south-dakota.

[16] The White House. "President Donald J. Trump Secures a Historic Deal with Mexico to Combat the Crisis at the Border," Whitehouse.gov, June 10, 2019. https://www.whitehouse.gov/briefings-statements/president-donald-j-trump-secures-historic-deal-mexico-combat-crisis-border.

[17] Tom Hebert. "Top 5 Wastes of Money in Nancy Pelosi's 'HEROES Act,'" Americans for Tax Reform, June 2, 2020. https://www.atr.org/top-5-wastes-money-nancy-pelosi-s-heroes-act.

Chapter 13: Will the Real Joe Biden Please Stand Up?

[1] The White House. "President Trump Sends a Letter on Border Security to Congress," Whitehouse.gov, January 4, 2019. https://www.whitehouse.gov/articles/president-trump-sends-letter-border-security.

[2] Andrew Kaczynski. "Joe Biden once said a fence was needed to stop 'tons' of drugs from Mexico," CNN Politics, May 10, 2019. https://www.cnn.com/2019/05/10/politics/kfile-biden-drugs-fence-2006/index.html.

[3] Andrew Kaczynski. "Joe Biden once said a fence was needed to stop 'tons' of drugs from Mexico," CNN Politics, May 10, 2019. https://www.cnn.com/2019/05/10/politics/kfile-biden-drugs-fence-2006/index.html.

[4] Andrew Kaczynski. "Joe Biden Was Opposed to Driver's Licenses for Undocumented Immigrants in 2008," Buzzfeed, September 28, 2015. https://www.buzzfeednews.com/article/andrewkaczynski/joe-biden-was-opposed-to-drivers-licenses-for-undocumented-i.

[5] "Fact-Checking the Democratic Debate," New York Times, September 12, 2019. https://www.nytimes.com/2019/09/12/us/politics/fact-check-democratic-debate-september.html.

[6] "Fact-Checking the Democratic Debate," New York Times, September 12, 2019. https://www.nytimes.com/2019/09/12/us/politics/fact-check-democratic-debate-september.html.

[7] Max Greenwood. "Trump knocks Dems for tweeting 2014 images of children in cages at border," The Hill, May 29, 2018. https://thehill.com/homenews/administration/389658-trump-knocks-dems-for-tweeting-2014-images-of-children-in-cages-at.

[8] Miriam Valverde. "Fact-checking Biden on use of cages for immigrants during Obama administration," Politifact, September 13, 2019. https://www.politifact.com/factchecks/2019/sep/13/joe-biden/fact-checking-biden-use-cages-during-obama-adminis.

[9] "Unaccompanied Immigrant Children," C-SPAN, June 12, 2014. https://www.c-span.org/video/?319951-1/dhs-secretary-johnson-unaccompanied-immigrant-children.

[10] "Unaccompanied Immigrant Children," C-SPAN, June 12, 2014. https://www.c-span.org/video/?319951-1/dhs-secretary-johnson-unaccompanied-immigrant-children.

[11] Joseph A. Wulfsohn. "Media outlets attribute Obama-era child-detention stats to Trump, issue retractions," Fox News, November 19, 2019. https://www.foxnews.com/media/obama-era-child-detention-statistics-trump-retractions.

[12] Joseph A. Wulfsohn. "Media outlets attribute Obama-era child-detention stats to Trump, issue retractions," Fox News, November 19, 2019. https://www.foxnews.com/media/obama-era-child-detention-statistics-trump-retractions.

[13] Allison Graves. "Fact-check: Did top Democrats vote for a border wall in 2006?," Politifact, April 23, 2017. https://www.politifact.com/factchecks/2017/apr/23/mick-mulvaney/fact-check-did-top-democrats-vote-border-wall-2006.

[14] Zachary B. Wolf. "Yes, Obama deported more people than Trump but context is everything," CNN Politics, July 13, 2019. https://www.cnn.com/2019/07/13/politics/obama-trump-deportations-illegal-immigration/index.html.

[15] Andrew Kaczynski. "Joe Biden once said a fence was needed to stop 'tons' of drugs from Mexico," CNN Politics, May 10, 2019. https://www.cnn.com/2019/05/10/politics/kfile-biden-drugs-fence-2006/index.html.

[16] Marc A. Thiessen. "Democrats were for a wall before they were against it," *Washington Post*, January 10, 2019. https://www.washingtonpost.com/opinions/democrats-were-for-a-wall-before-they-were-against-it/2019/01/10/9d114048-14f1-11e9-90a8-136fa44b80ba_story.html.

[17] Marc A. Thiessen. "Marc A. Thiessen: Democrats were for a wall it before they were against it," *Mail Tribune*, January 13, 2019. https://mailtribune.com/opinion/columns/marc-a-thiessen-democrats-were-for-a-wall-it-before-they-were-against-it.

[18] Marc A. Thiessen. "Democrats were for a wall before they were against it," *Washington Post*, January 10, 2019.https://www.washingtonpost.com/opinions/democrats-were-for-a-wall-before-they-were-against-it/2019/01/10/9d114048-14f1-11e9-90a8-136fa44b80ba_story.html.

[19] Dennis Romero. "Attorney General Sessions: Elite 'lunatic fringe' wants security for itself but not for U.S.," NBC News, June 26, 2018. https://www.nbcnews.com/politics/white-house/attorney-general-sessions-elite-fringe-wants-security-itself-not-u-n886831.

[20] Cheryl K. Chumley. "Border hypocrisies of the left," *Washington Times*, June 28, 2018. https://www.washingtontimes.com/news/2018/jun/28/border-hypocrisies-of-the-left.

[21] Cheryl K. Chumley. "Border hypocrisies of the left," *Washington Times*, June 28, 2018. https://www.washingtontimes.com/news/2018/jun/28/border-hypocrisies-of-the-left.

[22] Cher. "I understand helping struggling immigrants, but my city (Los Angeles) isn't taking care of its own." Twitter, April 14, 2019. https://twitter.com/cher/status/1117491420934365185?lang=en.

[23] Sarah Sanders. "Statement from the Press Secretary," The White House, February 15, 2018. https://www.whitehouse.gov/briefings-statements/statement-press-secretary-27.

[24] Heidi Przybyla. "Joe Biden's long evolution on abortion rights still holds surprises," NBC News, June 5, 2019. https://www.nbcnews.com/politics/2020-election/biden-s-long-evolution-abortion-rights-still-holds-surprises-n1013846.

[25] Tessa Stuart. "Joe Biden's Anti-Abortion Past (and Present) Is Haunting His Candidacy," *Rolling Stone*, June 5, 2019. https://www.rollingstone.com/politics/politics-news/joe-biden-anti-abortion-past-present-president-candidate-842314.

[26] Edward-Isaac Dovere. "How Biden's Campaign Confronted Him on Abortion," *The Atlantic*, June 7, 2019. https://www.theatlantic.com/politics/archive/2019/06/biden-abortion-hyde/591241.

[27] Joe Perticone. "Joe Biden's running as a bipartisan moderate, but he keeps flip-flopping on key policy issues to please the Democratic base," *Business Insider*, June 12, 2019. https://www.businessinsider.com/joe-biden-flip-flopping-key-policy-issues-2019-6.

[28] Joe Perticone. "Joe Biden's running as a bipartisan moderate, but he keeps flip-flopping on key policy issues to please the Democratic base," *Business Insider*, June 12, 2019. https://www.businessinsider.com/joe-biden-flip-flopping-key-policy-issues-2019-6.

[29] Christopher Cadelago. "Biden appears to be softening his stance on the death penalty," *Politico*, June 20, 2019. https://www.politico.com/story/2019/06/20/joe-biden-death-penalty-1371932.

[30] Sheryl Gay Stolberg and Astead W. Herndon. "'Lock the S.O.B.s Up': Joe Biden and the Era of Mass Incarceration," *New York Times*, June 25, 2019. https://www.nytimes.com/2019/06/25/us/joe-biden-crime-laws.html.

[31] Paris Dennard. "Joe Biden questions my blackness one moment, defends racist 1994 crime bill the next," *USA Today*, May 25, 2020. https://www.usatoday.com/story/opinion/2020/05/25/joe-biden-you-aint-black-racism-trump-column/5254434002.

[32] David Harsanyi. "The Real Reason Joe Biden Won't Release His Papers," *National Review*, May 4, 2020. https://www.nationalreview.com/2020/05/joe-biden-papers-would-reveal-flip-flops-notable-policy-stances.

[33] David Harsanyi. "The Real Reason Joe Biden Won't Release His Papers," *National Review*, May 4, 2020. https://www.nationalreview.com/2020/05/joe-biden-papers-would-reveal-flip-flops-notable-policy-stances.

[34] Katie Glueck and Thomas Kaplan, "Biden Adds a Claim to His Biography: An Arrest in South Africa," *New York Times*, February 21, 2020.

[35] Caitlin Oprysko. "Biden admits he was never arrested in South Africa," *Politico*, February 28, 2020. https://www.politico.com/news/2020/02/28/biden-south-africa-arrest-118134

Chapter 14: No Clue, No Resolve

[1] CBS News. "Maxine Waters Spars with Bernanke," YouTube, February 24, 2010. https://www.youtube.com/watch?v=jORdN7voejo.

[2] CBS News. "Maxine Waters Spars with Bernanke," YouTube, February 24, 2010. https://www.youtube.com/watch?v=jORdN7voejo.

[3] Jill Schlesinger. "Is Maxine Waters Really as Dumb as She Seems?," CBS News, February 25, 2010. https://www.cbsnews.com/news/is-maxine-waters-really-as-dumb-as-she-seems-25-02-2010.

[4] Mike Bibb. "Sometimes, you just can't fix stupid," *Eastern Arizona Courier*, April 17, 2019. https://www.eacourier.com/opinion/sometimes-you-just-can-t-fix-stupid/article_bcc3be8c-6098-11e9-902a-1f12d7d3bc3f.html.

[5] Fox Business. "Waters failed to pin student loan crisis on Bank CEOs during hearing," YouTube, April 10, 2019. https://www.youtube.com/watch?v=u_ByD_UVZmk.

[6] Mike Bibb. "Sometimes, you just can't fix stupid," *Eastern Arizona Courier*, April 17, 2019.https://www.eacourier.com/opinion/sometimes-you-just-can-t-fix-stupid/article_bcc3be8c-6098-11e9-902a-1f12d7d3bc3f.html.

[7] "Representative Maxine Waters (1938–) in Congress 1991–Present," Congress.gov. https://www.congress.gov/member/maxine-waters/W000187?q={%22search%22:[%22maxine%20waters%22],%22within%22:[%22maxine%20waters%22]}&searchResultViewType=expanded.

[8] Michelle Ye Hee Lee. "Bernie Sanders's misleading comparison of mortgage rates and student loan interest rates," *Washington Post*, January 19, 2016. https://www.washingtonpost.com/news/fact-checker/wp/2016/01/19/bernie-sanderss-misleading-comparison-of-mortgage-rates-and-student-loan-interest-rates.

[9] Trump War Room. "Bernie Sanders and Joe Biden are two sides of the same extreme coin.," Twitter, March 8, 2020. https://twitter.com/TrumpWarRoom/status/1236732032799117313?s=20.

[10] John Kartch. "Joe Biden: 'We Are Going to Get Rid of Fossil Fuels,'" Americans for Tax Reform, February 8,

2020. https://www.atr.org/joe-biden-we-are-going-get-rid-fossil-fuels.

[11] John Kartch. "Joe Biden: 'We Are Going to Get Rid of Fossil Fuels,'" Americans for Tax Reform, February 8, 2020. https://www.atr.org/joe-biden-we-are-going-get-rid-fossil-fuels.

[12] Americans for Tax Reform. "Biden: 'Yes' We Should End Fracking," Atr.org, January 25, 2020. https://www.atr.org/biden-yes-we-should-end-fracking.

[13] Stephen Moore. "Democrats' War on Fracking Will Cost Them in Battleground States," *Wall Street Journal*, January 22, 2020. https://www.wsj.com/articles/democrats-war-on-fracking-will-cost-them-in-battleground-states-11579734852?mod=opinion_lead_pos6.

[14] Grow America's Infrastructure Now. "Hypocrisy Watch: Joe Biden Changes His Tune on Energy," Gainfactchecker.org, December 30, 2019. https://gainfactchecker.org/hypocrisy-watch-joe-biden-changes-his-tune-on-energy.

[15] Grow America's Infrastructure Now. "Hypocrisy Watch: Joe Biden Changes His Tune on Energy," Gainfactchecker.org, December 30, 2019. https://gainfactchecker.org/hypocrisy-watch-joe-biden-changes-his-tune-on-energy.

[16] The Oprah Winfrey Show. "Donald Trump Teases a President Bid During a 1988 Oprah Show," YouTube, June 25, 2015. https://www.youtube.com/watch?v=SEPs17_AkTI.

[17] Matt Schlapp. "Five Ways America Would Take a Hard Left Under Joe Biden," *The Hill*, June 10, 2020. https://thehill.com/opinion/campaign/501986-five-ways-america-would-take-a-hard-left-under-joe-biden.

[18] Matt Schlapp. "Five Ways America Would Take a Hard Left Under Joe Biden," *The Hill*, June 10, 2020. https://thehill.com/opinion/campaign/501986-five-ways-america-would-take-a-hard-left-under-joe-biden.

[19] Louis Woodhill. "Obama Wins the Gold for Worst Economic Recovery Ever," *Forbes*, August 1, 2012. https://www.forbes.com/sites/louiswoodhill/2012/08/01/obama-wins-the-gold-for-worst-economic-recovery-ever/#473ed36a3ca2.

[20] Branko Marcetic. "Joe Biden's Budget-Cutting Dogma Is a Threat to Public Health," *Jacobin*, March 16, 2020. https://www.jacobinmag.com/2020/03/joe-biden-public-health-record-coronavirus-debate.

[21] Robert Oliver. "An Open Letter to Rev. Jesse Jackson, Rev. Al Sharpton, and Congresswoman Maxine Waters Regarding Racist White Presidents," *Westside Gazette*, March 20, 2019. https://thewestsidegazette.com/an-open-letter-to-rev-jesse-jackson-rev-al-sharpton-and-congresswoman-maxine-waters-regarding-racist-white-presidents.

[22] DailyGraze. "Jesse Jackson praises and thanks Donald Trump for a lifetime of service to African Americans - 1998," YouTube, August 29, 2016. https://www.youtube.com/watch?time_continue=97&v=J5lcART6TTE&feature=emb_logo.

[23] Jillian Kay Melchior. "Trump's Pal Al," *National Review*, September 1, 2015. https://www.nationalreview.com/2015/09/trumps-pal-al-sharpton.

Chapter 15: Biggest Losers

[1] Donald Trump Jr., *Triggered* (New York: Center Street, 2019, Kindle Edition), 286.

[2] "Rick Wilson 'Confederate Cooler' and Wife's Racist Tweets Go Viral After GOP Strategist Self-Owns," Dateway, June 2020. https://dateway.net/rick-wilson-confederate-cooler-and-wifes-racist-tweets-go-viral-after-gop-strategist-self-owns.

[3] "Rick Wilson 'Confederate Cooler' and Wife's Racist Tweets Go Viral After GOP Strategist Self-Owns," Dateway, June 2020. https://dateway.net/rick-wilson-confederate-cooler-and-wifes-racist-tweets-go-viral-after-gop-strategist-self-owns.

[4] Felicia Sonmez. "Kellyanne Conway says her husband changed his mind about administration job, contradicting Trump," *Washington Post*, March 31, 2019. https://www.washingtonpost.com/politics/kellyanne-conway-says-her-husband-changed-his-mind-about-administration-job-contradicting-trump/2019/03/31/e489f8e0-53f6-11e9-8ef3-fbd41a2ce4d5_story.html.

[5] Ariane de Vogue. "George Conway pulls out of consideration for Justice Department job," CNN Politics, June

2, 2017. https://www.cnn.com/2017/06/02/politics/george-conway-justice-department-kellyanne/index.html.

[6] Felicia Sonmez. "Kellyanne Conway says her husband changed his mind about administration job, contradicting Trump," *Washington Post*, March 31, 2019. https://www.washingtonpost.com/politics/kellyanne-conway-says-her-husband-changed-his-mind-about-administration-job-contradicting-trump/2019/03/31/e489f8e0-53f6-11e9-8ef3-fbd41a2ce4d5_story.html.

[7] Josephine Harvey. "Kellyanne Conway Rails Against Husband's Anti-Trump Group on Fox News," HuffPost, May 8, 2020. https://www.huffpost.com/entry/kellyanne-george-conway-lincoln-project-anti-trump-ad_n_5eb488c0c5b6a6733540083a.

[8] Brooke Singman. "Trump lashes out at attack ad by George Conway's Lincoln Project: 'Disgrace to Honest Abe,'" Fox News, May 5, 2020. https://www.foxnews.com/politics/trump-lashes-out-at-attack-ad-by-george-conways-lincoln-project-disgrace-to-honest-abe.

[9] Kevin Breuninger. "Robert Mueller's Russia probe cost nearly $32 million in total, Justice Department says," CNBC, August 2, 2019. https://www.cnbc.com/2019/08/02/robert-muellers-russia-probe-cost-nearly-32-million-in-total-doj.html.

[10] Ebony Bowden. "FBI lovebirds Lisa Page, Peter Strzok conspired in Michael Flynn case: docs," *New York Post*, March 7, 2020. https://nypost.com/2020/05/07/fbi-lovebirds-lisa-page-peter-strzok-conspired-in-michael-flynn-case.

[11] Gregg Re. "Strzok claims anti-Trump texts protected by First Amendment, administration violated his rights," Fox News, December 31, 2019. https://www.foxnews.com/politics/strzok-claims-anti-trump-texts-protected-by-1st-amendment-administration-violated-his-rights.

[12] Gregg Re. "Strzok claims anti-Trump texts protected by First Amendment, administration violated his rights," Fox News, December 31, 2019. https://www.foxnews.com/politics/strzok-claims-anti-trump-texts-protected-by-1st-amendment-administration-violated-his-rights.

[13] Julia Musto. "Hannity takes on FBI lovebirds: Lisa Page is 'neither innocent nor a victim,'" Fox News, December 3, 2019. https://www.foxnews.com/media/hannity-lisa-page-neither-innocent-nor-victim.

[14] Julia Musto. "Hannity takes on FBI lovebirds: Lisa Page is 'neither innocent nor a victim,'" Fox News, December 3, 2019. https://www.foxnews.com/media/hannity-lisa-page-neither-innocent-nor-victim.

[15] Catherine Herridge and Gregg Re. "Strzok-Page texts suggested using post-election briefing to gather information on Trump team," Fox News, April 25, 2019. https://www.foxnews.com/politics/strzok-page-texts-suggested-using-post-election-briefing-information-trump-team.

[16] Catherine Herridge and Gregg Re. "Strzok-Page texts suggested using post-election briefing to gather information on Trump team," Fox News, April 25, 2019. https://www.foxnews.com/politics/strzok-page-texts-suggested-using-post-election-briefing-information-trump-team.

[17] Tho Bishop. "Forget Security Clearance, John Brennan Should Be Prosecuted," Mises Institute, August 16, 2018. https://mises.org/power-market/forget-security-clearance-john-brennan-should-be-prosecuted.

[18] Tho Bishop. "Forget Security Clearance, John Brennan Should Be Prosecuted," Mises Institute, August 16, 2018. https://mises.org/power-market/forget-security-clearance-john-brennan-should-be-prosecuted.

[19] Ian Schwartz. "Tucker Carlson: John Brennan Lied to Congress about Steele Dossier, Why Is He Not Facing Perjury Charges?," RealClear Politics, December 11, 2019. https://www.realclearpolitics.com/video/2019/12/11/tucker_carlson_john_brennan_lied_to_congress_about_steele_dossier_why_is_he_not_facing_perjury_charges.html.

[20] Jonathan Turley. "James Clapper's perjury, and why DC made men don't get charged for lying to Congress," *USA Today*, January 19, 2018. https://www.usatoday.com/story/opinion/2018/01/19/james-clappers-perjury-dc-made-men-dont-get-charged-lying-congress-jonathan-turley-column/1045991001.

[21] Jonathan Turley. "James Clapper's perjury, and why DC made men don't get charged for lying to Congress," *USA Today*, January 19, 2018. https://www.usatoday.com/story/opinion/2018/01/19/james-clappers-perjury-dc-made-men-dont-get-charged-lying-congress-jonathan-turley-column/1045991001.

[22] Fox News. "Hannity: Clapper is proud of spying on the Trump campaign," YouTube, May 19, 2018. https://www.youtube.com/watch?v=SQgm9DHELWg.

[23] Liam Pritchett. "Billie Eilish Explains to 63 Million Fans Why 'All Lives Matter' Is Racist," LIVEKINDLY, June 11, 2020. https://www.livekindly.co/billie-eilish-explains-why-all-lives-matter-racist.

[24] Lee Brown. "Harvard grad says she'll 'stab' anyone who says 'all lives matter,' later reveals death threats over 'joke,'" Fox News, July 1, 2020. https://www.foxnews.com/us/harvard-grad-stab-all-lives-matter-death-threats-joke.

[25] Mark Joyella. "'Hannity' Leads Cable News Ratings but CNN Beats Fox in Key Demo," *Forbes*, June 9, 2020. https://www.forbes.com/sites/markjoyella/2020/06/09/hannity-leads-cable-news-ratings-but-cnn-beats-fox-in-key-demo/#216488aa60f6.

Chapter 16: Not a Beautiful Day in Your Neighborhood

[1] Derrick Bryson Taylor. "George Floyd Protests: A Timeline," *New York Times*, July 10, 2020. https://www.nytimes.com/article/george-floyd-protests-timeline.html.

[2] Caroline Bettinger-Lopez and Alexandra Bro. "A Double Pandemic: Domestic Violence in the Age of COVID-19," Council on Foreign Relations, May 13, 2020. https://www.cfr.org/in-brief/double-pandemic-domestic-violence-age-COVID-19.

[3] Amy Hollyfield. "Suicides on the rise during stay-at-home order, Bay Area medical professionals say," ABC 7News, May 21, 2020. https://abc7news.com/suicide-COVID-19-coronavirus-rates-during-pandemic-death-by/6201962.

[4] Evan Hill, Ainara Tiefenthäler, Christiaan Triebert, Drew Jordan, Haley Willis and Robin Stein. "How George Floyd Was Killed in Police Custody," *New York Times*, July 8, 2020. https://www.nytimes.com/2020/05/31/us/george-floyd-investigation.html.

[5] Scottie Andrew. "Derek Chauvin: What we know about the former officer charged in George Floyd's death," CNN, June 1, 2020. https://www.cnn.com/2020/06/01/us/derek-chauvin-what-we-know-trnd/index.html.

[6] Derrick Bryson Taylor. "George Floyd Protests: A Timeline," *New York Times*, July 10, 2020. https://www.nytimes.com/article/george-floyd-protests-timeline.html.

[7] Andrew Young. "OPINION: Lives must matter in a most-serious time for us all," *AJC, May 31,* 2020. https://www.ajc.com/news/opinion/opinion-lives-must-matter-most-serious-time-for-all/7iTWmC6UxZ5s53voGaE1eO.

[8] "'I'm thinking I want to cry': Andrew Young reacts to violent protests in Atlanta," WSB-TV News, https://www.wsbtv.com/video/local-video/im-thinking-i-want-cry-andrew-young-reacts-violent-protests-atlanta/7BWDE4W NLNAVM35X5UKOCZSUQQ.

[9] Derrick Bryson Taylor. "George Floyd Protests: A Timeline," *New York Times*, June 22, 2020. https://www.nytimes.com/article/george-floyd-protests-timeline.html.

[10] Jordan Heck. "Former ESPN NBA reporter criticized for hypocritical tweets about George Floyd protests," Sporting News, June 1, 2020. https://www.sportingnews.com/us/nba/news/espn-nba-reporter-tweets-george-floyd-protests/1eefhr1gpdx7910xlllizoun9i.

[11] Jordan Heck. "Former ESPN NBA reporter criticized for hypocritical tweets about George Floyd protests," Sporting News, June 1, 2020. https://www.sportingnews.com/us/nba/news/espn-nba-reporter-tweets-george-floyd-protests/1eefhr1gpdx7910xlllizoun9i.

[12] Jordan Heck. "Former ESPN NBA reporter criticized for hypocritical tweets about George Floyd protests," Sporting News, June 1, 2020. https://www.sportingnews.com/us/nba/news/espn-nba-reporter-tweets-george-floyd-protests/1eefhr1gpdx7910xlllizoun9i.

[13] Stanley Kurtz. "Massive Government Overreach: Obama's AFFH Rule Is Out," *National Review,* July 8, 2015. https://www.nationalreview.com/corner/massive-government-overreach-obamas-affh-rule-out-stanley-kurtz.

[14] Stanley Kurtz. "Attention America's Suburbs: You Have Just Been Annexed," National Review, July 20,

2015. https://www.nationalreview.com/corner/attention-americas-suburbs-you-have-just-been-annexed-stanley-kurtz.

[15] Stanley Kurtz. "Biden and Dems Are Set to Abolish the Suburbs," National Review, June 30, 2020. https://www.nationalreview.com/corner/biden-and-dems-are-set-to-abolish-the-suburbs.

[16] Philip Bump. "Trump keeps claiming that the most dangerous cities in America are all run by Democrats. They aren't." Washington Post, June 25, 2020. https://www.washingtonpost.com/politics/2020/06/25/trump-keeps-claiming-that-most-dangerous-cities-america-are-all-run-by-democrats-they-arent.

[17] "VA Police Chief: FFs Blocked from House Fire with Child Inside," Firehouse.com News, June 1, 2020. https://www.firehouse.com/operations-training/news/21140391/va-police-chief-firefighters-blocked-from-house-blaze-with-child-inside.

[18] "VA Police Chief: FFs Blocked from House Fire with Child Inside," Firehouse.com News, June 1, 2020. https://www.firehouse.com/operations-training/news/21140391/va-police-chief-firefighters-blocked-from-house-blaze-with-child-inside.

[19] "VA Police Chief: FFs Blocked from House Fire with Child Inside," Firehouse.com News, June 1, 2020. https://www.firehouse.com/operations-training/news/21140391/va-police-chief-firefighters-blocked-from-house-blaze-with-child-inside.

[20] Ebony Bowden. "More than 700 officers injured in George Floyd protests across US," New York Post, June 8, 2020. https://nypost.com/2020/06/08/more-than-700-officers-injured-in-george-floyd-protests-across-us.

[21] Ebony Bowden. "More than 700 officers injured in George Floyd protests across US," New York Post, June 8, 2020. https://nypost.com/2020/06/08/more-than-700-officers-injured-in-george-floyd-protests-across-us.

[22] Willis L. Krumholz. "Here's a List of the Police Killed or Injured in the Last Week's Violence," The Federalist, June 5, 2020. https://thefederalist.com/2020/06/05/heres-a-list-of-the-police-killed-or-injured-in-the-last-weeks-violence.

[23] Willis L. Krumholz. "Here's a List of the Police Killed or Injured in the Last Week's Violence," The Federalist, June 5, 2020. https://thefederalist.com/2020/06/05/heres-a-list-of-the-police-killed-or-injured-in-the-last-weeks-violence.

[24] Willis L. Krumholz. "Here's a List of the Police Killed or Injured in the Last Week's Violence," The Federalist, June 5, 2020. https://thefederalist.com/2020/06/05/heres-a-list-of-the-police-killed-or-injured-in-the-last-weeks-violence. https://twitter.com/joeborellinyc/status/1267962405117706245?s=21.

[25] "Deadly unrest: Here are the people who have died amid George Floyd protests across US," Fox News Channel, June 8, 2020. https://fox6now.com/2020/06/08/deadly-unrest-here-are-the-people-who-have-died-amid-george-floyd-protests-across-us.

[26] "Deadly unrest: Here are the people who have died amid George Floyd protests across US," Fox News Channel, June 8, 2020. https://fox6now.com/2020/06/08/deadly-unrest-here-are-the-people-who-have-died-amid-george-floyd-protests-across-us.

[27] Wikipedia. "Violence and controversies during the George Floyd protests," Wikipedia.org, July 4, 2020. https://en.wikipedia.org/wiki/Violence_and_controversies_during_the_George_Floyd_protests.

[28] Ebony Bowden. "More than 700 officers injured in George Floyd protests across US," New York Post, June 8, 2020. https://nypost.com/2020/06/08/more-than-700-officers-injured-in-george-floyd-protests-across-us.

[29] Ebony Bowden. "More than 700 officers injured in George Floyd protests across US," New York Post, June 8, 2020. https://nypost.com/2020/06/08/more-than-700-officers-injured-in-george-floyd-protests-across-us.

[30] Becket Adams. "AOC: Defund the police means defund the police," Washington Examiner, June 30, 2020. https://www.washingtonexaminer.com/opinion/aoc-defund-the-police-means-defund-the-police.

[31] Becket Adams. "AOC: Defund the police means defund the police," Washington Examiner, June 30, 2020. https://www.washingtonexaminer.com/opinion/aoc-defund-the-police-means-defund-the-police.

[32] "'Rotten to the Root': Rep. Ilhan Omar Defends Support of Dismantling Minneapolis Police," CBS Minnesota,

June 14, 2020. https://minnesota.cbslocal.com/2020/06/14/rotten-to-the-root-rep-ilhan-omar-defends-support-of-dismantling-minneapolis-police.

[33] Brooke Singman and Allie Raffa. "Biden comes out against defunding police, as movement gains traction," Fox News, June 8, 2020. https://www.foxnews.com/politics/biden-comes-out-against-defunding-police-as-movement-gains-traction.

[34] Morgan Phillips. "Biden says some funding should 'absolutely' be redirected from police," Fox News, July 8, 2020. https://www.foxnews.com/politics/biden-says-some-funding-should-absolutely-be-redirected-from-police.

[35] Amber Phillips. "The potentially dangerous politics of 'defund the police' for Democrats," *Washington Post*, June 12, 2020. https://www.washingtonpost.com/politics/2020/06/12/potentially-dangerous-politics-defund-police-democrats.

[36] Law Officer. "Police Officer Mocks 'Defund the Police' Protesters after They Request Security," Lawofficer.com, July 1, 2020. https://www.lawofficer.com/police-officer-mocks-defund-the-police-protesters-after-they-request-security.

[37] Evan Bush. "Protesters Push out Officers, Take over Seattle Police Precinct," Officer.com, June 11, 2020. https://www.officer.com/tactical/news/21141776/protesters-push-out-officers-take-over-seattle-police-precinct.

[38] Elizabeth Vaughn. "Seattle Mayor Has Had Portable Toilets Delivered and Sent Clean-up Crews to Assist the 'Patriots' of CHAZ," RedState, June 12, 2020. https://www.redstate.com/elizabeth-vaughn/2020/06/12/seattle-mayor-has-portable-toilets-delivered-to-chaz.

[39] Louis Casiano. "'Squad' Dems Tlaib, Pressley introduce bill to defund police, give reparations," Fox News, July 7, 2020. https://www.foxnews.com/politics/squad-dems-tlaib-pressley-introduce-bill-bill-to-defund-police-give-reparations.

[40] Tom Winter and Andrew Blankstein. "Police describe anarchists' extensive prep for violence, including 'bicycle scouts,'" NBC News, May 31, 2020. https://www.nbcnews.com/politics/justice-department/law-enforcement-plays-catch-stop-violence-radical-groups-protests-n1220486.

[41] Tom Winter and Andrew Blankstein. "Police describe anarchists' extensive prep for violence, including 'bicycle scouts,'" NBC News, May 31, 2020. https://www.nbcnews.com/politics/justice-department/law-enforcement-plays-catch-stop-violence-radical-groups-protests-n1220486.

[42] Tom Winter and Andrew Blankstein. "Police describe anarchists' extensive prep for violence, including 'bicycle scouts,'" NBC News, May 31, 2020. https://www.nbcnews.com/politics/justice-department/law-enforcement-plays-catch-stop-violence-radical-groups-protests-n1220486.

[43] Merriam-Webster. "Anarchy," Merriam-Webster.com, July 10, 2020. https://www.merriam-webster.com/dictionary/anarchy.

[44] KMOV.com Staff. "Central West End couple explains why they pointed guns at protesters who demanded Krewson's resignation," KMOV.com, July 14, 2020. https://www.kmov.com/news/st-louis-couple-seen-pointing-guns-at-protestors/article_afbb1b2c-b98e-11ea-ba7e-b3452007bfc8.html.

[45] KMOV.com Staff. "Central West End couple explains why they pointed guns at protesters who demanded Krewson's resignation," KMOV.com, July 14, 2020. https://www.kmov.com/news/st-louis-couple-seen-pointing-guns-at-protestors/article_afbb1b2c-b98e-11ea-ba7e-b3452007bfc8.html.

[46] Jordan Michaels. "Sheriff Vows to Deputize Gun Owners to Protect Citizens from Rioters," GunsAmerica, July 2, 2020. https://www.gunsamerica.com/digest/sheriff-vows-to-deputize-gun-owners-to-protect-citizens-from-rioters/?utm_source=email&utm_medium=20200703_FridayDigest_285&utm_campaign=/digest/sheriff-vows-to-deputize-gun-owners-to-protect-citizens-from-rioters.

[47] Jordan Michaels. "Sheriff Vows to Deputize Gun Owners to Protect Citizens from Rioters," GunsAmerica, July 2, 2020. https://www.gunsamerica.com/digest/sheriff-vows-to-deputize-gun-owners-to-protect-citizens-from-rioters/?utm_source=email&utm_medium=20200703_FridayDigest_285&utm_campaign=/digest/sheriff-vows-to-deputize-gun-owners-to-protect-citizens-from-rioters.

[48] Ed Mahon. "Biden brings campaign to Lancaster, but remains out of sight." *PA Post*, June 25, 2020. https://

papost.org/2020/06/25/biden-brings-campaign-to-lancaster-but-remains-out-of-sight.

[49] The White House. "Executive Order on Safe Policing for Safe Communities," Whitehouse.gov, June 16, 2020. https://www.whitehouse.gov/presidential-actions/executive-order-safe-policing-safe-communities.

[50] The White House. "'We need to bring law enforcement and communities closer together, not to drive them apart.' — President @realDonaldTrump," Twitter, June 21, 2020. https://twitter.com/whitehouse/status/1274849595286323200?lang=en.

[51] Countable. "President Trump Signs Executive Order to Increase De-Escalation Training for Police, Ban Chokeholds in Most Instances," *Countable.us*, June 16, 2020. https://www.countable.us/articles/44990-president-trump-signs-executive-order-increase-de-escalation-training-police-ban-chokeholds-instances.

[52] Countable. "President Trump Signs Executive Order to Increase De-Escalation Training for Police, Ban Chokeholds in Most Instances," *Countable.us*, June 16, 2020. https://www.countable.us/articles/44990-president-trump-signs-executive-order-increase-de-escalation-training-police-ban-chokeholds-instances.

[53] Countable. "President Trump Signs Executive Order to Increase De-Escalation Training for Police, Ban Chokeholds in Most Instances," *Countable.us*, June 16, 2020. https://www.countable.us/articles/44990-president-trump-signs-executive-order-increase-de-escalation-training-police-ban-chokeholds-instances.

PART III:
Chapter 17: Promises Kept

[1] Prisons Bureau. "Annual Determination of Average Cost of Incarceration," Federal Register, April 30, 2018. https://www.federalregister.gov/documents/2018/04/30/2018-09062/annual-determination-of-average-cost-of-incarceration.

[2] Sintia Radu. "Countries with the Highest Incarceration Rates," *U.S. News & World Report*, May 13, 2019. https://www.usnews.com/news/best-countries/articles/2019-05-13/10-countries-with-the-highest-incarceration-rates.

[3] Henry Olsen. "Trump has had a lot of policy successes. You just don't hear about them," *Washington Post*, January 10, 2020. https://www.washingtonpost.com/opinions/2020/01/10/trump-has-had-lot-policy-successes-you-just-dont-hear-about-them.

[4] Henry Olsen. "Trump has had a lot of policy successes. You just don't hear about them," *Washington Post*, January 10, 2020. https://www.washingtonpost.com/opinions/2020/01/10/trump-has-had-lot-policy-successes-you-just-dont-hear-about-them.

[5] Goldwater Institute. "Jackson Silva," RightToTry.org, September 21, 2017. https://righttotry.org/jackson-silva.

[6] Ariel Cohen. "Making History: U.S. Exports More Petroleum Than It Imports in September and October," *Forbes*, November 26, 2019. https://www.forbes.com/sites/arielcohen/2019/11/26/making-history-us-exports-more-petroleum-than-it-imports-in-september-and-october/#88d11935f3b3.

[7] The White House. "President Trump's Energy Independence Policy," Whitehouse.gov, March 28, 2017. https://www.whitehouse.gov/briefings-statements/president-trumps-energy-independence-policy.

[8] The White House. "President Trump's Energy Independence Policy," Whitehouse.gov, March 28, 2017. https://www.whitehouse.gov/briefings-statements/president-trumps-energy-independence-policy.

[9] The White House. "President Trump's Energy Independence Policy," Whitehouse.gov, March 28, 2017. https://www.whitehouse.gov/briefings-statements/president-trumps-energy-independence-policy.

[10] Natalie Gross. "Trump recently signed two veterans bills into law. Here's how they'll affect you," Military Times Rebootcamp, January 17, 2019. https://rebootcamp.militarytimes.com/news/transition/2019/01/17/trump-recently-signed-two-veterans-bills-into-law-heres-how-theyll-affect-you.

[11] Robert Wilkie. "A Breakthrough in Health Care for Veterans," The White House, May 13, 2019. https://www.whitehouse.gov/articles/breakthrough-health-care-veterans.

[12] Nikki Wentling. "VA to expand veterans' access to private medical care," *Stars and Stripes*, June 5, 2019. https://www.stripes.com/va-to-expand-veterans-access-to-private-medical-care-1.584717.

[13] Isabelle Morales. "List: 817 Regulations Waived to Help Fight COVID-19," Americans for Tax Reform, July 15,

2020. https://www.atr.org/rules.

[14] The White House. "President Donald J. Trump Has Delivered Record Breaking Results for the American People in His First Three Years in Office," Whitehouse.gov, December 31, 2019. https://www.whitehouse.gov/briefings-statements/president-donald-j-trump-delivered-record-breaking-results-american-people-first-three-years-office.

[15] The White House. "President Donald J. Trump Has Delivered Record Breaking Results for the American People in His First Three Years in Office," Whitehouse.gov, December 31, 2019. https://www.whitehouse.gov/briefings-statements/president-donald-j-trump-delivered-record-breaking-results-american-people-first-three-years-office.

[16] The White House. "President Donald J. Trump Has Delivered Record Breaking Results for the American People in His First Three Years in Office," Whitehouse.gov, December 31, 2019. https://www.whitehouse.gov/briefings-statements/president-donald-j-trump-delivered-record-breaking-results-american-people-first-three-years-office.

[17] The White House. "President Donald J. Trump Has Delivered Record Breaking Results for the American People in His First Three Years in Office," Whitehouse.gov, December 31, 2019. https://www.whitehouse.gov/briefings-statements/president-donald-j-trump-delivered-record-breaking-results-american-people-first-three-years-office.

[18] Yun Li. "This is now the longest US economic expansion in history," CNBC, July, 2, 2019. https://www.cnbc.com/2019/07/02/this-is-now-the-longest-us-economic-expansion-in-history.html.

[19] Christopher Condon and Steve Matthews. "Economy Breaks Records on Trump's Watch. He Wants All the Credit," *Bloomberg*, June 16, 2019. https://www.bloomberg.com/graphics/2019-the-longest-expansion.

[20] Christopher Condon and Steve Matthews. "Economy Breaks Records on Trump's Watch. He Wants All the Credit," *Bloomberg*, June 16, 2019. https://www.bloomberg.com/graphics/2019-the-longest-expansion.https://twitter.com/realDonaldTrump/status/1003738744061603843?ref_src=twsrc%5Etfw%7Ctwcamp%5Etweetembed%7Ctwterm%5E1003738744061603843%7Ctwgr%5E&ref_url=https%3A%2F%2Fwwwbloomberg.com%2Fgraphics%2F2019-the-longest-expansion%2F.

[21] Maggie Fitzgerald. "Trump stock market rally is far outpacing past US presidents," CNBC, December 26, 2019. https://www.cnbc.com/2019/12/26/trumps-stock-market-rally-is-far-outpacing-past-us-presidents.html.

[22] The White House. "President Donald J. Trump Has Delivered Record Breaking Results for the American People in His First Three Years in Office," Whitehouse.gov, December 31, 2019. https://www.whitehouse.gov/briefings-statements/president-donald-j-trump-delivered-record-breaking-results-american-people-first-three-years-office.

[23] The White House. "President Donald J. Trump Has Delivered Record Breaking Results for the American People in His First Three Years in Office," Whitehouse.gov, December 31, 2019. https://www.whitehouse.gov/briefings-statements/president-donald-j-trump-delivered-record-breaking-results-american-people-first-three-years-office.

[24] Alex Hendrie. "Trump tax cuts and the middle class: Here are the facts," Fox Business, January 13, 2019. https://www.foxbusiness.com/economy/trump-tax-cuts-and-the-middle-class-here-are-the-facts.

[25] Lori Robertson. "Democrats' Misleading Tax Line," FactCheck.org, January 26, 2018. https://www.factcheck.org/2018/01/democrats-misleading-tax-line.

[26] John Kartch. "List of Tax Reform Good News," Americans for Tax Reform, July 8, 2020. https://www.atr.org/list.

[27] Felix Richter. "Has the Stock Market Moved on from COVID-19?," Statista, June 11, 2020. https://www.statista.com/chart/20939/year-to-date-performance-of-major-us-stock-market-indices.

[28] Jeff Cox. "Record jobs gain of 4.8 million in June smashes expectations; unemployment rate falls to 11.1%," CNBC, July 2, 2020. https://www.cnbc.com/2020/07/02/jobs-report-june-2020.html.

[29] Natasha Turak. "Trump becomes first sitting US president in history to cross border into North Korea," CNBC, July 2, 2019. https://www.cnbc.com/2019/06/30/rtrs-190630-trump-kim-quotes-dmz-eu.html.

[30] Elise Labott, Nicole Gaouette, and Kevin Liptak. "US sent plane with $400 million in cash to Iran," CNN Politics, August 4, 2016. https://www.cnn.com/2016/08/03/politics/us-sends-plane-iran-400-million-cash/index.html.

[31] The Bureau of Investigative Journalism. "Obama's Covert Drone War in Numbers: Ten Times More Strikes Than Bush," Thebureauinvestigates.com, January 17, 2017. https://www.thebureauinvestigates.com/stories/2017-01-17/obamas-covert-drone-war-in-numbers-ten-times-more-strikes-than-bush.

[32] The White House. "Remarks by President Trump on the Death of ISIS Leader Abu Bakr al-Baghdadi," Whitehouse.gov, October 27, 2019. https://www.whitehouse.gov/briefings-statements/remarks-president-trump-death-isis-leader-abu-bakr-al-baghdadi.

[33] Jeanine Santucci. "The Washington Post faces backlash for headline calling ISIS terrorist 'austere religious scholar,'" USA Today, October 28, 2019. https://www.usatoday.com/story/news/politics/2019/10/28/abu-bakr-al-baghdadi-washington-post-austere-headline/2483340001/

[34] U.S. Department of Defense. "Statement by the Department of Defense," Defense.gov, January 2, 2020. https://www.defense.gov/Newsroom/Releases/Release/Article/2049534/statement-by-the-department-of-defense.

[35] Jim Geraghty. "Nancy Pelosi: Killing Soleimani Was 'Provocative and Disproportionate,'" National Review, January 3, 2020. https://www.nationalreview.com/corner/nancy-pelosi-killing-soleimani-was-provocative-and-disproportionate.

[36] Jim Geraghty. "Nancy Pelosi: Killing Soleimani Was 'Provocative and Disproportionate,'" National Review, January 3, 2020. https://www.nationalreview.com/corner/nancy-pelosi-killing-soleimani-was-provocative-and-disproportionate.

[37] Carisa Nietsche and Martijn Rasser. "Washington's Anti-Huawei Tactics Need a Reboot in Europe," Foreign Policy, April 30, 2020. https://foreignpolicy.com/2020/04/30/huawei-5g-europe-united-states-china.

[38] Robin Emmott. "In gesture to Trump, US allies close to deal to pay more for NATO running costs," Reuters, November 26, 2019. https://www.reuters.com/article/us-nato-summit-defence-budget/in-gesture-to-trump-us-allies-close-to-deal-to-pay-more-for-nato-running-costs-idUSKBN1Y01WY.

[39] The White House. "Remarks by President Trump in a Fox News Virtual Town Hall," Whitehouse.gov, May 4, 2020. https://www.whitehouse.gov/briefings-statements/remarks-president-trump-fox-news-virtual-town-hall.

[40] Jack Wilson. "Wilson: From Hope and Change to Broken Promises and Empty Words: The Joe Biden Story," Roanoke Times, June, 26 2020 https://roanoke.com/opinion/commentary/wilson-from-hope-and-change-to-broken-promises-and-empty-words-the-joe-biden-story/article_26e22ebb-53fa-5532-9788-9551eccoc2f2.html.

Chapter 18: He Did It Before and He Can Do It Again

[1] Brian Ross and Rehab El-Buri. "Obama's Pastor: God Damn America, U.S. to blame for 9/11," ABC News, May 7, 2008. https://abcnews.go.com/Blotter/DemocraticDebate/story?id=4443788&page=1.

[2] "Killing Jobs—The Biden Record on Trade," Donaldjtrump.com, July 1, 2020. https://www.donaldjtrump.com/media/killing-jobs-the-biden-record-on-trade.

[3] "Remarks by President Trump at South Dakota's 2020 Mount Rushmore Fireworks Celebration, Keystone, South Dakota," The White House, July 4, 2020. https://www.whitehouse.gov/briefings-statements/remarks-president-trump-south-dakotas-2020-mount-rushmore-fireworks-celebration-keystone-south-dakota.

Appendix: The Best of the Worst Joe Biden Quotes

[1] Ryan Grim. "Freshman Sen. Joe Biden Didn't Like Roe v. Wade in 1974," Huffington Post, October 1, 2015. https://www.huffingtonpost.ca/entry/joe-biden-abortion-1974_n_560c5ee3e4b076812700b4d6.

[2] Alana Goodman. "Joe Biden embraced segregation in 1975, claiming it was a matter of 'black pride,'" Washington Examiner, February 5, 2019. https://www.washingtonexaminer.com/politics/joe-biden-embraced-segregation-in-1975-claiming-it-was-a-matter-of-black-pride.

NOTES

[3] Congressional Record. October 21, 1975.

[4] Brianna Rhodes. "Joe Biden: 5 things to know about his surprising views on school desegregation," The Grio, March 14, 2019. https://thegrio.com/2019/03/14/joe-biden-school-desegregation.

[5] Laura Barron-Lopez. "Bobby Rush rips Biden as 'woefully ignorant,'" *Politico*, June 21, 2019. https://www.politico.com/story/2019/06/21/bobby-rush-biden-ignorant-1376557.

[6] Virtue News, June 23, 2019. https://virtue.news/home/oxvs8wqeuk5gx1vnocribbfcyzk85w.

[7] Ben Dreyfuss. "That Time Joe Biden Lied about His Academic Credentials," *Mother Jones*, May 3, 2019. https://www.motherjones.com/politics/2019/05/that-time-joe-biden-lied-about-his-academic-credentials

[8] Matt Viser, Dino Grandoni, Jeff Stein. "Joe Biden's campaign acknowledges lifting language from other groups for its policy plans," *Washington Post*, June 4, 2019. https://wapo.st/2XvME0U.

[9] Ryan Grim. "Fact check: Joe Biden has advocated cutting social security for 40 years," The Intercept, January 13, 2020. https://theintercept.com/2020/01/13/biden-cuts-social-security.

[10] Alana Goodman. "Six times Biden described major events in his life that never happened," *Washington Examiner*, August 19, 2019. https://www.washingtonexaminer.com/news/six-times-biden-described-major-events-in-his-life-that-never-happened.

[11] Rebecca Klar. "Biden says he doesn't view abortion 'as a choice and a right' in unearthed video," *The Hill*, June 13, 2019. https://thehill.com/homenews/campaign/448473-biden-says-he-doesnt-see-abortion-as-a-choice-and-a-right-in-unearthed-2006.

[12] "The Screwups of Campaign '08," Time.com, 2019. http://content.time.com/time/specials/2007/article/0,28804,1643290_1643292_1643323,00.html.

[13] Andrew Kaczynski. "Joe Biden once said a fence was needed to stop 'tons' of drugs from Mexico," CNN, May 10, 2019. https://www.cnn.com/2019/05/10/politics/kfile-biden-drugs-fence-2006/index.html.

[14] "Joe Biden: moron, racist, or poorly transcribed?," *Economist*, January 31, 2007. https://www.economist.com/democracy-in-america/2007/01/31/joe-biden-moron-racist-or-poorly-transcribed.

[15] "Panel on Joe Biden's Clinton Comment," Real Clear Politics, September 11, 2008. https://www.realclearpolitics.com/articles/2008/09/panel_on_joe_bidens_clinton_co.html.

[16] Cal Thomas Tribune Content Agency. "Cal Thomas: Biden's record reveals a disturbing pattern," *Winston-Salem Journal*, May 31, 2020. https://www.journalnow.com/opinion/columnists/cal-thomas-bidens-record-reveals-a-disturbing-pattern/article_84678a49-d6d3-51ad-8304-c3a56969ee1e.html.

[17] Mackenzie Weinger. "GOP slams Biden 'chains' remark," *Politico*, August 15, 2012. https://www.politico.com/story/2012/08/gop-lashes-biden-chains-remark-079717.

[18] Pres Office Ted Cruz. "FACT CHECK//Democrats Deny Biden Corruption," Cruz.senate.gov, January 22, 2020. https://www.cruz.senate.gov/?p=press_release&id=4883.

[19] Jack Crowe. "Biden Fabricates Emotional War Story While Campaigning in New Hampshire," *National Review*, August 29, 2019. https://www.nationalreview.com/news/biden-fabricates-emotional-war-story-while-campaigning-in-new-hampshire.

[20] Breck Dumas. "Watch: Joe Biden gets testy with Iowa college student, grabs her by the arm over question about gender," *The Blaze*, August 9, 2019. https://www.theblaze.com/news/watch-joe-biden-gets-testy-with-iowa-college-student-grabs-her-by-the-arm-over-question-about-gender.

[21] Miranda Devine. "Joe Biden's bias comes through in trying to outwoke competition: Devine," *New York Post*, January 26, 2020. https://nypost.com/2020/01/26/joe-bidens-bias-comes-through-in-tweet-devine/.

[22] Tristan Justice. "The Biden Gaffe Machine: A Running List of Joe Biden's Best Slip-Ups," *The Federalist*, September 2, 2019. https://thefederalist.com/2019/09/02/biden-gaffe-machine-running-list-joe-bidens-best-slip-ups.

[23] Tristan Justice. "Joe Biden Claims He Started Out at a Historically Black College. He Didn't," *The Federalist*, October 28, 2019. https://thefederalist.com/2019/10/28/joe-biden-claims-he-started-out-at-a-historically-black-

college-he-didnt.

[24] Gregg Re. "Biden, in New Hampshire, jokingly calls student 'a lying dog-faced pony soldier,'" Fox News, February 9, 2020. https://www.foxnews.com/politics/biden-new-hampshire-lying-dog-faced-pony-soldier.

[25] Quint Forgey and Myah Ward. "Biden apologizes for controversial 'you ain't black' comment," Politico, May 22, 2020. https://www.politico.com/news/2020/05/22/joe-biden-breakfast-club-interview-274490.

[26] Ian Schwartz. "Biden: '10 to 15 Percent' of Americans Are Not Very Good People," RealClear Politics, June 4, 2020. https://www.realclearpolitics.com/video/2020/06/04/biden_10_to_15_percent_of_americans_are_not_very_good_people.html.

[27] Yaron Steinbuch. "Joe Biden says there are '120 million dead from COVID,'" New York Post, June 26, 2020. https://nypost.com/2020/06/26/joe-biden-wrongly-says-we-have-120-million-dead-from-covid.

[28] Ben Smith. "Biden garbles Depression history," Politico, September 23, 2008. https://www.politico.com/blogs/ben-smith/2008/09/biden-garbles-depression-history-012167.

[29] Bob Franken. "Age-old gaffes," Venice Florida Weekly, August 8, 2019. https://venice.floridaweekly.com/articles/age-old-gaffes.

[30] Jeffrey A. Rendall. "Assault on America, Day 264: Democrats have more to worry about than Joe Biden's flubs," ConservativeHQ, September 23, 2019. https://www.conservativehq.com/article/31055-assault-america-day-264-democrats-have-more-worry-about-joe-biden's-flubs.

[31] The Wall Street Journal. "Biden: 30 Percent Chance We'll Get It Wrong," Fox News, February 7, 2009. https://www.foxnews.com/politics/biden-30-percent-chance-well-get-it-wrong.

[32] Shane Croucher. "Joe Biden's Biggest Gaffes: Quotes, Blunders That Could Hurt a 2020 Presidential Campaign," Newsweek, February 9, 2019. https://www.newsweek.com/joe-biden-gaffes-quotes-2020-election-1323905.

[33] Lucy Madison. "Biden: Obama's bin Laden mission was 'audacious' plan in 500 years," CBS News, September 24, 2012. https://www.cbsnews.com/news/biden-obamas-bin-laden-mission-was-most-audacious-plan-in-500-years.

[34] Eric Randall. "Joe Biden's Comedy Tour Continues: 'Pretend You Like Me!'," The Atlantic, April 27, 2012. https://www.theatlantic.com/politics/archive/2012/04/joe-bidens-comedy-tour-continues/328801.

[35] Ben Baker. "Joe Being Joe," Politico, March 4, 2014. https://www.politico.com/magazine/story/2014/02/joe-biden-bidenisms-103689.

[36] Talia Buford. "Biden: 'A gaffe is when you tell the truth,'" Politico, June 20, 2012. https://www.politico.com/blogs/politico44/2012/06/biden-a-gaffe-is-when-you-tell-the-truth-126866.

[37] Dwight Adams. "A baker's dozen of Bidenisms," IndyStar, October 21, 2015. https://www.indystar.com/story/news/2015/10/21/bakers-dozen-bidenisms/74338682.

[38] Julia Manchester. "Biden tell supporters 'I'm not going nuts,'" The Hill, August 26, 2019. https://thehill.com/homenews/campaign/458817-biden-tells-supporters-after-flub-im-not-going-nuts.

[39] Tim Hains. "Joe Biden in Keene, New Hampshire: What's Not to Like about Vermont? What a Neat Town," RealClear Politics, August 25, 2019. https://www.realclearpolitics.com/video/2019/08/25/joe_biden_in_keene_new_hampshire_whats_not_to_like_about_vermont_what_a_neat_town.html.

[40] Emma Kinery. "Biden Misdates 2018 Parkland Shooting in His Latest Blunder," Bloomberg, August 10, 2019. https://www.bloomberg.com/news/articles/2019-08-10/biden-says-he-was-vice-president-during-the-parkland-shooting.

[41] Gene Veith. "We Choose Truth over Facts," Patheos, August 13, 2019. https://www.patheos.com/blogs/geneveith/2019/08/we-choose-truth-over-facts.

[42] "Joe Biden's record-player moment," Axios, September 13, 2019. https://www.axios.com/joe-biden-record-player-democratic-debate-0cab34f7-510e-4408-9a92-b7af814e2e77.html.

[43] Zack Beauchamp. "The weird, telling Joe Biden debate moment that didn't get enough attention," Vox, September 13, 2019. https://www.vox.com/policy-and-politics/2019/9/13/20864328/democratic-debate-september-abc-biden-iraq-afghanistan.

[44] Max Greenwood. "Biden forgets Harris exists," The Hill, November 20, 2019. https://thehill.com/homenews/

campaign/471434-crowd-erupts-after-harris-points-out-biden-mistaken-claim-to-have-support.

[45] Chris Riotta. "Joe Biden confuses Nevada with New Hampshire in speech after second primary vote," *Independent,* February 12, 2020. https://www.independent.co.uk/news/joe-biden-nevada-new-hampshire-primary-state-confusing-gaffe-a9330701.html.

[46] Tristan Justice. "Joe Biden Claims Bolivia Is on the Border of Venezuela. It's Not," *The Federalist,* January 10, 2020. https://thefederalist.com/2020/01/10/joe-biden-claims-bolivia-is-on-the-border-of-venezuela-its-not.

[47] James Crowley. "Biden Suggests Coal Miner Learn to Code to Be Prepared for 'Jobs of the Future,'" *Newsweek*, December 31, 2019. https://www.newsweek.com/joe-biden-new-hampshire-campaign-code-1479913.

[48] Tristan Justice. "Joe Biden Confuses Wife and Sister on Super Tuesday Stage," *The Federalist,* March 4, 2020. https://thefederalist.com/2020/03/04/joe-biden-confuses-wife-and-sister-on-super-tuesday-stage.

[49] Tristan Justice. "Joe Biden Says He's Running for the Senate: 'Don't Like Me? Vote for the Other Biden," *The Federalist,* February 25, 2020. https://thefederalist.com/2020/02/25/joe-biden-says-hes-running-for-the-senate-dont-like-me-vote-for-the-other-biden.

[50] Alex Shephard. "Joe Biden Should Thank the Media for His Super Tuesday Win," *New Republic*, March 4, 2020. https://newrepublic.com/article/156749/joe-biden-thank-media-super-tuesday-win.

[51] M. Dowling, "Biden lied during his calamitous town hall," *Independent Sentinel*, March 14, 2020. https://www.independentsentinel.com/biden-lied-during-his-calamitous-mini-town-hall/.

[52] Bradford Betz. "Joe Biden botches Declaration of Independence," Fox News, March 2, 2020. https://www.foxnews.com/politics/joe-biden-declaration-of-independence.

[53] Becket Adams. "Biden berates construction worker with threats and anti-gun propaganda," March 10, 2020. https://www.washingtonexaminer.com/opinion/biden-berates-construction-worker-with-threats-and-anti-gun-propaganda.

[54] Howie Carr. "Howie Carr: Trust the man, Joe Biden is going to beat Joe Biden," *Boston Herald*, May 23, 2020. https://www.bostonherald.com/2020/05/23/trust-the-man-joe-biden-is-going-to-beat-joe-biden.

I hope you will stay connected through
social media!

Facebook: DonaldJTrumpJr

Twitter: @DonaldJTrumpJr

Instagram: donaldjtrumpjr